I0003371

The Perfect Programmer

The Perfect Programmer

A Christian Computer Programming Curriculum

The Perfect Programmer
Joseph Stephen

© 2014 by Joseph K. Stephen. All rights reserved.

ISBN: 978-0-9924875-3-9

No part of this book may be reproduced without written permission from the publisher or copyright holder, except in the case of brief quotations embodied in critical articles and reviews. All Scriptures are taken from The *King James Version* of the Holy Bible.

Contents

ANSWERS

Foreword

Joseph Stephen's book is a concise guide to take students through the elements of C++ programming, and it briefly introduces the Windows GUI programming world. What makes this book special is the author knows that good teaching should be founded upon good philosophy—and good philosophy is needed because there is so very much poor philosophy in the world today.

The student following this course will discover what every good programmer knows: That good software is always created by intelligent and skilful hard-working minds who are able to visualise the completed process before committing to build it, and the importance of attention to detail. For Joseph, visualisation is especially pertinent as his total blindness forces him to exercise exceptional visualisation. It is my prayer that students of this book will similarly visualise beyond what can be "seen," and know the Creator who is the greatest programmer - Our physical bodies are still going well 6,000 years after they were programmed! Only a couple of my programs are still used after 20 years!

Ray Lakeman - High school Science and Maths Teacher (16 years), Software Engineer (21 years).

Aims and Objectives

This course is designed for students from thirteen years and up, and assumes good mathematic skills and language comprehension. No prior programming experience is necessary, however, the supervisor or student should have basic computer skills in order to be able to download and install software and samples as described in Appendix 6. It is recommended that you purchase Visual Studio student edition or download the free Visual C++ Express development environment included with the samples for this course.

Unlike any other Computer Science course to our knowledge, this curriculum begins with the Creator, the *Perfect Programmer* who had prior claim to the Programmable Computer. This is a Computer Science curriculum from a Christian worldview.

This course will introduce you to:

- A brief history of the computer from a Providencial perspective;

- The architecture of the computer and its periferals;

- Basic principles of programming;

- Introduction to the C++ programming language;

- A brief introduction to Object Oriented Programming;

- Number systems: binary and hexadecimal;

- Algorithms: The recipe of programming instructions;

- Debugging: Discovering why things aren't working as you expect.

At the end of this course you will be able to:

- Identify the various components of a computer system;

- Read and follow the flow of a computer program;

- Understand the basics of object oriented programming;

- Trace through and understand a real computer program;

- Write a simple computer program;

- Understand several of the most important programming algorithms;

- Work with other number systems such as Binary and Hexadecimal;

- Gain insight into how to debug or troubleshoot a program that doesn't work as you expect;

- Understand why it is impossible for even a single living cell to evolve from nothing;

- Begin to appreciate the power of the Almighty God who created all things by His Word!

The historical chapter is written as much for the supervisor as for the student since it is likely that even the supervisor will not have learned this history from a Christian perspective, nor perhaps have thought through the implications of atheistic presuppositions. The supervisor may thus need to discuss some of this content with the student, if the student's ability to follow logic is still immature. Also, while the latter lessons on Data Structures may appear complex and the learning curve rather steep, it is not mandatory to fully understand everything before delving into programming. You will over time understand and there is no substitution for experience and perseverance. Feel free to skip over these chapters and come back to them once you've had a bit more experience experimenting with some simple examples. The beauty of home education means that at the point this book becomes too difficult, you can revise and repeat it in subsequent years. I envisage that this book will be useful for several years rather than necessarily being completed in one.

Rationale

One might ask why I chose to teach C++ as opposed to C# or another more "modern" programming language. While C# is similar in syntax to C++ and generally easier to learn, there is still far more C++ code in the world than C# code and this is not likely to change for many years to come. C++ has been around a long time and has been used on virtually all operating systems while C# is predominantly used only on the Windows platform so far. I will, however, devote an appendix to the comparison between C++ and C# so that if you choose to learn C#, the transition won't be too difficult. In all likelihood, sometime in your programming career, or the journey leading to that career, you'll need to work with C or C++. C++ is a mature, well understood, well used, flexible and powerful language. While no language is suited to every programming task, hence the development of many languages, it is a good general purpose language with many resources available to help you in your learning journey. Languages such as C# and JAVA borrow heavily from C++ syntactically so once you know C++, the transition to C# or JAVA should be easy. Think of this process as like learning to drive a manual car before you learn to drive an automatic. While an automatic may be easier in the long run, some of the skills learned through driving a manual are simply good skills every driver should learn in order to understand and better handle their vehicle.

Acknowledgments

- I'd like to thank all of the patient people who have read programming manuals and other technical gobledegook to me over the years. Though perhaps meaningless and boring to the reader, it was the key to my learning.

- I'd like to thank my life savers, my wife Florence and my children (the ones old enough to read), who patiently dictate the long strings of seemingly meaningless numbers and letters to me when my computer crashes without speech.

- Much thanks to my wife Florence who researched photos and illustrations for this curriculum.

- I thank Ray Lakeman, my high school science teacher who was partially responsible for setting me on the course to programming. Mr Lakeman lost both of his hands and much of his arms in an accident when he was a child. He without hands and me without eyes made a curious working team at school. I also thank him for writing the forword to this book.

- I thank Alex Grant, a peer who taught me assembly code programming when I was in my early teens.

- I thank David Wright, another student at the same school who contributed greatly to me taking both Christianity and programming seriously.

- I thank Mark George, a long-time friend whilst growing up, who spent hours programming with me.

- I thank Assoc. Prof. Paul Calder, who often went out of his way to help me during my computer science degree at Flinders University.

- I thank Carl Wise and Glen Gordon, two senior programmers at Freedom Scientific, who have taught me much over the past fifteen years.

- I thank my Lord Jesus Christ to whom I owe everything.

    Unless otherwise stated, all images are royalty free.

From Creation to Computation

Why study history? Why should we worry about the origin of computers? Why not get straight into programming? History is *His Story*, God's story. Humanists of the past few decades have purposefully tried to remove God from history or to simply encourage history not to be taught. It is vitally important to look at origins to see just how everything fits into God's great plan for mankind. It is also important to understand the motivation behind such great inventions as the computer. Even though the canon of Scripture is complete, you and I are part of God's story for mankind. Your life can be used of Him to impact mankind for good or ill, just as God used great scientists of the past to impact man for good. Studying history helps us see where we fit in God's grand scheme of things.

One might also ask what the beliefs of scientists of the past have to do with their scientific discoveries. The truth is that our worldview and beliefs directly affect what we do and motivate why we do what we do. Scientists wise enough to acknowledge the existence of the Almighty, omniscient God of absolutes, smart enough to see that God is a God of order, and observant enough to see God's immutable laws at work in nature, had a solid foundation on which to make scientific inquiry. Science cannot be built upon irrational, purposeless, random chaos as is implied by the evolutionary presuppositions of Atheism. While atheists study science, they must borrow from the Christian Worldview to do so. I hope this becomes clear as you study this course.

Man-made computers are such an integral part of our lives today, it is hard to imagine life without them. The truth is, we have not always needed them. God created the first super computer when He created the first living cell on day three as He spoke into existence every original plant species. While Charles Darwin may have thought that the cell was a simple organism, we now know it to be more complex than a modern city—self repairing, self-reproducing, functional powerhouses of utility, even able to communicate intelligently with its neighbours.[1] God created the first ultra-super computer on day six when he created man in His own image and endowed him with an incredible brain made up of hundreds of billions of cells. This ultra-super-computer was able to teach itself, repair and update itself, and had the most incredibly powerful memory, not to mention its speed and accuracy at speech and image recognition, language translation, and creativity. Its ability to precisely control limbs and fingers to perform the most delicate of tasks or the most strenuous of manoeuvers makes all man-made robotic arms look clumsy.[2] The Bible teaches us that mankind is the most privileged of all creatures, created in the very image of Almighty God himself.[3] Yet with all of our intelligence, nothing we do comes close to God's handiwork. Modern computers may have been built by man, but like most of our inventions, God had the prior claim. Even the smallest of our computer chips today still does not approach the complexity of a single living cell.

Man-made computers or computing devices have been around for a very long time. The Puzzle of Ancient Man by Dr Donald E Chittick Ph.D reveals archaeological evidence of computing devices and other technology from periods of history thought to be times of ignorance. We can deduce from Scripture that man has degenerated and not become smarter as evolution has lead us to believe. Let us consider for a moment the purpose of technology from the printing press to today's powerful pocket-sized computers. Of course every tool discovered by man can be and is often used for evil, however understanding the sovereignty of God in all things, there is a greater reason for such discovery and an explanation as to why we do not read of such technology in the early chapters of the Scriptures.

At creation, Adam was created perfect. His knowledge was perfect, his memory perfect and his reason and intellect perfect. He was able to name every animal and remember every name.[4] Even after the fall, for many generations, God's Word and will for man was entirely communicated from one generation to the next via spoken word and easily memorized.[5] This would have been amply sufficient since our mental capacity had not yet degenerated to its state of today. There was literally no need for the printing press, no need for computers or even calculators for that matter, man was smarter. We learn from history that children were taught to memorize the entire first five books of the Bible plus the Psalms and Proverbs, and even more. This seems impossible to us today and yet Scripture memorization should be a part of all of our daily routines.[6] When we look at history, we cannot explain the building of the ark, the tower of Babel, the pyramids or many other wonders of the ancient world. Yet from a biblical standpoint, it is easy to explain—man has degenerated from a perfect being, not risen from a cave man. Today it is thought that we use but a fraction of our brain's capacity. Adam, being perfect, had the capacity to use all of his brain, after all, God made no mistakes nor made anything without purpose—no vestigial organs. All His creation was very good![7] As sin took hold and man's memory degenerated

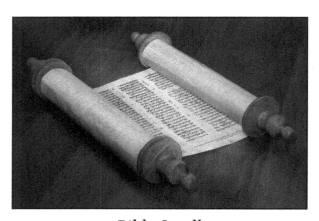

Bible Scrolls

through genetic degradation because of sin, God in His wisdom made provision. We see this provision to compensate man's degenerating state as He writes His law upon tablets of stone and then commands man to write His Word in books to ensure its preservation.[8] God then allowed man to develop the printing press and ultimately digital memory for global disemination of His Word as man's mental abilities degenerated further. Nothing is an accident. God allows and wills all things for His own purposes![9] May we use this expression of God's grace for His own glory!

We see God's providential hand all the way through the history of Science from creation up until the modern era of powerful, pocketsized computers. Humanist textbooks will not tell you that most of the major scientific advances of today are directly attributable to scientists who believed in and worshipped the God of the Bible. Humanists have rewritten history to remove God. They will not tell you that the first message transmitted by Samuel Morse, the inventor of Morse Code, was "What hath God wrought!" Many of the greatest scientists of all time attributed their discoveries to the God of the Bible. Indeed, the Bible gave them the very motivation, foundation and framework in which to inquire. You see if evolution were true, and everything that we see is the result of random chance, then there would be no point doing scientific experiments because without absolutes there would be no guarantee that the result we obtain today would be the same tomorrow. We could not use induc-tion or deduction, in fact, we couldn't use logic at all. If evolution

Samuel Morse

were true, and the universe only contained matter, then logic, which is immaterial, wouldn't exist. Scientists who believed in the God of absolutes expected laws in creation to reflect the absolutes of the God who created them which is why they even attempted experimental science at all. Scientists who believed in the rational God of the Bible believed that His creation would reflect his rationality. They then looked for His laws in nature and of course found them. While atheistic scientists do conduct scientific inquiry, they do so by borrowing from the Christian's assumptions; they are being inconsistent to the assumptions of evolution.

Johannes Gutenberg (c.1398-1468), invented the printing press in 1440. Its first main use was the publication of the world's first Holy Bible! Gutenberg said, "God suffers in the multitude of souls whom His word can not reach. Religious truth is imprisoned in a small number of manuscript books which confine instead of spread the public treasure. Let us break the seal which seals up holy things and give wings to Truth in order that she (truth) may win every soul that comes into the world by her word no longer written at great expense by hands easily palsied, but multiplied like the wind by an untiring machine."

As Gutenberg contemplated the adaptation of his printing press from a wine press, he reflected, "Yes, it is a press, certainly, but a press from which shall flow inexhaustible streams—the most abundant and most marvelous liquor that has ever flowed to relieve the thirst of men. Through it, God will spread His word; a spring of pure truth shall flow from it; like a new star it shall scatter the darkness of ignorance, and cause a light hithertofore unknown to shine among men."[10]

It was no coincidence that the printing press was invented in perfect time for the great reformation which saw the spread of the Word of God and the gospel of the Lord Jesus Christ around the world. Martin Luther's 95 theses were published using the printing presss less than seventy years after the printing of the Gutenberg Bible, making his defense of the Word of God one of the first news stories to be globally disseminated using this new technology.

Johannes Kepler (1571-1630), developed three famous laws of planetary motion.

Kepler did not hide the motivations for his work under a bushel. He understood his discoveries and writings as hymns to his Creator and Redeemer and he often punctuated his writings with prayers and psalms of praise to God as illustrated from The *Harmonice mundi* (The Harmonies of the World), published in 1619.[11]

Kepler wrote, "Great is our Lord and great His virtue and of His wisdom there is no number praise Him, ye heavens, praise Him, ye sun, moon, and planets.

Use every sense for perceiving, every tongue for declaring your Creator.

Johannes Kepler

Praise him, ye celestial harmonies, praise Him, ye judges of the harmonies uncovered … and thou my soul, praise the Lord thy Creator, as long as I shall be: for out of Him and through Him and in Him are all things…"[12]

He said, "God is the *beginning* and *end* of scientific research and striving…"[13]

Galileo Galilei (1564-1642), discovered the laws of falling bodies and of the parabolic path of projectiles. He studied the motions of pendulums, and he investigated mechanics and the strength of materials.

Galileo demonstrating telescope

He said, "God is known … by Nature in His works, and by doctrine in His revealed word."[14]

… the glory and greatness of Almighty God are marvellously discerned in all his works and divinely read in the open book of heaven. For let no one believe that reading the lofty concepts written in that book leads to nothing further than the mere seeing of the splendour of the sun and the stars and their rising and setting, which is as far as the eyes of brutes and of the vulgar can penetrate…[15]

Blaise Pascal

Blaise Pascal (1623-1662), was the founder of Hydrostatics and Hydrodynamics.

Blaise Pascal was a great mathematician after whom the Pascal programming language was named. Pascal made the following profound observation about man's deepest needs, recognizing that without God, all the knowledge in the world cannot satisfy the longing of the human heart.

He said, ""What else does this craving, and this helplessness, proclaim but that there was once in man a true happiness, of which all that now remains is the empty print and trace?

This he tries in vain to fill with everything around him, seeking in things that are not there the help he cannot find. In those that are, though none can help, since this infinite abyss can be filled only with an infinite and immutable object; in other words by God himself."[16]

Gottfried Wilhelm Von Leibniz (1646-1716), invented Binary Mathematics, the foundation of all digital computers. He also invented a binary calculator which was a forerunner of modern computational machines. He was a devout Lutheran who refused opportunistic advancement which would have required him to convert to Roman Catholicism.[17]

Leibniz said, "There must be a sufficient reason [often known only to God] for anything to exist, for any event to occur, for any truth to obtain…"[18]

Leibniz

Leibniz asserted that the truths of theology (religion) and philosophy cannot contradict each other, since reason and faith are both "gifts of God" so that their conflict would imply God contending against himself.[19]

Sir Isaac Newton (1642-1727), is universally ranked as the greatest mathematician of all time. Newton not only did work in mathematics and science; he also wrote volumes of material expositing Bible passages which in volume was comparable to The *Principia*.

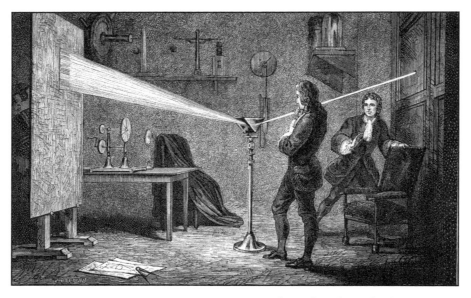

Isaac Newton using prism to break white light into spectrum

In the third edition of *The Principia*, Newton explained the true source of the beautiful system of the universe. He wrote, "The most beautiful system of sun, planets, and comets could only proceed from the counsel and dominion of an intelligent and powerful Being... This Being governs all things, not as the Soul of the world, but as Lord over all; and on account of his dominion he is wont to be called Lord God ..."[20]

Sir Michael Faraday (1791-1867), was the founder of Electronics and Electro-magnetics. Such technology formed the foundation of circuitry and magnetic storage media such as tape and hard disks, both fundamental for modern computers.

He said, "I bow before Him who is Lord of all, and hope to be kept waiting patiently for His time and mode of releasing me according to His Divine Word and the great and precious promises whereby His people are made partakers of the Divine nature."[21]

In one of his sermons (London, 7 July 1861), Sir Michael Faraday said, "And therefore, brethren, we ought to value the privilege of knowing God's truth far beyond anything we can have in this world. The more we see the perfection of God's law fulfilled in Christ, the more we ought to thank God for His unspeakable gift."[22]

Michael Faraday lecturing on electricity and magnetism

Charles Babbage

Charles Babbage (1791 to 1871), was an English mathematician, analytical philosopher, mechanical engineer and the first "computer scientist" who thought of the idea of a programmable computing device.

In 1837, responding to the official eight Bridgewater Treatise "On the Power, Wisdom and Goodness of God, as manifested in the Creation", he published his ninth Bridgewater Treatise putting forward the thesis that God had the omnipotence and foresight to create as a divine legislator, making laws (or programs) which then produced species at the appropriate times, rather than continually interfering with ad hoc miracles each time a new species was required.

George Boole (1815-1864), is the father of Boolean Algebra, upon which digital circuits and digital computer logic are founded. By his teens, Boole had learned Latin, Greek, German, Italian, and French. With these languages, he was able to read a wide variety of Christian theology. Combining his interests in mathematics and theology, he compared the Christian trinity of Father, Son, and Holy Ghost with the three dimensions of space, and was attracted to the Hebrew conception of God as an absolute unity. At the age of 17, he felt the conviction of God to explain how the mind processes thought. He decided to do this

George Boole

in a mathematical form, for the Glory of God. The personal character of Boole inspired all his friends with the deepest esteem. He was marked by true modesty, and his life was given to the single-minded pursuit of truth.[23] On his death bed, Boole repeated Psalm 119:89, "For ever, O LORD, thy word is settled in heaven." For Boole, it "expressed for him the excellence of mathematical truth."[24]

James Maxwell

Sir James Clerk Maxwell (1831-1879), was the founder of Statistical Thermodynamics.

According to the Encyclopaedia Britannica (1997): "James Clerk Maxwell is regarded by most modern physicists as the scientist of the 19th century who had the greatest influence on 20th-century physics; he is ranked with Sir Isaac Newton and Albert Einstein for the fundamental nature of his contributions." Like Sir Isaac Newton, Kepler and Galileo, he was unashamed in his open praise of Almighty God. He wrote, "Almighty God, who hast created man in Thine own image, and made him a living soul that he might seek after Thee and have dominion over Thy creatures, teach us to study the works of Thy hands that we may subdue the earth to our use, and strengthen our reason for Thy service; and so to receive Thy blessed Word, that we may believe on Him whom Thou hast sent to give us the knowledge of salvation and the remission of our sins. All which we ask in the name of the same Jesus Christ our Lord."[25]

Sir John Ambrose Fleming (1849-1945), was the eldest of 7 children born to a Congregational minister.[26]

He was not only a Christian Creationist,[27] but a first-class pioneer in electronics, inventor of the "bridge" and the "thermionic valve" or vacuum tube which were both essential to the development of the field. His thermionic valves made Marconi's radio, the television, and early computers possible. His thermionic valves are still used today in some applications but in many, they have now been superceded by the transistor.

John Fleming

Vacuum tubes and transistors

He said, "The theory of evolution is totally inadequate to explain the origin and manifestation of the inorganic world... Evolution is baseless and quite incredible."[28]

Sir John Ambrose Fleming not only wrote books on electronics, but is the author of *The Evidence of Things Not Seen*[29] and *Evolution or Creation?*[30]

Guglielmo Marconi

Guglielmo Marconi (1874-1937), received the 1909 Nobel Prize in Physics for his invention of the first successful system of wireless telegraphy. Marconi is the inventor of the radio; his revolutionary work made possible the wireless communications of the modern world.

He said, "The more I work with the powers of Nature, the more I feel God's benevolence to man; the closer I am to the great truth that everything is dependent on the Eternal Creator and Sustainer; the more I feel that the so-called science, I am occupied with, is nothing but an expression of the Supreme Will, which aims at bringing people closer to each other in order to help them better understand and improve themselves."[31]

He also said, "I am proud to be a Christian. I believe not only as a Christian, but as a scientist as well. A wireless device can deliver a message through the wilderness. In prayer the human spirit can send invisible waves to eternity, waves that achieve their goal in front of God."[32]

John Von Neumann (1903-1957), *was the computer scientist* largely responsible for the architecture of the first modern computers which bore his name—Von Neuman Architecture. Von Neuman acknowledged the existence of God and understood consciousness of the individual to be non-physical.[33] In the late 1940's Von Neumann studied the theory of self-reproducing automata. He was the first to provide an algorithmic model of a self-reproducing automaton. He proved that in order for an entity to reproduce itself, it is first necessary to resolve four problems:

John Von Neumann

1. To store instructions in a memory.

2. To duplicate these instructions.

3. To implement a factory to read the instructions from the memory and create a new instance of the entity using the instructions stored.

4. To manage all of these functions via a central controler.

A self-reproducing system must contain the *program of its own construction*. What Von Neuman proved, whether he wished to admit it or not, was that self reproduction requires *intelligent design,* not just the material from which to construct the new entity, but the controller and instructions to do it—hardware and software, i.e., a programmed computer.[34] This was later discovered to be exactly what is built into every living cell! Irriduceable complexity means that the something must be created in its entirety and cannot evolve from its constituent components. Von Neumon showed that anything which reproduces itself, required a programmer. Nothing evolved by chance. Trillions of years can not solve the irriduceable complexity problem.

Donald Knuth

Professor Donald Knuth is one of the fathers of modern Computer Science. He is responsible for much of the Computer Science and Software Engineering theory and instructional material taught in universities today. Knuth is the inventor of TeX the typesetting system used to produce much of the world's scientific literature as well as having done a lot of other work in digital typography. Even though Knuth has received numerous awards and recognition for his contribution to computer science, he has also humbly yet boldly proclaimed his faith in God in what is typically a hostile environment, proving as did the other great scientists of the past that science and faith are not at odds but in fact science is built upon faith.[35] True science is built upon God's immutable laws. Indeed any branch of science without the law of God would not be science but random and unpredictable folly.

Dennis Ritchie

Dennis M Ritchie (September 9, 1941–October 12, 2011), was the inventor of the C programming language from which Bjarne Stroustrup created C++. He was also the co-author of the UNIX operating system from which most modern operating systems are derived. His death in 2011 was almost missed by the mainstream media, even though it was within a few days of the death of Steve Jobs, the founder of Apple. Dennis's contribution however dwarfs the contribution of Steve Jobs because everything Jobs invented was built upon Ritchie's work at some level. Ritchie's contribution to programming is as significant as the programmable computer itself. Almost every computer's operating system not to mention almost every hand-held device such as a mobile telephone, is programmed in C or a derivative of C, or is built upon a derivative or cloan of UNIX. Basically all the worlds computers directly or indirectly benefit from Ritchies language and/or operating system. 90% of the world's software is either written in C or a direct descendent. Among many awards, Ritchie received the Turing Award in 1983 for his enormous contribution to the fields of computing and operating systems. The Turing Award is the highest distinction given to anyone for their contribution to Computer Science.

There are indications that Ritchie was a Christian, and though I have not been able to verify this[36], many concur that he was not only brilliant, but humble, gracious and generous, certainly a testimony to the Christian values he espoused and which knowingly or unknowingly undergirded his work.

"… Mr. Ritchie lived a life full of goodness, generosity and love … he spent his life in the Lord's work … Like a true humble Christian, Mr. Ritchie always stayed behind the scenes, taking pride in his work, but never being boastful. He was the true innovator and pioneer …"[37]

Two such stories of his humility come from those who met him in person.

David Madeo wrote, "I met Dennis Ritchie at a Usenix without knowing it. He had traded nametags with someone so I spent 30 minutes thinking "this guy really knows what he's talking about." Eventually, the other guy walked up and said, "I'm tired of dealing with your groupies" and switched the nametags back. I looked back down to realize who he was, the guy who not only wrote the book I used to learn C in freshman year, but invented the language in the first place …"[38]

Tim Pierce wrote, "… not just brilliant, but humble, gracious and generous. I happened to find myself at a reception with him at Usenix many years ago, and cornered him by the drinks table just so I could have a few words with him. I was nobody, just a young geek a few years out of college, and yet he could hardly have been kinder to me. Humble and gracious indeed. I may never have met Steve Jobs, but between you and me, I think I got the better deal."[39]

"As Dennis's siblings, Lynn, John, and Bill Ritchie—on behalf of the entire Ritchie family—we wanted to convey to all of you how deeply moved, astonished, and appreciative we are of the loving tributes to Dennis that we have been reading. We can confirm what we keep hearing again and again: Dennis was an unfailingly kind, sweet, unassuming, and generous brother—and of course a complete geek. He had a hilariously dry sense of humor, and a keen appreciation for life's absurdities—though his world view was entirely devoid of cynicism or mean-spiritedness. We are terribly sad to have lost him, but touched beyond words to realize what a mark he made on the world, and how well his gentle personality—beyond his accomplishments—seems to be understood."[40]

Dr Bjarne Stroustrup

Dr Bjarne Stroustrup (1950-), is the inventer of C++ so it would be remiss of me not to include him in a book on C++. Dr. Stroustrup is a Distinguished Professor and holder of the College of Engineering Chair in Computer Science at Texas A&M University. He has received numerous honours. He did not want to comment on his beliefs, saying in an email to me, "I consider religious views private, and best kept out of scientific and engineering matters."[41] This is in stark contrast to Newton, Kepler, Galileo, Faraday and others who openly professed their faith, as we have seen.

It is clear however that like Ritchie and many other scientists, he has been influenced by Christian values, saying in another email, "… being able to help people do good is one of the main things that keeps me going with C++ …"[42]

This is the fruit of unbelievers living in a culture shaped by Christianity. They desire to do "good" without acknowledging that the "good" that they like to do comes from the God of "goodness" who created us in His image; and with a conscience which knows "good" and "evil." (Atheism cannot invent good and evil, since both good and evil are immaterial, and an atheist's world only consists of matter they can see and touch. They also have no absolute standard by which to define such terms.) This is a reminder that while salt and light may not always bring about conversion to Christ, it does still produce valuable fruit in a culture.

Dr Stroustrup, like Ritchie, is very humble in light of his incredible accomplishments and I am extremely grateful that he even took the time to respond to my email.

Professor David Powers is a pioneer in the area of Natural Language Learning at the Flinders University of South Australia. As a computer scientist, his focus is to research ways to get a computer to learn natural language like a baby. He invented the fastest known PRAM (Parallel Random Access Memory) sorting algorithm as well as having lead extensive research into Natural Language Learning by machines.

David Powers

"I did the SIL/Wycliffe training course for how to be a Bible translator and my whole research career is focussed around getting a computer to be able to learn in a way similar to the way we were taught there, largely inspired by and based on the work of (Christian and founder of Tagmenics) Ken Pike as well as Jean Piaget (Christian and founder of Psycholinguistics) ... Imagine taking your laptop to deepest darkest Africa, opening it up and letting it with its webcam start monitoring, learning and understanding the village language, including developing dictionaries, grammars and an orthography (writing system), literacy materials and a first draft of a Bible translation ... My current research has the computer/talking/thinking/teaching head both learning and teaching languages (including English, German and Mandarin at the moment) as well as providing other kinds of assistive technology ..."[43]

Like many other scientists, explorers and inventors, Dr Powers' motivation is rooted in his faith in the God of the Bible, and a vision to see science applied to the furtherance of the gospel of the Lord Jesus Christ. He also exemplifies multigenerational faithfulness, being the son of B. Ward Powers, theologian, Dean, and board member of Tyndale College, New South Wales, Australia.

All of the scientists and inventors above were used of God to bring modern science (minus the devolution of evolution) to where it is today. While I do not necessarily endorse the doctrinal positions of some of these men, nevertheless, they were honest enough to see that without God, science would not make sense. I do not claim that every man who contributed to and ultimately realized the development of modern computers or programming languages were God-fearing, I do claim that these men stood upon the shoulders of the ones who were, just as the godless society of today reaps the benefits of the God-fearing generations which preceded them.

If there is one lesson I'd like readers to learn from this book on Computer Programming, it is this: No amount of random typing on a computer keyboard for any length of time, whether billions or trillions of years will ever produce software which does anything meaningful.

Just as most of the scientists and inventors above acknowledged the God of the Bible as the creator and sustainer of all, I hope this book makes it abundantly clear that everything has a designer and must be crafted with thoughtful design for it to be of any use. As you embark on a journey of learning, you will come face-to-face with the reality of man's fallibility.

Though computers were theoretically designed to execute tasks without error—the computer executing your errors with lightning speed and accuracy—you'll see that in developing software, You will realize your own limitations as you battle with the problem of debugging your code in order to make it work as you expect. As you begin on your journey of programming, may you have a deeper appreciation of the creator of everything in the universe who made everything perfect first time. As you begin to design and craft solutions to problems, may you grow in gratitude and faith in the person, work and Word of the Lord Jesus Christ, the *Perfect Programmer.*

Jude 1:25, "To the only wise God our Saviour, be glory and majesty, dominion and power, both now and ever. Amen."

Questions to Introduction:

1. Why were there no computers mentioned in the book of Genesis?

2. Why did God tell man to write words down after the fall?

3. If there is no God of absolutes, why is experimental science impossible?

4. What do logic, love, kindness and faithfulness have in common?

5. Can evolution explain such things as logic, love, kindness or faithfulness?

6. Evolution claims that non-living matter became living matter able to reproduce itself, why is this impossible?

7. How many years would it take a monkey to write a functioning computer program to print out the 23rd Psalm on the computer's screen? (I do not expect most students to know how to calculate this, but do want them to think about the likelihood of it occurring in terms such as certain, probable, possible, impossible, crazy, etc. See answers for a detailed solution to this problem.)

8. What did many of the world's greatest scientists have in common?

9. Science and faith are not incompatible but science is_____upon faith, either the faith in the theory of evolution or faith in the absolutes of the God of the Bible.

10. Why did God allow the printing press to be invented when it was, and what was its first main use?

Lesson 1

An Introduction to Computers

Vocabulary:

computer, input, output, data, processor, storage, memory, keyboard, monitor, peripheral.

Memory Verse:

Colossians 3:20, "Children, obey your parents in all things: for this is well pleasing unto the Lord."

Computers are a major part of our life today. Almost all modern electronic devices contain some kind of computing device. In its most simple form, a computer is a device which can follow instructions coded in a special language which the device can understand. A computer program is a recipe which defines a set of steps required to accomplish a task. The computer, however, is more than the electronics which do the calculations; it must be able to receive information containing the instructions and then communicate the results of following the instructions back to us in a form we can understand.

Classic shot of ENIAC

1

The first man-made computers were gigantic machines which took up entire rooms and even buildings. These huge machines were far less powerful than even the simplest modern calculator and only had a few pages worth of memory. Today, a memory card the size of your fingernail can hold as much information as the text in sixteen thousand Bibles. A mobile phone with a built-in camera can run special software to take a photo of printed text, interpret that text and read it back in a human-like voice. A mobile phone with a built-in GPS (Global Positioning System) receiver can also run software, which can tell you how to get from your home to a location across the country, instructing you when to turn and which roads to take. It can even tell you what shops you are passing along the way. Computers are indeed amazing, but even more amazing is the God who designed us humans and gave us the ability to design and build such devices.

God made you to be able to follow instructions. He gave you parents to instruct you. You are far more amazing than any computer because you can learn wisdom. Wisdom is the right use of knowledge. Wisdom is the ability to make right choices when faced with many decisions. It is easy to receive and learn knowledge, but only through the fear of the Lord can you also learn wisdom.[44]

Your memory is also far more vast than even the most powerful computer. When you, for example, follow a recipe to bake bread, you are reading information (through your eyes), interpreting the instructions (understanding the names of ingredients and measures), following the instructions (executing the instructions) and yielding a result.

Input is the process of gathering information. We have five inputs, the five senses, touch, taste, smell, sight and hearing. Actually, our sixth sense is our conscience, which God has given us to know right from wrong. A computer also has inputs; typically a home computer has a keyboard, microphone, mouse, perhaps a scanner and camera.

Output is the means of communicating information to others. We have at least two outputs, our voice and our facial expressions. A home computer typically has a monitor (screen), printer and speakers.

Our brain is our processor; the part that makes sense of information entering our inputs. It is what allows us to understand what we hear and see. The computer's processor, called a Central Processing Unit (or CPU) is the device that processes the information coming from the inputs, and sends the results to the outputs. Our brain also contains storage for later recollection of data.

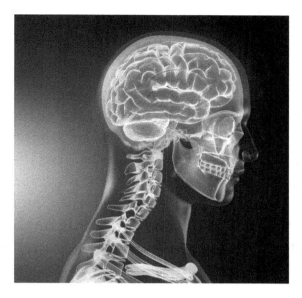

Brain   CPU Close up

Data is simply information. For example, when you read words on a page or hear words spoken to you by your parents, data is entering your inputs. Similarly, typing on the keyboard, speaking into the microphone or moving and clicking the mouse is sending data to the computer that is processed by the currently running program.

Just as we have short term memory and long term memory, a computer has memory for short term recall and permanent storage for longer term safekeeping. Short term memory for a computer remains only while the power to the computer remains connected and the power switch left on. This is called RAM (Random Access Memory). We'll talk about the meaning of this in Lesson 2. Permanent storage is where information is maintained even when the power is disconnected or the switch is turned off. This storage is usually in the form of a CDROM, Hard disk, Flash Memory or even printed text. We'll look at the different kinds of storage in Lesson 2.

Memory Chip

A peripheral is simply any other general device attached to your computer system such as a camera, printer, scanner, etc.

Activity:

Instruct a blindfolded person how to walk across the room and sit on a chair. In the middle of the room is a table. Between the table and the chair is a toy truck left by your baby brother. On the table is a glass bowl. You need to give instructions to cross the room, going around the table and around the truck to a chair. You do not want the blindfolded person to slip on the truck or trip over the table and break the glass bowl. You also do not want the blindfolded person to sit on someone else's lap who is sitting on the chair next to the vacant one you must direct them to. Write down a list of instructions that you might give this person, for example, walk forward so many steps, turn right, etc. With your parent's permission, set up your living room (without the breakable glass bowl) and Practise reading your instructions to a blindfolded sibling, and see how well you can give accurate instructions, and how accurately the sibling can follow them.

Lesson 2

Memory and Storage - Everything has a Home

Vocabulary:

Address, random access, sequential access, byte, kilobyte, megabyte, gigabyte, terabyte.

Memory Verse:

1 Corinthians 14:33a, "For God is not the author of confusion…"

God is a God of order, not confusion. Imagine each time you went out for a walk if you decided that today you'd return to your neighbour's house instead of returning to your own address. One of the first things you probably get taught as a little child is to put things away in their correct place. Imagine the confusion a library would be in if books were not ordered and catalogued! How would you know which books you had or where they were? So too, order is extremely important when it comes to memory and storage used for keeping data which must be processed by a CPU.

Memory is the ability to remember information. A computer has two kinds of memory, RAM (Random Access Memory) and permanent storage. RAM is memory that is only maintained while the power is connected and stored in silicon chips, which contain millions of tiny electronic components called transistors. RAM by itself would be pretty useless, since each time you turned the computer on you'd have to somehow remind it what you were working on previously. Hard disks, CDROMs, Flash Memory sticks or cards, tapes and other devices are used for permanent storage. They store information that is not lost when the power is disconnected.

CD   Floppy disk   Hard disk   inside computer

The simplest way to imagine how a computer's memory works is to think of a very tall skyscraper. Each floor can hold exactly the same amount of information. In your home computer, there may be up to 4,000,000,000 floors. Each floor can hold exactly one value. That value may be a letter, number or a fragment of a picture, sound, video, etc. Each floor is said to have an address. For instance, the word "hello" would be stored on five floors, say from address 1 through 5 of your computer's memory. In order to display this word on your screen, instructions would read each address and copy the value to the device, which displays the visible characters on your screen or monitor.

Memory is not just used for text though, the instructions themselves also must be stored on floors. A special address inside the CPU is used to keep track of which memory address needs to be read from or written to, much like an elevator services the floors of a giant skyscraper. Imagine a postman delivering mail to people living on different floors. He must know who lives at what address in order to deliver the right mail to the right person.

We said that the computer's memory was called Random Access Memory. This simply means that using the address in the CPU, any address in the main memory can be accessed in any order. Some storage devices like tapes are said to be sequential access. This means that rather than being able to access any address in any order, the information on the tape must be read from first address to last address in the same order. In other words, you can't just read the last address, then an address in the middle and then the first address. You must read the first address, then the second, then the third, etc. Imagine walking down your street giving out gospel tracts. You can't go from house 2 to house 10 without passing by house 4, 6 and 8 first, this is sequential access.

You may have heard of some common words describing memory including kilobyte, megabyte, gigabyte, terabyte etc. A value such as a letter of the alphabet or a small number (less than 128) is one byte. A thousand bytes is a kilobyte, a thousand kilobytes is a megabyte, a thousand megabytes is a gigabyte and a thousand gigabytes is a terabyte. (What a mouthful; let's not byte [I mean bite] off more than we can chew right now.)

You may wonder why we need RAM and why we can't just use permanent storage directly. The main reason is that permanent storage is much, much, much slower to access than RAM which would slow the whole processing time down thousands of times. Hard disks are getting faster but they are still thousands of times slower than RAM. CDROMs are slower again. It is thus much faster to read a large amount of data into the computer's RAM and allow the computer to process that data in RAM. Once the data has been modified, the whole lot is then written out to the permanent storage, which is again a much slower process.

Activity:

1. With your supervisor's permission, order your bookshelf in alphabetical order. Imagine that each book's location takes up one address. With the leftmost book taking up address 0, work out how many addresses your entire shelf contains. What is the address of the last book on your shelf.

2. Ask your sibling or parent to retrieve the book from the fifth address. (Remember, the first book is address 0, so the book retrieved should have been in address 4). Was the book retrieved the book you expected?

3. What happens if the book is wrongly placed back in the shelf and you go to retrieve the book from its expected location:

    a. If the book was inserted before its correct address?

    b. If it was inserted after its correct address?

    Will you get the right book? If not, is it possible to tell which one you will get? (Knowing this may one day help you debug an errant program by investigating the content of consecutive memory addresses.)

4. What is the difference between Random Access Memory and sequential access memory?

Lesson 3

Instructions, Instructions

Vocabulary:

instruction, compiler, machine code, divide and conquer, high level, programming language.

Memory Verse:

Proverbs 6:23, "For the commandment is a lamp; and the law is light; and reproofs of instruction are the way of life:"

Have you ever thought about how you are able to follow instructions? When your father tells you to take out the rubbish, your ears hear the instruction, your brain translates the instruction into hundreds more instructions, which are individually sent to muscles to tie the rubbish bag, open the door, walk through the door and close it behind you, walk to the bin, lift the lid, place the bag inside the bin, shut the bin lid, walk back to the house, open the door, walk through the door and close it behind you, replace the bin liner, wash your hands etc. You do not think of each individual instruction that made up the completed task, nor did you think about each muscle you needed to exercise in order to obey the instruction. At some point, however, you were trained or programmed to know that "take out the rubbish" meant all of the actions you just performed. Without this training, the instruction would have been meaningless to you.

Today, computers are programmed by writing a series of instructions in a human readable language, called a high level computer programming language. A programming language is called high level because that language must then be translated into a much simpler language with far more numerous and specific instructions, which the CPU can interpret, known as machine code. Just as your finger doesn't understand the command to open the door, that command has to be translated into electrical pulses that cause your muscles to react, so too the CPU cannot understand English, and thus the language we write the instructions in must be translated into the simpler instructions, which the CPU can follow. Also, just as your father doesn't give the hundreds of instructions to do each part of the task to take out the rubbish, that would be too time consuming, we too generally do not program the computer in the CPU's native instructions because they are too numerous. Instead, we use a special tool which translates the human like instructions into the far more numerous instructions required for the CPU to execute (or perform). This tool is called a language compiler.

Let's look at a simple example. I want the computer to print "hello." I might program this as follows:

```
Printf ("hello");
```

Don't worry about the parentheses, quotes and semicolon, we'll explain that later. For now, just think of the way we write English, we use grammar rules and punctuation (syntax), and words with meaning (semantics). PrintF happens to be a C and C++ command to print formatted information to the screen. In other languages such as BASIC, the command might be print("hello.")

Of course the CPU can't understand this and so we would use our special language compiler which might translate this as follows (again, this is an example only, a real translator would use loops and other optimizations to reduce the repetition):

read data address 1

write screen address 1

read data address 2

write screen address 2

read data address 3

write screen address 3

read data address 4

write screen address 4

read data address 5

write screen address 5

return

You can see that our English-like instructions are much easier to read and write for us humans.

Just as there are many languages spoken by humans today, many human-like languages have been developed to program computers. We will look at one main language throughout this course, one of the most popular and powerful languages, C++. One difference between human languages and programming languages is that programming languages must be much more precise. Think of the following question:

"Where did you hurt your leg?"

This could mean,

"Where were you when you injured your leg?"

or

"Which part of your leg did you injure?"

A programming language statement must always have the same meaning; it can't be ambiguous.

The key to programming a computer lies in the skill of being able to break down a large task into smaller, more manageable tasks, each of which can be expressed in the programming language you are using. This process of dividing a task up into smaller tasks, and then recombining the smaller tasks is known as divide and conquer. The Divide and Conquer principle was first described in the scriptures in Genesis 2:18 where God gave a helper to Adam, his wife, to help him with his dominion mandate described in Genesis 1:28. Man's role was in the leadership of his home, discipling of his children, providing and protecting his family, and also often contributing to the leadership of the community. The wife's role was to keep the home, nurture the young children and help her husband in his dominion work.[45]

Activity:

1. Think of a task you do regularly like brushing your teeth or making your bed. Write down all of the steps you need to do in order to complete that task.

2. Look at your list and see if any of the instructions can be misinterpreted. Give it to a sibling or parent to read, and see if they can find any statement that could be wrongly executed, i.e. ambiguous.

3. Why don't we usually program a computer in the native language of the CPU?

4. What is the name of one kind of tool which translates the English-like instructions into machine code understood by the CPU?

5. What does divide and conquer mean in the context of programming?

6. Who first presented the Divide and Conquer concept to the world?

Review of Lessons 1 through 3

1. What is a computer?

2. What is memory?

3. What are the two kinds of memory?

4. What is each slot or memory location called?

5. Why do we need both kinds of memory?

6. Define the following terms:

   a. byte

   b. kilobyte

   c. megabyte

   d. gigabyte

7. What is data?

8. What is the process of getting data into a computer called?

9. What is the process of getting the results out of a computer called?

10. What is the tool called that translates English-like programming languages into the native language understood by the CPU?

11. Why do we need English-like programming languages, rather than just writing our programs directly in the native language understood by the CPU?

12. What important skill is required in order to program a computer (hint, d_____ and c_____)?

13. Think of a task you do frequently such as pouring a drink, and write down the subtasks involved in this task.

14. A programming statement must always have the same m_____.

15. What is wrong with the following English statement: "The lion ate off the boy's hand."

16. God is a God of _____. Why is _____ important in a library. Why do you think _____ is so important when programming a computer?

17. What two things does a computer's memory hold? (Hint: i_____ and d____.)

18. Name as many input devices as you can think of.

19. Name as many output devices as you can think of.

20. Who invented the world's most powerful computer and when was it invented?

Intro to Programming Language Constructs 1 – Syntax, Statements, Execution, Loops, Branches

Vocabulary:

syntax, grammar, statement, execution, sequential, flow, loop, iteration, branch

Memory Verse:

Proverbs 3:19, "The LORD by wisdom hath founded the earth; by understanding hath he established the heavens."

Every language has rules of grammar that define how it is to be understood. The grammar of a language is also called its syntax. Computer programming languages are no exception. In this lesson, rather than learning the specifics of a particular programming language, we will look at some introductory constructs that are applicable to most programming languages you may come across.

When your mother follows a recipe method, it is usually important that the sequence of steps given is followed in the order they are written. For example, she couldn't roll the dough into biscuits before the dough had been prepared to the right consistency. She must preheat the oven prior to mixing the ingredients or there will be an unwanted delay whilst the oven reaches its correct cooking temperature. She must mix all of the dry ingredients before adding the wet ones. This sequence of steps in programming terms is called the "flow of execution." This simply means, the order in which instructions are followed. We read a recipe from top to bottom, left to right on the page, so too, a computer usually executes its instructions from start to end.

Let's look at a simple example. I want to write a program that asks the user of the computer for a number, and then print that number multiplied by 10. Here are the instructions (in English):

1. Ask user for a number.

2. Multiply that number by 10.

3. Print the result on the screen.

The computer must follow this sequence of instructions in order. The flow of execution is instruction 1, instruction 2, instruction 3. The flow of execution is said to be sequential because the instructions are followed in sequence, or, one after the other, none are skipped. Each complete instruction and its associated data is called a statement. A statement is made up of keywords, function calls, data and punctuation. A keyword is a word with a specific meaning, which the compiler can translate into machine code instructions. The punctuation helps the compiler to understand each statement by indicating the end of the statement or clarifying which part of the statement should be translated or calculated first.

Suppose now that we want to ask the user if they would like to type another number so that we can multiply that number by 10 also. We will need to stop if the user doesn't wish to type another number. The instructions, or statements, might be written as follows:

1. Ask user for a number.

2. Multiply that number by 10.

3. Print the result on the screen.

4. Ask user if they want to type another number.

5. if the user types yes, then go to 1.

6. otherwise, stop.

Now, the flow of execution has two possible paths. It can stop at 6 if the user types no or it can go back to 1 and start again. If the execution goes back to 1, this is called a loop. A loop means that one or more instructions must be repeated. In this case instructions 1 through 4 are repeated.

Each time a loop body is executed is known as an iteration.

Instruction 5 is also a branch; there are two possibilities, go back to 1 or go to 6. What do you think would happen if statement 5 simply said, "go to 1"? If you said, "never stop," you'd be right. This is called an infinite loop, and is one very common and nasty error programmers make while writing programs. This means the loop would keep executing forever until the programmer somehow forceably stopped the execution.

Activity:

1. Think of a task which you must repeatedly do, and write down the instructions in the form of a loop. For example, when you brush your teeth, you must move the toothbrush up and down a certain number of times. Can you think of how you might add instructions to set the number of times the loop runs (iterations)? We will look at controlled loops in our next lesson.

2. Write a list of instructions that asks the user for a temperature, and then prints one of the following results: If the temperature entered is 0, print freezing! If the temperature is between 1 and 15 print cold; if it is 16 to 27 print warm and if it is 28 to 40 print hot. Use English like instructions in a similar manner to our example above with branches to handle each temperature range. Hint: at the end of each branch you may need instructions to skip the other branches and go straight to the end.

3. Extend your answer in 2 to add the ability to ask the user if they wish to enter another temperature and if they answer yes, loop back to the beginning or if no, stop.

Intro to Programming Language Constructs 2 – Loops Continued, Comments, Variables

Vocabulary:

do, while, comment, declare, variable, assignment.

Memory Verse:

Psalms 90:2, "Before the mountains were brought forth, or ever thou hadst formed the earth and the world, even from everlasting to everlasting, thou art God."

In our last lesson, we introduced sequential execution, following instructions one after the other, and loops, iterating or repeating a sequence of instructions over and over again. In practice, we need to have more control over the execution of instructions. In this lesson we will introduce the controlled loop.

In your prior activity, we asked if you could think of a way of controlling how many times a loop ran. The answer is the controlled loop. An example follows:

1. start counter at 1.
2. do something.
3. add 1 to the counter.
4. if counter equals 5 then go to 6.
5. go to 2.
6. stop.

Trace through this code by pointing at each instruction and thinking about what it is doing.

Set counter to 1.

Do something.

Add 1 to the counter, now counter equals 2.

The counter doesn't equal 5, so go back to 2 and do something, and then add 1 to the counter. Now the counter equals 3. It is still not equal to 5, so go back and do something again and add 1 again. Now the counter is 4. It is still not 5, so go back and do something again and add 1 again. Now the counter is 5, so stop. You have just executed the "something" 5 times.

Another form of a controlled loop is known as a *while* loop. The idea is that while a given condition is true, execute the instructions in the loop.

An example:

while condition statement.

let counter start at 1

while counter does not equal 5

　　do something

　　add 1 to counter.

end of while block

This should be read: Starting at 1, while the counter is not 5, do something and add one to the counter.

another form of the while statement is

do statement while condition.

e.g.

do

add one to counter

while counter less than 10.

The difference is that the former checks the condition before executing the statement (or block of statements), whereas the second executes the statement (or block of statements) and then checks the condition. Thus, the former may never execute the statement at all, whereas the latter is guaranteed to execute the statement at least once.

In real programming languages, these constructs are even simpler. For example, in C++ the first type of loop can be written:

```
for (int n=1; n <=5; n++)
{
    cout << "The counter is" << n << "." << endl;
}
```

This says, let n be an integer and set it to 1. While n is less than or equal to 5, execute what is in the {}, and then add one to n. The statement within the {} is called the body of the loop. Don't worry too much about how it looks; basically it prints the following output to the console (display) of the computer:

The counter is 1.

The counter is 2.

The counter is 3.

The counter is 4.

The counter is 5.

The "++" after the letter n in the loop declaration means add one to n, i.e. n++ is equivalent to n=n+1; you take what is in n, add one to it and store it back in n. You guessed it, n—- is the opposite, i.e. n=n-1 or take what is in n, subtract one from it and store it back in n.

Notice that once the counter gets to 6, the test condition at the top of the loop (n <=5) is now false, which is why the loop stops. The C++ while loop could be written like this:

```
int n=1;
while (n <= 5)
{
    cout << "The counter is" << n << "." << endl; /* display the
    output */
    n++; // Add 1 to the counter.
}
```

Note the // after the statement on some of the lines. This simply means that what follows (to the end of the line) should be ignored by the compiler, because it is for us humans to read. It is called a program comment and is to clarify the meaning of the computer program instructions for someone who may need to understand an unfamiliar computer program. Normally, the comments would not restate what the instructions are doing, since the instructions would be clear enough to a programmer used to programming in C++. However, the comments would be used to clarify a set of instructions whose meaning is unclear.

If you want to write a longer comment, you can also enclose a paragraph within /* and */ as follows:

```
/* This is all a comment and ignored by the compiler. It is only here
for humans to read. It is a long comment to demonstrate the method of
writing a longer comment. In this case the comment finishes at the final
star slash, below.
*/
```

Every C++ statement must be terminated by a semicolon ";". The {} surround a sequence of statements, grouping them into a block of statements, which must be kept together. In the example above, the {} mark the statements that are repeated by the loop (the loop body).

Another programming construct snuck in during the last two lessons was the assignment operator "=".

The C++ statement:

```
x=5;
```

means that the letter x has been assigned a value of 5. In programming terms, x is a variable that can hold any value. (It is like putting something into the correct sized box.) In most modern languages, the value must be of a particular data type; if x is defined as an integer then it can hold only an integer value. Other kinds of variable types include characters (alphabetic, numeric, punctuation symbols etc.), strings of letters, dates, times, decimal values, etc. Don't worry too much what an integer is. Simply put, it is a whole number; a variable declared as an integer can't hold a number of the form 2.5 or 3.9. It can only hold a whole number, e.g. 3, 4, 5000, ... We'll deal more with data types in Lesson 9. Put simply, you can't put a round peg in a square hole or vice versa.

Before a variable can be used for the first time, in many languages, it must first be declared. This simply means that you need to tell the compiler what data type this variable is to hold. You saw in the above example:

```
int x=1;
```

This declares x to be an integer whose initial value is set to 1. It is good practise to always set variables to an initial value when they are declared. Some languages do not enforce variable initialization. If you do not initialize a variable in some languages, it might have a random value assigned to it (whatever happens to be at the memory address used for that variable), which means that when your code is executed, the results will be unpredictable.

Put simply, x is a box that can hold a value. In lesson two, we learned about the computer's memory being divided into addresses. A variable in real terms is a memory address used to hold a value, or the starting address of a series of addresses used to hold a value (in the case of strings, arrays, or data types requiring more than a single address). We, however, refer to this address by a useful name as it makes our computer program easier to read. Just like when your friend visits you, he might say, "I'm going to Joseph's house" rather than saying, "I'm going to 27 Fred Street, Newtown". The name "Joseph's house" is more understandable to those familiar with this person than stating his address. Note that the enforcement of the correct data being stored in the correct variable type is enforced by the compiler. The raw computer's memory has no concept of integers, characters or anything else; raw memory addresses hold a binary value (a bunch of 1s and 0s). The exact number of 1s and 0s depends on the architecture of the computer. Your home PC's memory address is typically 32 or 64 bits wide. A single 32-bit address can hold a number with maximum value 2147483648. To hold a larger number, multiple addresses must be combined together.

For example:

int x=1; // x is an integer variable which is initially set to the value 1.

x=x+1; /* now x holds 2, therefore, we take what is in x and add 1 to it, and then store that value back in x. */

x=x+1; // now x will be three.

x=x*x; /* now x will be 9, the * symbol is used by most programming languages to mean multiply. */

Note that the "equals sign" is being used to assign a value to x, and is not the same as the equality operator ==, meaning, x does not equal x+1. We'll learn about the equality operator == in a later lesson.

The variable x might be stored at address 5000 in the computer's RAM. But the compiler takes care of the detail. Usually we name variables something meaningful which helps us understand the purpose of the variable.

Activity:

1. Describe in English sentences what the following program code does:

```
int i=1;
int j=0;
while (i <=5)
{
        j=(j+i);
        i++;

}
```

2. What does j equal after the code has finished executing?

3. Read the below code and calculate the value of totalChildren.

```
int totalChildren=0;
int myChildren=7;
int yourChildren=5;
int hisChildren=8;
totalChildren=yourChildren+myChildren+hisChildren;
```

4. What does the * symbol mean in most programming languages when placed between two numbers or variables holding numbers?

5. Consider the following code fragment:

```
int n=2;
while (n < 50)
{
        n=n*n;
}
```

    a. Write down the values of n after each time the body of the loop is executed.

    b. How many times will the body of the loop be run?

    c. What will the value of n be at the end.

6. Write a loop construct that calculates the 7 times tables. (Hint: each time through the loop, the value of a variable must be multiplied by the loop counter.) Use similar syntax to question 5.

7. What is the difference between the

        do {statements} while (condition)

    and

    while (condition) {statements}

    forms of the while loop?

Intro to Programming Language Constructs 3 – Conditional Branches, Functions, Naming Convention, Logical Operators

Vocabulary:

if then else, switch, case, default, function, return value, Hungarian Notation, argument, parameter, logical operator, and, or, not.

Memory Verse:

Joshua 24:15, "And if it seem evil unto you to serve the LORD, choose you this day whom ye will serve; whether the gods which your fathers served that were on the other side of the flood, or the gods of the Amorites, in whose land ye dwell: but as for me and my house, we will serve the LORD."

We have briefly discussed how program flow can be controlled using a loop construct of some sort. It repeats a set of instructions until some condition becomes true. In this lesson we will look at some other constructs, which allow us to change the flow of execution in a program.

One of the most common constructs is known as the "if ... then ... else" construct. It is used like this:

if something is true then

    do something.

else

    do something different

In some languages such as C++, the word "then" is omitted.

The condition may also be a set of conditions linked together such as:

if (condition or condition2) then

or

if (condition1 and condition2) then

Here is an example code fragment written in the programming language C++:

```
BOOL bPassWordMatches=GetUserPassword();
if (bPassWordMatches)
{
    cout << "You are permitted to run this program." << endl;
    // print a message to the console
    DoMainTask();
}
else
{
    cout << "Your password is incorrect. The program will now exit."
        << endl;
}
cout << "Program exiting" << endl;
```

1. This program declares a variable called bPassWordMatches to be a boolean variable; it can either have the value TRUE or FALSE. It is preceded by a b, so that we can easily tell later in the program that the variable is a boolean variable. The rest of the variable's name tells us its purpose; it holds a value that indicates if the user entered the correct password or not. Remember, variable names are completely arbitrary as long as they don't conflict with a built-in language keyword (such as if, else, return, etc.). Of course, as already mentioned, variable names should be clearly chosen to reflect their usage and purpose in the program. The practise of preceding the meaningful part of the variable name by a letter or group of letters to indicate the scope and type of the variable is known as Hungarian Notation (see Appendix 8).

2. The program calls a function, GetUserPassword. If the user enters the correct password, the function will return true, if they enter a different password, the function returns false. The result of the function is assigned to the variable. You can tell that GetUserPassword is a function name by the () following it. This is how you can tell the difference between a function name and a variable name in C++. The detail of the function is not listed, but from its name you can tell that its purpose is to ask the user to enter a password and, depending on whether the password is correct or not, returns a TRUE or FALSE value. A function is simply a named set of instructions to calculate or perform some task and returns (passes back) a result to the caller of the function. Again, like variables, we give functions human readable names, but they are really just stored in the computer's memory like any other sequence of instructions. The compiler hides this detail from us as we really don't

need to know the underlying details. The process of hiding unnecessary details is called information hiding or abstraction.

3. The if ... then ... else construct is executed. This simply says, if the value of the bPasswordMatches variable is TRUE then print the message to tell the user that they are permitted to run the program. Then the main task is run after which Execution then jumps to the instruction printing the exit message. Note again the function calls to print the various messages. We'll look closer at the cout statement in chapter 10, Simple Input and Output.

4. If the user didn't enter the correct password and the value of the bPasswordMatches variable was FALSE, execution would instead jump to the statement after the "else," which prints the error message and then the program exit message.

It is always a good rule to keep the conditions as easy to understand as possible so if multiple conditions are needing to be tested, put them in a separate function and just test the function's result. For example:

```
bool ComplexTest()
{
      return condition1 && (condition2 || condition3);
}

if (ComplextTest())
      DoSomething();
```

Note the "&&" and the "||". "&&" is the C++ "and" logical operator and the "||" is the c++ logical "or" operator. Another logical operator, "Not," may also be used to negate the test. The ComplextTest function says that if condition 1 is true and either condition 2 or condition 3 are also true, then return true, otherwise return false.

If we wanted to test if ComplexTest() was false, we could have written:

```
if (!ComplextTest())
      DoSomething();
```

The exclamation mark is the C++ "not" operator. The test above says that if the ComplextTest function returns false, then do something.

Also note the abbreviated condition, we did not write, if (ComplexTest()==true) we simply wrote if (ComplextTest()). This is the same thing, since the condition evaluates to a true or false result.

if ... then ... else statements are useful for a small set of choices, and though they can be nested to make more complex constructs for handling more choices, a more efficient and easily understood construct for more than a couple of choices is the switch statement. Again, this is specific to the C and C++ languages but other languages have an equivalent construct for handling multiple choices:

Consider the below example:

```
cout << "Enter your age and press Enter:";
int nAge=0;
cin >> nAge; /* wait for the user to type a number followed by
        the Enter key. */
switch (nAge)
{
    case 0:
        cout << "Newborn: Children are a blessing from the Lord
            (Ps 127:3-5" << endl;
        break;
    case 2:
        cout << "Toddlers are very cute! The Lord Jesus carried
            young children in His arms (Mark 9:36)." << endl;
        break;
    case 3:
        cout << "Samuel was probably between 3 and 5 when he was
            taken to Eli to serve the Lord (1 Sam 1:24)." <<
            endl;
        break;
    case 12:
        cout << "The Lord Jesus was a responsible 12 year old and
            was known for his growth in wisdom, He is our
            example (Luke 2:42-52)." << endl;
        break;
    default:
        cout << "So teach us to number our days and apply our hearts
            unto wisdom (Psalm 90:12)." << endl;
        break;
}
```

What do you think happens if the user entered the following ages? 0, 1, 2, 3, 4, 5, 11 and 12?

For ages 0, 2, 3 and 12, a specific message for that age is printed. For all other values, the default branch of the switch statement is executed. The break statement tells the program to continue execution after the closing brace "}" of the switch statement, i.e., to break out of the switch statement. Unlike the if ... then ... else statement where the choice is either or, the switch statement may optionally still execute subsequent instructions in the list. Remember to put a break statement after each choice's instructions to prevent the following case statement from being executed.

As mentioned above, a function is a named set of instructions. Many useful functions have already been defined in libraries that are distributed with the compiler, so you won't have to write code to do many common tasks (see Appendix 9).

In order to pass information to a function so it can perform its calculation, you will often pass a parameter or argument into a function. The argument or parameter (or list of parameters) go between the () in the function call. Consider the following program fragment:

```
int Max(int a, int b)
{
    if (a > b)
        return a;
    else
        return b;
}

void Test()
{
    int x=0;
    int y=0;
    cout << "Enter first number: ";
    cin >> x;
    cout << "Enter second number: ";
    cin >> y;
    cout << "The maximum of " << x << " and " << y << " is "
        << Max(x,y) << endl;
}
```

The max function takes two arguments or parameters. the list of parameters in the function definition (in this case "a" and "b") are called Formal parameters whereas the parameters actually passed to the function when it is called from the Test procedure (in our case "x" and "y") are called the Actual parameters. We'll learn more about parameters in Lesson 11. Our Max function returns an int (the maximum of its two Formal parameters). An int is simply an integer, i.e. a positive or negative whole number. See Lesson 9 for an introduction to data types.

Activity:

1. What is a function?

2. Describe in a paragraph what the following program does. (Don't worry about the bits you haven't seen before such as the word "void" or "int" before the function names. They simply tell us what kind of data type the function returns, see Lesson 9.)

Start by looking at the main function; this is where execution always begins. Though we haven't looked at input and output yet (see Lesson 10), cin waits for the user to enter input at the keyboard, followed by the Enter key and cout prints a message to the screen (or console as it is also known).

```cpp
/* Include some other headers necessary to make this a real working
program. */
#include "stdafx.h"
#include <iostream>
using namespace std; /* allow us to access the standard C++ library
called std. */

void CalcPerimeter()
{
    int nWidth=0;
    int nLength=0;
    cout << "Enter width: ";
    cin >> nWidth;
    cout << "Enter length: ";
    cin >> nLength;
    int nPerimeter=2*nWidth + 2*nLength;
    cout << "The perimeter is " << nPerimeter << " units. " << endl;
}

void CalcArea()
{
    int nWidth=0;
    int nLength=0;
    cout << "Enter width: ";
    cin >> nWidth;
    cout << "Enter length: ";
    cin >> nLength;
    int nArea=nWidth*nLength;
    cout << "The area is " << nArea << " units squared." << endl;
}
```

```
void CalcVolume()
{
    int nWidth=0;
    int nLength=0;
    int nHeight=0;
    cout << "Enter width: ";
    cin >> nWidth;
    cout << "Enter length: ";
    cin >> nLength;
    cout << "Enter height: ";
    cin >> nHeight;
    int nVolume=nWidth*nLength*nHeight;
    cout << "The volume is " << nVolume << " units cubed." << endl;
}

int main(int argc, char* argv[])
{
    cout << "Please choose one of the following:" << endl;
    cout << "1. Calculate perimeter." << endl;
    cout << "2. Calculate area." << endl;
    cout << "3. Calculate volume." << endl;
    cout << "4. Exit." << endl;
    int nChoice=0;
    while (nChoice != 4)
    {
        cout << "Please choose a number from 1 to 4 followed by
        Enter: ";
        cin >> nChoice;
        switch (nChoice)
        {
            case 1:
                CalcPerimeter();
                break;
            case 2:
                CalcArea();
                break;
            case 3:
                CalcVolume();
                break;
            case 4:
                cout << "Goodbye." << endl;
                break;
            default:
                cout << "You made an invalid choice, try again."
                    << endl;
                break;
```

```
            }
        }

        return 0;
}
```

3. This calculator program is comprised of 4 functions. Write down as many reasons you can think of as to why you think programmers divide up their programs into separate functions.

4. What are the declarations between the () after a function name called?

5. Why are the declarations between the () after a function name used?

6. What is the difference between Formal and Actual parameters?

7. How might we have divided the above program into more functions to make it easier to read and follow? (Hint: look at the body of the loop.)

8. In the following program fragment,

    a. list the variable names.

    b. list the function names,

    c. list the arguments or parameters in any function calls.

    d. list the parameters in any function definitions.

    e. list the return type of any functions.

    f. list the return value of any function call.

```
int average(int n1, int n2)
{
        return (n1+n2)/2;
}

int max(int a, int b)
{
        if (a > b)
        return a;
        else
        return b;
}
```

```
void main()
{
      int x=5 ;
      int y=9;
      int nAverage=average(x,y) ;
      int nMax=max(x,y) ;
}
```

Review of Lessons 5 through 7

In Lessons 5 through 7 we briefly introduced some of the basic building blocks of a computer program. We also introduced you to some C++ code. Answer the following questions:

1. What do the following programming terms mean?

    a. statement,

    b. branch,

    c. loop,

    d. syntax,

    e. variable,

    f. declaration,

    g. assignment,

    h. data type,

2. a. What are two of the branching constructs discussed in Lessons 5 through 7?

    b. Describe why you would choose one construct over the other.

3. What is one common error that programmers make when writing loops?

4. What is a program comment used for?

5. What is a function?

6. In C++, how can you tell the difference between a variable name and a function name?

7. What goes between the parenthesis () in a function call?

8. a.   What does it mean that a function returns a result?

    b.   Who does the function return the result to?

9. Why are variables and functions given names?

10. a.   What is Hungarian notation?

    b.   What does this naming convention accomplish?

11. In the following program fragment,

    a. List the variable names.

    b. List the function names.

    c. List the arguments or parameters in any function calls.

    d. List the parameters in any function definitions.

    e. List the return type of any functions.

    f. List the return value of any function call.

```
int average(int n1, int n2)
{
     return (n1+n2)/2;
}

int max(int a, int b)
{
     if (a > b)
          return a;
     else
          return b;
}

void main()
{
     int x=25;
     int y=17;
     int nAverage=average(x,y);
     int nMax=max(x,y);
}
```

Lesson 9

Simple Data Types – int, string, array, float, struct, bool, pointer, object, variant

Vocabulary:

int, string, array, float, struct, bool, pointer, object, variant, void.

Memory Verse:

1 Corinthians 15:39, "All flesh is not the same flesh: but there is one kind of flesh of men, another flesh of beasts, another of fishes, and another of birds."

As we begin to move into writing real programming code, it is time to introduce simple data types. As we mentioned in Lesson 7, a variable is a box with a label in which some data is stored. We already introduced the integer (or int) data type, which is simply a box which can hold a whole number. To be precise, the box can hold a positive number, zero, or a negative number. (Don't worry too much if you have not yet been introduced to negative numbers in your mathematics just yet; I'm stating this here for completeness, but you don't need to know what a negative number is, if you don't yet know.)

Every programming language has simple or built-in data types. More complex data types can then be constructed from these simple ones as you'll learn later in this course. In this lesson we will be looking at the intrinsic data types built in to the C and C++ languages.

One of the main reasons why computer languages require variables to be declared as of a particular data type is to ensure program integrity; i.e., to ensure that the variable is used as it was intended throughout the life of the program. When writing small programs this is not such an issue. However, when writing very complex programs that are maintained over several years, and where the person maintaining the program is not necessarily the one who wrote it and who may not know the mindset of the original programmer, providing a mechanism for ensuring that variables are only used for their intended purpose is very important. For example, a program offers a choice of options to the user, say three options. You would want the variable holding the user's choice to be an integer, and not some data type, which could hold a letter of the alphabet or a decimal value such as 2.5. This could lead to a misuse of the variable and erroneous or unpredictable results in the program. Languages that enforce type checking are called Strongly Typed languages.

Note that the type checking is only done by the compiler during the translation of the high level language into the machine code instructions. Any inconsistencies or errors in the variable usage, such as attempting to assign an integer to a string, results in the compiler issuing an error message and stopping the compilation. Once the program is compiled into machine code, variables are simplified into single memory addresses or consecutive blocks of addresses to hold the actual data. For example, an int typically is stored in a single memory address. A string of characters is usually stored in a consecutive block of addresses, one for each letter in the text and one for a NULL character (0) marking the end of the text.

Let's look at some other data types. These types are specific to the C and C++ languages but most of these types have equivalent types in other languages.

The char (short for character) data type can hold a single alphabetical, numerical or punctuation symbol.

A float can hold a decimal number (such as 2.5, 3.141592654 etc.) For greater precision you can use a double.

A bool holds a value that is either true or false. In C or C++, this is non-zero for true and 0 for false to be precise.

An array is simply a contiguous collection of another data type. For example, a string is an array of characters. Strings allow the storage of text (rather than a single character as in a char). You can recognize an array by the [] after the variable name. Don't get this confused with the () denoting a function call or {} marking a block of statements.

A struct (short for structure) allows us to define a variable that can hold several different data types in a single box. For example, you could create a variable that holds information about a person, such as their age and name in a single variable.

A pointer is a special type that simply holds the address of another variable. We'll deal with these very powerful, but potentially dangerous data types in future lessons.

A variant is a data type that can hold one of any number of data types. On the surface, this might seem like it circumvents the need to have a data type at all, since a variant can hold most kinds of data. Of course the consumer of the variant must query the variant to determine what kind of data it holds. The primary use of variants is to pass parameters of arbitrary data between functions. We'll not deal with variants in this course.

An object is actually more than just a data type. Rather than a box that holds a single value of a given type, an object is a package containing data and functions to query or manipulate that data. We'll look in depth at objects starting in Lesson 12. Objects are the heart of the C++ language.

The special type "void" means nothing. A function that returns void does not return anything to the caller. Indeed, if you declare a function that returns void, and you try and return a value from the function, you'll get a compilation error.

Here are some examples. Note the syntax of the declaration in C/C++.

```
int nChoice=5; // nChoice is an integer initialy assigned a value of 5.
char chGrade='a'; /* chGrade is a single character initially assigned
a value of 'a'. */
char szName[25]="Joseph"; /* szName is a string which can hold up to
25 characters and which is initialy assigned a value of "Joseph". */
```

(Note the " around character values and the "" around string values when initializing variables of these types such as above. Also note the [25] specifying the maximum number of characters in the character array or string.)

To access each character in the string, we must refer to it by its index or position, starting at position 0 up to the number of characters minus 1. For example, in the string above, the variable is declared to be able to hold 25 characters. This is actually 24 characters pluss what we call a 0 or null character to mark the end. the letter 'j' is at position 0, 'o' at position 1, 's' at position 2 and so on. To refer to a character or for that matter any element in an array, we reference it as follows:

```
char chTest=szName[0]; // chTest holds 'j'
chTest=szName[1]; // chTest is now 'o'
chTest=szName[5]; // chTest is now 'h'.
```

Arrays are particularly efficient when you want to access an item directly by its index, but are not so good when you need to insert an element into the middle and shift the rest of the elements to make room for it. We'll explain more about this in Lesson 25.

```
float fWidth=2.54; // fWidth is a float which is initially set to 2.54.
bool bResult=true; /* bResult is a boolean value which is initially
set to true. */

struct
{
    char name[25];
    int age;
} sPersonInfo; /* sPersonInfo is a structure which can hold a string
and an integer. */
```

```
int n=5; /* n is a variable of type int which is initialized to the
value of 5. */
int* pn=n; /* pn is a pointer to an integer. It actually points to the
same memory as the variable n above. If we now change the contents
of what pn points to, we will actually change the value of what is
stored in n. */
```

For example:

```
*pn=6; /* now the value of n is 6 because pn is pointing to the same
memory as n. */
```

Note that if we change pn it would no longer point at n, which is why we used the * to dereference the pointer. It refers to the memory pointed to by pn, rather than the address stored in pn itself which is, of course, the address of the variable n. Don't worry if this isn't too clear yet; it will become clearer as we go along. I said that pointers were dangerous and we've just shown why; you can change what they point to which may change other variables. They are, however, very very useful as you'll see.

Declaring variables of a particular data type helps ensure program integrity because it is not possible, for example, to mathematically multiply a string and an integer, it doesn't make sense. Thus the programmer can't accidentally mix up their variables and cause difficult to find errors, especially if they have not used the suggested Hungarian notation mentioned in Lesson 7.

Example:

```
int a=5;
char b[25]="hello";
int nAnswer=a*b; /* error the compiler will tell you you can't do
this! You can't multiply hello by 5. */
nAnswer=a+a; /* this is okay; you're adding an integer to an integer,
remember, a is an int variable initialized to 5. (Though Hungarian
notation was not used when naming the variable "a"). */
```

Warning: if a mathematical expression contains operands of different types, but the operands can be coerced or converted to equivalent types, the compiler will go ahead and convert one of the operands so that the expression can be evaluated. For example, when adding a float and an int, the int will be converted to a float. Generally This is intuitive but be careful, however, as a char is also stored as a numerical value so adding a char to an int will compile without complaint. For example, 'A' + 1 is 'B.' This works because internally, the computer represents characters using a predefined table of values known as ANSI or ASCII values. The letter 'A' has the ANSI value 65 and 'B' 66. Thus,

'A' +1 is converted to 65 + 1 = 66. If the result is stored in a variable of type char, the value 66 is interpreted as the letter 'B'. If the result is stored in a variable of type int, the value would just be 66.

Activity:

1. Identify the data types of the following declarations:

```
int nCounter=0;
char chMiddleInitial='K';
char szFirstName[25]="Joseph";
char chWidth;
char chLength;
float fWidth=2.54;
float fHeight=3.17;
int arrBookmarks[50];
```

2. Identify the errors below:

```
a. int nAnswer=nCounter+5;
b. int nResult=chMiddleInitial+nCounter;
c. int nRet=szFirstName+chMiddleInitial;
d. int nArea=chWidth*chLength;
```

3. What do you think the value of the following variables would be?

```
a. char* pszTemp=szFirstName;
b. int nResult=fWidth*fHeight;
c. float fResult=fWidth*fHeight;
```

4. We declared pszTemp above as a pointer to a character string, what do you think pszTemp points to after each instruction below:

```
a. pszTemp=pszTemp+1;
b. pszTemp=pszTemp+1;
c. pszTemp=pszTemp+4;
d. pszTemp=pszTemp+30; // careful with this one!
```

5. Add comments to the following short program to describe what each line does:

```
void MysteryFunction()
{
    int nCounter=9;
    char szFirst[12]="hello world";
    char szSecond[12="";
    for (int nIndex=0; nIndex < 10; nIndex++)
    {
        szSecond[nIndex]=szFirst[nCounter];
```

```
        nCounter--;
    }
    printf(szSecond);
}
```

6.

    a. What is an array?

    b. How do you recognize an array from the variable declaration in C++?

7. How do you access the values in an array?

8. Write a loop using C++ syntax that initializes an array of 50 integers increasing from 0 to 49, i.e., position 0 is set to 0, position 1 is set to 1, etc. (Hint: first declare a variable which is an array of integers.)

9. What happens if you try to access memory beyond the end of the array?

10. Write down as many advantages and disadvantages of using the array data type.

Lesson 10

Simple Input and Output

Vocabulary:

stream, library, include, compiler directive, namespace, token.

Memory Verse

Mark 7:15, "There is nothing from without a man, that entering into him can defile him: but the things which come out of him, those are they that defile the man."

Now that we've introduced some simple data types, we can begin to write programs that actually do something. We briefly introduced input and output in an earlier lesson, and our simple calculator program demonstrated how you could obtain input from the user's keyboard, and display messages on the user's display.

In order to write real programs, we often need to use functions to do basic operations, such as input and output that we should not have to implement from scratch. You will have noticed some strange lines at the top of some of the programs, which we did not explain. For example:

```
#include <iostream>
```

The #include is called a compiler directive and tells the compiler to include the content of a file called iostream located in the compiler's standard include path. This file happens to contain the declarations for our input and output stream handling; the library that enables us to read from the keyboard and display text on the console. This library also allows you to read from and write to files on disk or other devices. (See Lesson 35 for more on compiler directives.)

You may also have noticed the statement:

```
using namespace std;
```

Often, a group of related functions are stored in a library. To avoid the names of these functions from clashing with other functions by the same name in an unrelated library, the functions are placed within a namespace. If you don't have the "using namespace std;" at the top of your file, you will have to prefix each and every function in the std namespace with std::.

:: is the namespace or class qualifier. You'll see this more in Lesson 12. For example, std::cout rather than just cout. Of course, if you need to refer to functions with the same name in different namespaces, then you'll need to qualify one of the functions with its namespace prefix to disambiguate which function you are referring to. Because we don't have any clashing names in our program, we can simply put the "using" statement at the top, and save us having to disambiguate functions by preceding their name with the namespace prefix.

A stream (like a stream of water) implies a flow of information to or from an object. You may have noticed syntax like the following:

```
cout << "God created the heavens and the earth." << endl;
```

The << shows the direction of the flow of information. It shows that the stream of text is flowing to cout which is the console output. The special keyword "endl" just means to ensure a newline is started after the end of the text displayed, otherwise a subsequent cout statement would continue to display text on the same line.

The other flow symbol >> shows information flowing from an object. For example:

```
cin >> x;
```

Says that input from the keyboard is going to the variable x. Basically, the computer will read input from the keyboard until the Enter is pressed and place the first token into the variable, which is the target of the stream. This implies, of course, that the variable can hold the data typed by the user. You must thus ensure that the variable type matches the data expected.

Note the ">>" and "<<" operators usually perform bitwise shifting when used with numeric variables, rather than stream objects. These operators have been overloaded for the stream object to provide a conceptual equivalent. Rather than shifting bits in a number, they shift data to and from a stream. (See Lesson 15 for a brief discussion of the overloading of operators, and see Lesson 19 for a brief discussion of binary and bitwise shift operators.)

As mentioned above, cin only copies the first token on the line into the given variable, unless you supply multiple variables to the stream. A token is basically a piece of text delimited by a space. If you want to get an entire line from the user into a string, use the following C++ syntax:

```
char szName[256]="\0"; /* declare string to hold text, up to 255
characters. */
cout << "Enter your name: ";
cin.getline (szName,256);
```

This will copy up to 255 characters (or until the user presses the Enter key) to a string. Remember, the last character of a string must always be the NULL or 0 character to mark the end which is why we said that this string can hold a maximum of 255 and not 256 characters.

As well as writing to the console, we can create a file and write text to a file. In order to write or read files we must first open them and then after reading or writing, close them. Here is a simple example.

(Note: The starting procedure of any program is the Main procedure. It takes parameters that can be supplied from the command line, i.e., arguments following the program name when the program is started. Int argc holds the number of parameters supplied on the command line and argv is an array of strings, one string for each parameter supplied. argv[0] will be the name of the program and thus argc will always be at least 1.)

```
#include "stdafx.h"
#include <iostream>
#include <fstream>
using namespace std;

int main(int argc, _char* argv[])
{
    cout << "Enter some text you want saved to a file: ";

    char szText[255]="\0";
    cin.getline(szText,255);
    if (strlen(szText) < 1) // Test length of string.
    {
        cout << "You didn't enter any text." << endl;
        return 0;
    }
    cout << "You entered: " << szText << endl;
    cout << "Saving this text to example.txt." << endl;
    fstream fTest; // create a file output stream
    fTest.open ("example.txt", ios::out); /* Open a file for output
        only */
    fTest << szText << endl; /* Insert the text in szText into the
        file stream. */
    fTest.close(); // Close the file.
    return 0;
}
```

Here's an example of how to read a text file a line at a time, and display it one screenful at a time.

```cpp
// Reader Sample
#include "stdafx.h"
#include <iostream>
#include <fstream>
#include <string>
using namespace std;

int main(int argc, char* argv[])
{
    cout << "Enter filename (without the .txt extention, e.g. test
        for test.txt): ";

    char szText[255]="\0";
    cin.getline(szText,255);
    if (strlen(szText) < 1) // Test length of string.
    {
        cout << "You didn't enter a filename." << endl;
        return 0;
    }
    strcat(szText,".txt"); /* add the txt extention by using the
    strcat string concatination function. */
    cout << "You entered: " << szText << endl;
    fstream fTest; // create a file output stream
    fTest.open (szText, ios::in); //Open a file for input only
    if (fTest.is_open()==false)
    {
        cout << "I couldn't find " << szText << endl;
        return 0;
    }
    char szLine[32768]="\0";
    int nCounter=0;
    while (fTest.eof()==false) /* keep reading until we reach the
        end of file. */
    {
        fTest.getline(szLine, 32768); /* read a line (upto 32768
        characters) at a time. */
        cout << szLine << endl; // display the line of text
        nCounter++; // Count the lines.
        if (nCounter%20==0) /* modulo division: i.e. if nCounter
        divided by 20 has no remainder */
        {// every 20 lines we'll wait for a key to be pressed.
            cout << "Press Enter to continue, q then Enter to
```

```
                    quit.";
                    cin.getline(szText, 255);
                    if (strcmp(szText,"q")==0)
                         break; // break out of the while loop.
          }
     }
     fTest.close(); // Close the file.
     cout << endl << "Goodbye." << endl;

     return 0;
}
```

I mentioned above that you could grab the text typed at the command line, when the user ran your program. Below, we've modified the above reader program to do just that. If the user doesn't type a filename on the command line, we'll instruct them to do so.

```
// Reader Sample obtaining file from command line
#include "stdafx.h"
#include <iostream>
#include <fstream>
#include <string>
using namespace std;

int main(int argc, char* argv[])
{
     if (argc < 2)
     {
          cout << "Type " << argv[0] << " followed by the file name
          without its extention." << endl;
          return 0;
     }

     char szText[255]="\0";
     strcpy(szText,argv[1]); /* copy the filename from the command
          line into the szText variable so we can add the .txt
          extention.*/
     strcat(szText,".txt"); // add the txt extention by using the
     strcat string concatination function.
     cout << "You entered: " << argv[0] << " " << szText << endl;
     fstream fTest; // create a file output stream
     fTest.open (szText, ios::in); //Open a file for input only
     if (fTest.is_open()==false)
     {
          cout << "I couldn't find " << szText << endl;
          return 0;
     }
     char szLine[32768]="\0";
```

```
    int nCounter=0;
    while (fTest.eof()==false) /* keep reading until we reach the
        end of file. */
    {
        fTest.getline(szLine, 32768); /* read a line (upto 32768
            characters) at a time. */
        cout << szLine << endl; // display the line of text
        nCounter++; // Count the lines.
        if (nCounter%20==0) /* modulo division: i.e. if nCounter
        divided by 20 has no remainder */
        {// every 20 lines we'll wait for a key to be pressed.
            cout << "Press Enter to continue, q then Enter to
            quit.";
            cin.getline(szText, 255);
            if (strcmp(szText,"q")==0)
                break; // break out of the while loop.
        }
    }
    fTest.close(); // Close the file.
    cout << endl << "Goodbye." << endl;

    return 0;
}
```

In our first example, we used the keyboard and display as input and output streams. In our second two we used disk files. We can, however, use a string object as a stream, and either read multiple tokens from a string into variables, or send multiple variables to a string. Note that instead of using the basic C style string or character array data type as introduced in Lesson 9, we will now use a string object for simplicity. Don't worry too much about this now; we'll introduce objects in Lesson 12. For now, we'll just tell you that C++ comes with a standard library with a string object, which is easier to use than the one previously introduced. The important thing is the concept of being able to insert and extract data from a stream.

This example demonstrates the use of a string stream object for input and output. Similar to the way cin can be used to read information from the keyboard a token at a time, string streams can be used to feed data into a set of variables (or in this case, feed values into a single variable one at a time) from a string. This sample puts 7 numbers into the string stream, and then feeds each number from the stream into an int variable to output. You can even feed values from a stream into variables of different types, so long as the value you feed using the >> operator moves the right token into the right type variable.

```
#include <iostream>
#include <sstream>
```

```
using namespace std;

int main(int argc, char* argv[])
{
     int nVal=0;
     stringstream ss (stringstream::in | stringstream::out);

     ss << "123 456 789 777 54321 754 777";

     for (int n=0; n<7; n++)
     {
          ss >> nVal;
          cout << nVal << endl;
     }

     return 0;
}
```

You can also feed values back into a string stream as follows:

```
#include <iostream>
#include <string>
#include <sstream>
using namespace std;

int main(int argc, char* argv[])
{
     int nDay=25;
      int nYear=1971;
      string sMonth=" August ";
      stringstream ss (stringstream::in | stringstream::out); /* init
      the string stream for input and output. */

      ss << nDay << sMonth << nYear << endl; /* put my birthday into
          the string stream. */
      cout << ss.str(); // print it as a single string.

      return 0;
}
```

You might wonder what the point of doing this is. You do not need to convert the variables into strings, and then concatenate them into a single string; the conversion is done for you automatically. So, if you have all kinds of different data and want to put them all into a string for saving to disk or displaying on screen, this is one simple way of doing it.

The below example enables us to get a line and extract the various tokens with some error handling to avoid your program malfunctioning, if the user enters bad data:

```
#include "stdafx.h"
#include <iostream>
#include <sstream>
#include <string>
using namespace std;

int main(int argc, char* argv[])
{
     string sLine;
     cout << "Please enter your title, first and last name (e.g. Mr
     Joseph Stephen): ";
     getline (cin, sLine);
     /* using a stringstream, extract the title and last names into
     separate variables, skipping the first name. */
     stringstream ss (stringstream::in | stringstream::out); /* init
     the string stream for input and output. */
     ss << sLine; // send the line of text to the string stream.
     string sTitle;
     string sFirst;
     string sLast;
     ss >> sTitle >> sFirst >> sLast; /* Extract the first three tokens
     from the string stream data entered and put them into sTitle,
     sFirst and sLast. */
     cout << "Hello " << sTitle << " " << sLast << "." << endl;
     return 0;
}
```

Activity:

1. Study the following program carefully and answer the questions below.

```
#include "stdafx.h"
#include <iostream>
using namespace std;
int main(int argc, char* argv[])
{
     cout << "Hello, plese enter your name: ";
     char szName[255]="\0";
     char szTheirName[255]="\0";
     cin >> szName;
     cout << "Hello " << szName << " how old are you? ";
     int nAge=0;
     cin >> nAge;
     cout << szName << " is " << nAge << " years old." << endl;
```

```cpp
cout << "Do you have a sibling (y/n)? ";
char ch=0;
int nTheirAge=0;
cin >>ch;
if (ch=='y')
{
    cout << "How old is your oldest or youngest sibling? ";
}
else
    cout << "Enter the age of a friend or relative then: ";
cin >> nTheirAge;
cout << "What is their name? ";
cin >> szTheirName;
switch (nTheirAge)
{
    case 0:
        cout << "Newborn: Children are a blessing from the
        Lord (Ps 127:3-5" << endl;
        break;
    case 2:
        cout << "Toddlers are very cute! The Lord Jesus
        carried young children in His arms (Mark 9:36)."
        << endl;
        break;
    case 3:
        cout << "Samuel was probably between 3 and 5 when he
        was taken to Eli to serve the Lord (1 Sam 1:24)."
        << endl;
        break;
    case 12:
        cout << "The Lord Jesus was a responsible 12 year
        old and was known for his growth in wisdom, He is
        our example (Luke 2:42-52)." << endl;
        break;
    default:
        cout << "So teach us to number our days and apply
        our hearts unto wisdom (Psalm 90:12)." << endl;
        break;
}
if (nAge > nTheirAge)
    cout << "Remember, " << szName << " to disciple " << sz
            TheirName << " by setting a good example 1 Tim
            4:12." << endl;
else
    cout << "Even though you're younger than " << szTheirName
            << ", you can be a good example to them (1 Tim
            4:12)." << endl;
```

```
cout << "There are " << abs(nTheirAge-nAge) << " years difference
        between " << szName << " and " << szTheirName << "." <<
        endl;
cout << "Your combined age is " << nAge+nTheirAge << endl;
char szNameInReverse[255]="\0";
size_t nLen=strlen(szName); /* size_t is a typedef (or alias)
for unsigned int. An unsigned int is simply a whole number greater
than 0. See note in Lesson 24 on the typedef keyword, just before
the activity. */
for (size_t n=0; n < nLen; n++)
{
        szNameInReverse[n]=szName[nLen-n-1];
}
cout << "Your name backward is " << szNameInReverse << endl;

return 0;
}
```

    a. Which two header files does this sample program include?

    b. How many characters can szName hold (excluding the NULL character marking the end of the string)?

    c. What does the following fragment do:

```
size_t nLen=strlen(szName);
for (size_t n=0; n < nLen; n++)
{
        szNameInReverse[n]=szName[nLen-n-1];
}
```

    d. What do you think abs(nTheirAge-nAge) calculates?

    e. How many parameters are passed to the Main function?

    f. Add comments to the above program to describe what each line does.

2.   What is a file stream used for?

3.   What must you do before using a file stream to insert or extract data?

4.   What must you do after you've finished with a file stream?

5.   What is a string stream used for?

A Closer look at Functions, Procedures and Parameters

Vocabulary:

Function, Caller, Procedure, subroutine, Return Type, Parameter (or argument), Pass by Value, Pass by Reference, scope, const.

Memory Verse:

Philippians 2:14, "Do all things without murmurings and disputings:"

We've already briefly introduced functions in an earlier lesson, but in this lesson we take a closer look at a function, and explain the difference between a function and a procedure. We also look at two methods for passing information between the caller and callee.

A function is a named set of instructions, which is used to perform a calculation and return a result to the caller of the function. The caller is simply the instructions that call the function, and which usually acts upon its result. Note the "int" before the function name. This says the function returns a value, which must be assigned to or stored in a variable of type int. You'll notice that after the function name in the below example, there is a declaration of an integer variable, x. This special variable declaration is called a formal parameter, and allows us to pass something into the function. In other words, the function takes an int as a parameter (or argument) and returns an int to the caller.

```
int Square(int x)// x here is the formal parameter
{
        return x*x; // remember * means multiply if between two operands.
}
```

In the above example, the function takes an integer parameter; the caller can pass a value into the function in order for the function to do its calculation. The parameter is called x, and is only accessible inside the square function. The parameter is said to have function level scope. Any x variables in other functions or in the caller do not affect this x inside the square function. If we want to find the square of 5, we call the square function with the value 5 as follows:

```
int nResult=square(5);
```

What this says is, call the square function and pass it the value of 5. The 5 is known as the actual parameter. When execution begins inside the square function, the value of 5 is copied into the parameter x. Inside the function, the calculation 5 times 5 is executed, and the result passed back to the caller using the return statement. When the square function has done its calculation, the answer is copied to the nResult variable. Thus, after calling square, nResult equals 25.

To clarify, the formal parameter or parameters are the variables declared as part of the function definition, and the actual parameters (or arguments) are the values passed in to the function at the point where the function is actually called.

```
void Caller()
{
    int x=5;
    cout << "x squared is" << Square(x) << endl; /* x here is the
    actual parameter */
}
```

Note in the above procedure, the x is local to this procedure and is different to the x in the square function. Remember, x is simply the name of the memory we are using to hold an integer. We could have called it Fred, if we wanted to. Scoping allows us to use variables of the same name, but are only accesssible or relevant within the block defining their scope. A block is either a piece of code surrounded by {} or the function or procedure in which the variable is defined. You can define variables that have global scope; they are accessible to all functions in your program, but this is generally discouraged. Note that different languages use different grouping symbols to define a block, but several of the most used languages use the {} pair.

An example of scope:

```
void test(int x)
{
    x=5;
    {
        int x=3; // a different x to the outer block
        cout << x << endl; // x is 3.
    }
    cout << x << endl; /* x is 5 because this is the x in the outermost
    block */
}
```

To avoid confusion, it is always good to name your variables something meaningful that reflects their usage. For example, a variable used to count inside a loop could be called nCounter or nCount, whereas a variable used for storing someone's age might be nAge. To clarify the scope of a variable, look to its immediately enclosing block. If it is not declared there, work your way outward until you find the block where it is declared. Here's another example:

```
void testScope2()
{
    int x=2;
    {
        cout << x << endl; /* x is 2 because the outer scope is
        visible and no x is declared inside this block. */
    }
    {
        int x=5;
        cout << x << endl; /* x is 5 because this block declares
        a new x. */
    }
    {
        /* this x is 2 because the outer x is the only x declared
        at this block level. */
        cout << x << endl;
    }
}
```

A procedure is a set of instructions that does not return a result. The caller calls the procedure or subroutine to perform the set of instructions. The flow of execution after calling the procedure does not depend on the result of the procedure call. We can also pass values to procedures just like functions. A simple distinction is that a function is typically used to calculate a result, whereas a procedure is used to execute a series of related instructions.

For example:

```
void Main()
{
    Caller();
    // some more statements.
}
```

The main procedure calls the Caller procedure to print the square of 5. Of course, in this simple example, the main procedure could have simply called the square function directly.

The Square function takes an int parameter. The value of this parameter is passed by value, when the caller calls the Square function, the value of the parameter, 5, is copied directly into the function. Usually numeric variables are passed by value. Passing by value is the easiest method of passing information to a function, though it is not always suitable. If, for example, we want to pass an object into a function—since the object takes up much more memory—it might be more efficient to pass the address of the object to the function, so that the function can use the passed address to access the object. This method of passing a parameter is called Pass By Reference. This method of passing information between functions is very useful, but has its dangers. Consider the following:

```
void main()
{
    int y=5;
    cout << Square(y) << endl;
}

int Square(int x)
{
    x=x*x; /* multiply what is in x by itself and store the value
    back in x. */
    return x; // return the value stored in x to the caller.
}
```

After main calls Square, the value of y is still 5, because we passed the value of y to Square rather than the address of y. We copied the value stored in y to the function's formal parameter, rather than allowing the function to access our variable by its address directly.

If we now define Square to receive its data by reference as follows:

```
int Square(int& x)
{
    x=x*x; /* multiply what is stored in x by itself and store it
    back in x. */
    return x; // return the value stored in x back to the caller.
}
```

If main now calls our new version of Square, after this call y will not be 5 as expected. Since the reference to y was passed to Square, inside Square, x=x*x will actually change the value of y. This happens because, rather than just passing the value of y, we passed the address of y, which means whatever we do to x inside Square actually references the memory of the Y variable directly. In this case this is bad design (see Appendix 5, point 13).

Note the & symbol in the declaration of the Square function. In C++ this & means obtain the address of. Thus int& x means that the function takes the address of a variable which holds an int. Without the & symbol, the function simply takes an int value that is stored in x for use within the Square function, and which does not change the value of the memory outside the function.

Let us clarify this last point as it is a bit confusing. When we pass a parameter by value, we obtain the value in the variable and copy it to the function, thus the original variable from which we obtained the value is not changed. On the other hand, when we pass by reference, rather than copying the value of the variable, we pass the address of the variable, so that inside the function we actually access the same piece of memory, since we are using the address of the variable, rather than just copying its value. Imagine you want to paint your house, but first want to know what it will look like. You could take a picture of the house, copy the picture and colour the copy of the picture, or you could colour the original picture directly. If you color the original picture, you'll no longer have a picture of the original since you coloured it.

Note code which is called by other code is sometimes referred to as a subroutine. Subroutines are generally synonymous with procedures.

When a parameter is passed by reference due to its size, but you do not want it modified by the function, you can declare the function and the variable as const. If the programmer attempts to modify the variable inside the function unintentionally, the compiler will issue a warning. For example:

```
int JoesFunc(const int& x) const
{
     x=x+1; /* error, you can't modify x because the function and
               formal parameter are declared const. */
}
```

Activity:

1. What is the value stored in x after calling the Triple function.

    ```
    void main()
    {
          int x=10;
          int y=Triple(x);
    }

    int Triple(int k)
    {
          k=k*3;
          return k;
    }
    ```

2. What is the value stored in x after calling the Triple function in the below code fragment (using the Triple function above)? Why?

    ```
    void main()
    {
          int x=10;
          x=Triple(x);
    }
    ```

3. What is the value stored in x after calling MySpecialFunc? Why?

    ```
    void main()
    {
          int x=3;
          int y=MySpecialFunc(x);
    }

    int MySpecialFunc(int& z)
    {
          z=z+5;
    }
    ```

4. What is the value stored in x after calling YourSpecialFunc? Why?

    ```
    void main()
    {
          int x=3;
          x=YourSpecialFunc(x);
    }

    int YourSpecialFunc(int& z)
    ```

```
{
        z=z+9;
        return 5;
}
```

5. What is the value stored in x after calling AnotherFunc? Why?

```
void main()
{
        int x=7;
        int y=AnotherFunc(x);
}

int AnotherFunc(int& z)
{
        z=(z*z)+2;
        return z;
}
```

6. Looking carefully at the above questions, which one do you think is the worst coding design and why?

7. What does a variable's scope mean?

8. In the following procedure, write down the value of x at each cout statement.

```
void AnotherScopeTest()
{
        {
                int x=27;
                cout << x << endl;
        }
        cout << x << endl; // be careful!
        {
                int x=2;
                {
                        int x=3;
                        cout << x<< endl;
                }
                cout << x << endl;
        }
}
```

9. What is the difference between a function and a procedure?

10. What is meant by the return type of a function?

11. What is the difference between a formal parameter and an actual parameter?

12. When should you use pass-by-reference, rather than pass-by-value when passing parameters to a function?

13. What can you do to the function declaration to ensure that any variables passed by reference do not unintentionally get modified by the function into which they are passed?

Lesson 12

Introduction to Objects and Object Oriented Programming

Vocabulary:

Class, Object, encapsulation, reuse, state, interface, method, member, instantiation.

Memory Verse:

Psalms 119:105, NUN. "Thy word is a lamp unto my feet, and a light unto my path."

Now that we have introduced the basics of programming, functions, procedures, variables, statements and flow control, its time to put them all together. In the real world, we usually deal with objects—we read a book, build a house, pass a package to someone, etc. Since programming solutions are usually written to solve real-world problems, they also need to deal with objects. Writing programs in terms of objects is known as object oriented programming. Up until now, we have discussed procedural programming. Object Oriented programming is a major programming paradigm, and accounts for a very large proportion of code in the real world.

Put simply, an object is a way of encapsulating procedures, functions and variables relating to a particular concept into a single package. This package then exposes what we call an interface to the user of the object. The user of the object does not need to know how the internals of the object work, just how to interact with the object. In fact, to protect the user of the object from misusing the internals of the object, the user or caller can't access what is inside the object and is forced to only make use of the exposed interface. For example, if a user knew how we implemented the internals of the object and they made assumptions about our implementation, if the implementation was changed or updated later, the user's code may no longer work.

A simple example is a mobile phone. We interact with the phone via its keypad, the keypad or touch screen serves as an interface to the functionality of the phone. We do not need to know how many transistors or integrated circuits there are inside the case. We do not need to know how the software on the chips was programmed. All we need to know is how to use the external interface to operate the phone.

57

One of the great things about objects is that a programmer can distribute them to other programmers or put them into a library for reuse. Once an object has been written, debugged and tested, the user of the object need not worry about whether the object will malfunction since it should have already been thoroughly tested. This makes writing larger and more sophisticated programs easier, since a programmer need only obtain a library of objects and write code to interact with all of the objects. This ability to collect objects into a library for later usage is called object reuse. The process of packaging the functions, procedures and variables is called encapsulation. Another advantage to using objects is that their implementation can be changed without changing their interface, which means that other objects that rely on this object do not need to change.

Typically the object's interface is distributed as a header file and the implementation in a compiled library. The declaration of the interface is distributed in a separate file to the implementation or body of the object. This way, the user of the object cannot access the implementation, but is forced to use the object in accordance with its interface.

Most of the time spent researching how to program the solution to a problem will often be researching existing libraries of objects, rather than actually writing new code. Today, there are thousands of objects already distributed in just as many libraries and it can be a bit daunting just figuring out the best objects to use to solve your problem.

Let's consider an example in C++. In C++, an object definition is called a class. We want to create an object representing a lamp. It may have the following class definition. Note, this definition and the implementation below that define the object, but are not an instance of the object. To clarify this, we may define how a house looks, but until we build the house, the plan is simply a definition. Once the house is actually built, it is an instantiation of the plan. So to, in programming, the class definition defines the interface, the class implementation defines how the class actually works, but until we create an instance of the object, it remains simply a classs declaration.

```
// lamp.cpp : Defines the entry point for the console application.
//

#include "stdafx.h"
#include <windows.h>
#include <iostream>
using namespace std;
class CLamp
{
    public: // the public members accessible by users of this object.
            // constructor see below
            CLamp();
            // destructor see below
```

```
        ~CLamp();
        // methods for interacting with object (interface)
        void OnOffButton(); // turn the lamp on or off
        bool IsOn(); // test if the lamp is on.
        bool IsOff(); // tests if the lamp is off
        void SetBrightness(int nValue); // sets the lamps brightness
        int GetBrightness(); // gets the lamp's brightness
        void SetSleepTimer(int nSeconds); /* turns the lamp on for
              the specified number of seconds then turns it off. */
    // end of interface
        /* below here are protected members and variables
        only available within the object itself or objects that
        inherit from this object (see Lesson 14).
        */
    protected:
        void Wait(int nSeconds); /* note this is a private method
        to the CLamp class. */
        /* below here are private members and variables only
        available within the object itself.
        */
    private:
        bool m_bIsOn; /* variable to store whether the lamp is on
        or off. */
        int m_nBrightness; // variable to hold the brightness value
};
```

Let's look closely at our class definition above. In object oriented programming, procedures are known as methods, functions are known as Member Functions, and class variables are called member variables. The methods, functions and member variables are collectively called class members. Every object has two special methods. The first, the constructor, is usually called implicitly by the C++ runtime system when an object is instantiated; when an instance of this object is actually created. If an object has a public constructor requiring parameters, the user must explicitly call the constructor in order to supply it with the necessary parameters for construction. The destructor is called by the C++ runtime system at the time the object is destroyed. Every object has a life time, from the time it is created to the time it is destroyed, i.e., the time in which the instantiation of the object is valid.

The constructor is responsible for initializing the object to a useable state. The destructor is responsible for cleaning up or freeing any resources used by the object. In our example, the constructor would initialize all of the object member variables to 0. Member variables are simply variables that are defined inside the object. These should not be accessible to the user of the object directly, and should be declared private. Member functions or methods may be declared private, protected or public. We'll deal with these terms further in the next lesson. For now, public means that anyone using the object can access the member. Protected or private means that the member is only accessible by the implementation of the object itself, i.e., it is not visible outside the object. (We'll deal with the protected directive in Lesson 14 when we look at inheritance.) Note also in the class definition above that the member variables for brightness and on-off state are not initialized to any value, we only declare the variable type. The constructor must initialize the variables.

In our example above, if a user could access the internals of our object and perhaps refer directly to the private member variables, if we later updated our lamp and changed the names of these variables, the user's code would no longer work. The user's code must only interact with our example object via its public members, i.e., call OnOffButton(), IsOn(), IsOff(), SetBrightness(), GetBrightness, SleepTimer(). They can't call Wait nor refer to the member variables m_bIsOn or m_nBrightness. Only the class implementation itself (below) can refer to these private members. Did you note the m_ preceeding the member variables names? This is our Hungarian notation applied at the class level, so we know that m_something is a member variable.

The class implementation is distributed as a compiled library (machine code), not the source code below.

The declaration of a class is usually stored in a file by the same name as the class with a ".h" extension. The implementation of the class is stored in a file by the same name as the class with a ".cpp" extension. In our case, the declaration of CLamp would be stored in "lamp.h," and the implementation in "lamp.cpp." The lamp.cpp would contain a line near the top such as:

```
#include "lamp.h"
```

To ensure that the implementation of the class could reference its declaration.

The constructor implementation looks like this:

```
CLamp::CLamp()
{
    m_bIsOn=false; // initialize to off state
    m_nBrightness=5; // initialize brightness to half.
}
```

The first thing you'll notice is the double colon ::. This means that what follows is a member of the class preceding the double colon. The constructor's name is always the same as the class itself, as is the destructor, except that the destructor's name is preceded by a Tilde ~ character.

The destructor of the CLamp class would look like this (note the "~" after the ::):

```
CLamp::~CLamp()
{
      if (IsOn())
            OnOffButton(); // turn it off.
}
```

When the CLamp object is destroyed or goes out of scope, it turns itself off. (We discussed scope in Lesson 11.)

```
void CLamp::OnOffButton()
{// toggle the value
      if (m_bIsOn)
            m_bIsOn=false;
      else
            m_bIsOn=true;
}

bool CLamp::IsOn()
{
      return m_bIsOn;
}

bool CLamp::IsOff()
{
      return m_bIsOn==false;
}

void CLamp::SetBrightness(int nValue)
{
      if (nValue >=1 && nValue <=10)
          m_nBrightness=nValue;
}

int CLamp::GetBrightness()
{
      return m_nBrightness;
}

void CLamp::SetSleepTimer(int nSeconds)
{
      if (IsOff())
            OnOffButton(); // turn it on
      Wait(nSeconds); // leave it on for the requested time.
      OnOffButton(); // turn it off after the specified time has elapsed.
}
```

```
void CLamp::Wait(int nSeconds)
{
    /* GetTickCount() is a builtin function which obtains the time
  since the computer was started from the computer's clock measured
  in thousands of a second (milliseconds or ticks). We obtain the
  current time, add to it 1000 times the value of the parameter
  supplied to calculate a time in the future. We then wait in a loop
  continuously obtaining the current time until the current time
  reaches the time in the future which we calculated and then we exit
  the loop.
    Also note the DWORD variable which is a double word or four
  bytes. We'll talk about bytes and bits later. For now, think of it
  as a number much like an integer or int.
*/
    DWORD dwWaitTime=GetTickCount()+(nSeconds*1000);
    DWORD dwNow=GetTickCount();
    while (dwNow < dwWaitTime)
    {
        dwNow=GetTickCount(); /* get the current time and store in
        dwNow. */
    }
}
```

There is another special kind of method called a copy constructor, which we will not look at in detail here, but mention for completeness. When initializing a variable of a particular object to the value of another variable of the same class, this copy constructor is called to ensure that the copy of the object has the same internal state, i.e., ensures that the internal state of both objects match. For example, if a is of type CLamp and b is of type CLamp, and b is on, then initializing b to a: CLamp a(b); would ensure that a is on and set to the same brightness as b. A custom copy constructor is only necessary when your class has allocated resources on the heap (see Lesson 18), and a shallow copy of member variables would be insufficient to ensure that the initialized copy is the same as the original object. If you haven't specifically allocated any class resources on the heap, then you don't need to worry about declaring a copy constructor; the compiler will do it for you. Since our CLamp class does not allocate any resources on the heap, a copy constructor is not necessary. When a copy constructor is necessary, it would also be necessary to overload the assignment operator "=". To clarify the difference, the copy constructor is used when creating a new variable from an existing variable, whereas the assignment operator is used when assigning a variable to an existing variable (where the existing variable first needs to release its resources before the copy). Copy constructors and operator overloading are beyond the scope of this book, but an example for the above class is listed for completeness:

```
/* Declaration of copy constructor which would usually follow the
constructor in the class declaration */

CLamp (const CLamp& other);


// Implementation

CLamp ::CLamp (const CLamp& other)

{

   m_nBrightness=other.m_nBrightness;

   m_bIsOn=other.m_bIsOn;

}


/* declaration of assignment overload */

CLamp& operator=(const CLamp& other);


/* Assignment overload implementation */

CLamp& CLamp::operator=(const CLamp& other)

{

/* you'd normally first deallocate any resources before reallocating
with copy */

   m_nBrightness=other.m_nBrightness;

   m_bIsOn=other.m_bIsOn;

   return *this;

}
```

Now that we've declared our CLamp class, we need to make use of it. Below is a simple procedure that declares a variable of type CLamp and tests it out. Declaring a variable of the type CLamp instantiates the object; it creates an instance of the object.

```
int main(int argc, char* argv[])
{
     CLamp myLamp;
     myLamp.OnOffButton(); // toggle the lamp's state
     if (myLamp.IsOn())
          cout << "The lamp is on" << endl; /* print a message to
          the console */
```

```
else
      cout << "The lamp is off" << endl; /* print a message to
      the console */
int nBrightness=1; /* initialize the brightness to the lowest
setting */
while (nBrightness < 10)
{// loop until brightness is the maximum
      myLamp.SetBrightness(nBrightness);
      cout << "The brightness is " << myLamp.GetBrightness() <<
      endl;
      ::Sleep(1000);
      nBrightness++; /* ++ means add one to the value stored in
      this variable. */
}
myLamp.SetSleepTimer(30);
if (myLamp.IsOn())
      cout << "Now the lamp is on";
else
      cout << "Now the lamp is off";

      return 0;
}
```

If you run the main procedure, the lamp is turned on, and a message is printed to tell you that the lamp is on. It is turned on at its lowest brightness and gradually increases in brightness until after 10 seconds, the lamp reaches its full brightness. After it reaches its full brightness, it remains lit for 30 seconds, and then turns itself off. Finally a message is printed to tell you that the lamp is now off.

Activity:

1. What is an object?

2. What are some of the advantages of object oriented programming?

3. The user of the object interacts with the object via its i_____.

4. Why is the user of an object typically not permitted to know about the object's implementation?

5. How is an object typically distributed?

6. What is the difference between the object's declaration, its implementation and its instantiation?

7. a. What is the purpose of the constructor of the object?

   b. When is it called?

   c. What calls it?

8. a. What is the purpose of the destructor of the object?

   b. When is it called?

   c. What calls it?

9. What is the lifetime of an object?

10. What is the difference between procedural and object oriented programming?

Review of Lessons 9 through 12

In Lessons 9 through 12, we introduced data types, functions, procedures and objects.

* Data types specify the kinds of things we can store in memory, and refer to by human readable names. These named boxes for storing values are known as variables (as their contents may change).

* A Procedure is a named set of instructions.

* A function is a named set of instructions that returns a value to the caller.

* Procedures are also known as subroutines.

* Both procedures and functions may take parameters; they allow values of a particular data type to be passed to them to be used in the execution of the instructions.

* Parameters may be passed by value or by reference.

* An object is a named collection of related procedures (methods), functions (member functions) and variables (member variables).

Questions:

1. What is the main purpose of requiring variables to be declared of a particular data type?

2. a. What does it mean to pass a variable by value?

   b. What does it mean to pass a variable by reference?

   c. Why would you choose one method over the other?

    d. What design issue should we be careful of when passing variables by reference? (Hint: what happens when you change the variable inside the function or procedure when it is passed by reference?)

    e. How could you avoid the unintentional modification of an actual parameter when passed by reference?

3. Consider the declarations below:

```
int n=5;
int* pn=n;
int arrInts[100] ;
```

    a. What is the difference between a pointer to a variable of a particular type and a variable of the same type?

    b. What is stored in pn?

    c. What is stored in the memory pointed to by pn (i.e. *pn)?

    d. What is arrInts?

    e. Write a loop to fill arrInts with even numbers starting from 2. Remember that the first position is 0 and not 1.

    f. What happens if you attempt to write to memory beyond the end of arrInts?

4. What are some of the main advantages of object oriented programming?

5. a. Why do we usually separate an object's class definition (or interface) from its implementation (or body)?

    b. Why do we want a user of our class to only know the interface and not how we implemented the class?

    c. How is the implementation of the class distributed?

6. Consider the following class definition:

```
class cTalkingBible
{
public:
    cTalkingBible();
    ~cTalkingBible();
    void Play();
    void Stop();
    void NextBook();
    void PriorBook();
    void NextChapter();
    void PriorChapter();
```

```
        void NextVerse();
        void PriorVerse();

    private:
        LoadText();
        int m_nCurrentBook;
        int m_nCurrentChapter;
        int m_nCurrentVerse;
        bool m_bIsPlaying;
};
```

What are the

   a.   public members?

   b.   private members?

   c.   What can access the public members?

   d.   What can access the private members?

   e.   Describe the data types of the member variables, i.e., what can they hold, and what do you think they would be used for from their names?

7. What is the difference between an object's declaration, its implementation and its instantiation?

8. a.   What is an object's constructor for?

   b.   What is an object's destructor for?

   c.   Who calls the constructor and destructor?

9. What is an object's life-time?

10. What are the three categories of member visibility within a class declaration?

Inheritance

Vocabulary:

inheritance, derived, private, protected, public.

Memory Verse:

Romans 5:12, "Wherefore, as by one man sin entered into the world, and death by sin; and so death passed upon all men, for that all have sinned:"

One of the most powerful concepts of object oriented programming, which I now introduce is inheritence. Inheritence is the ability to pass on traits from one generation to the next. You inherit characteristics from your parents. You also inherit a sin nature from them. Your children will in turn inherit characteristics from you and, of course, will also inherit your sin nature.

Consider our CLamp class of Lesson 12. Suppose we now want to be able to have a flashing mode to be able to use our lamp as a warning light. Rather than creating a new CLamp object from scratch (which we could do), it would be better if we could reuse the code we've already written. It turns out that we can. The beauty of object oriented programming is the concept of inheritance. Consider our new CSuperLamp class below:

```
class CSuperLamp : public CLamp
{
    public:
    CSuperLamp (){}
    ~CSuperLamp (){}
    void FlashMode(int nSeconds); /* nSeconds is the length of time
    you want it to flash. */
};
```

Looking at the class definition above, we see that CSuperLamp inherits from CLamp, and makes whatever is available to the outside world from that class publicly available from this class. This means that anything public in CLamp is also public in CSuperLamp.

Rather than having to reimplement all of the methods declared in CLamp, we only need to implement the new methods not present in CLamp.

```
void CSuperLamp::FlashMode(int nSeconds)
{
      for (int n=0; n < nSeconds; n++)
      {// loop for the number of iterations specified,
      //toggling the lamp and waiting one second for each.
            OnOffButton();
            Wait(1);
      }
}
```

You'll note that all we did was inherit from our prior class and add one new member, FlashMode. Because this is a new object, and we need to distinguish this from our CLamp, it has its own constructor and destructor, though these do not do anything in this example. We put them inline in the declaration as well, since they do nothing. Now let's instantiate our new lamp:

```
void main()
{
      CSuperLamp yourLamp; // instantiate an instance of this new object
      yourLamp.FlashMode(20); // flash the lamp for 20 seconds.
      if (yourLamp.IsOn())
            yourLamp.OnOffButton(); /* since it was flashing, we're not
            sure if it is on or off. */
      /* Note, we didn't really have to turn it off because in the
      CLamp destructor, if it was on, when the object is destroyed, it
      will be turned off but I thought I'd turn it off anyway since
      this procedure might do other things before destroying the CLamp
      object.*/
      // do other things …
};
```

Our CSuperLamp has all of the methods of our CLamp plus a FlashMode method. Its implementation is also able to make use of our protected member function Wait(). It can't, however, access the other private member variables, but must use the public members to test if the lamp is currently on, off or to toggle it on or off.

You'll note if you look back at the CLamp declaration that the Wait member is declared as protected. Protected means objects that inherit from this class can access them but nothing else, i.e., the user of the object can't access the member. Thus, the three visibility types are:

* Public: Any user of the object as well as the object implementation itself are able to access this member.

* Protected: Only this object's implementation or objects that inherit from this object can access this member.

* Private: Only this object's implementation can access this member. No user of the object nor any object that inherits from this object can access this member.

Note that when you instantiate an object that inherits from another class, the constructor of the original object is called by the runtime system prior to the constructor of the inheriting object. Likewise, when an object is destroyed, its destructor is called by the runtime system prior to the object's destructor from which you inherit, i.e., in reverse order to construction.

A class that inherits from another class is called a derived class, because it derives its functionality from the class from which it inherits.

Activity:

1. What is inheritance?

2. What do the three visibility designations mean:

    a. public

    b. protected

    c. private

3. What is the main advantage of inheritance? Write some reasons why you might use inheritance in programming?

4. What do you think would happen, if your inherited class had a public member with the same name as a public member in the class you were inheriting from, but which did something different?

5. Write down the order of construction and destruction of the yourLamp object in the prior example. Hint: remember that myLamp is a CSuperLamp object that inherits from CLamp.

6. CSuperLamp is called a d_____ class because it inherits from CLamp.

Overriding Members

Vocabulary:

virtual member, base class, inline implementation, abstract class, polymorphism.

Memory Verse:

1 Corinthians 15:22, "For as in Adam all die, even so in Christ shall all be made alive."

In our last lesson, I asked what you thought would happen, if you had a public member with the same name as a public member in the class you were inheriting from. This turns out to be a very useful thing to be able to do. Imagine now that you want another lamp object that made a sound when turned on, so that a blind person could hear when it was being switched on. Do you need to create an entirely new object? No. You only need to override a class member. I need, however, to introduce a new modifier, the virtual modifier. When defining a class from which you want to inherit, any members that you want functionality to be modifiable, you need to declare with the virtual modifier. For now, consider our original CLamp object now declared with a virtual modifier for each public member:

```
class CLamp
{
    public: // the public members accessible by users of this object.
        // constructor see below
        CLamp();
        // destructor see below
        ~CLamp();
        // methods for interacting with object (interface)
        virtual void OnOffButton(); // turn the lamp on or off
        virtual bool IsOn(); // test if the lamp is on.
        virtual bool IsOff(); // tests if the lamp is off
        virtual void SetBrightness(int nValue); /* sets the lamps
                brightness */
        virtual int GetBrightness(); // gets the lamp's brightness
        virtual void SetSleepTimer(int nSeconds); /* turns the lamp
```

```
            on for the specified number of seconds then turns it off.
            */
            // end of interface
      protected: /* below here are protected members and variables
            only available within the object itself. */
            virtual void Wait(int nSeconds); /* note this is a private
            method to the CLamp class. */
      private: /* below here are private members and variables only
            available within the object itself. */
            bool m_bIsOn; /* variable to store whether the lamp is on
            or off. */
            int m_nBrightness; // variable to hold the brightness value
};
```

Note, we do not need to change the implementation of the CLamp object, only the class declaration.

The class from which other classes inherit from is often called a base class. Our new class, which has a beep builtin when we toggle the lamp on, would look like the following:

```
class CBeepingLamp : public CSuperLamp
{
      public:
            CBeepingLamp (){}
            ~CBeepingLamp() {}
            void OnOffButton(); /* this is our substitute for the base
            class member by the same name. */
};


void CBeepingLamp::OnOffButton()
{
      CLamp::OnOffButton(); /* call the base class implementation to
      press the button. */
      if (IsOn())
            Beep(1000,100); /* beep with a tone of 1000 for 100
            milliseconds. */
      else
            Beep(500,100); // Beep with a tone of 500 for 100 ms.
}
```

We declared our base class's public members to be virtual. Since we "overrode" the OnOffButton method, when we instantiate our new object and call its OnOffButton member, rather than calling the CLamp method, it will call our derived method. This indirectly calls our base class, but could have just as well not done that and done something totally different. This may seem obvious, but look carefully at our below example:

```
void main()
{
    CBeepingLamp bl;
    bl.OnOffButton(); // if off, turn on and beep as you would expect.
    // now look at the below line:
    bl.FlashMode(20); // what do you think this does?

}
```

This demo will flash the lamp for 20 seconds, beeping each time it goes on and off. Why? Because the FlashMode implementation in CSuperLamp calls the OnOffButton method. Since the base class declares this as virtual, and since it is overridden in our CBeepingLamp class, which was the object we instantiated, guess which implementation gets called? The CBeepingLamp implementation. Inheritance is very powerful.

To clarify:

* Your base class declares its public members as virtual. CLamp declared OnOffButton to be virtual.

* Your derived class inherits all the public members of your base class, and may optionally override some of the members, and/or add new functionality in new members. Our CSuperLamp added the FlashMode member that called OnOffButton in a loop.

* A subsequent class may then inherit from the intermediate class. CBeepingLamp inherited from CSuperLamp, but overrode OnOffButton to toggle the lamp on or off and if on, beep. Since this is now overridden, the FlashMode member declared in the class we inherited from (CSuperLamp) also now calls us (CBeepingLamp), rather than the base class from which it inherited (CLamp).

Consider another example:

```
class CShape
{
    public:
    CShape(){};
    ~CShape(){};
    virtual int Area()=0;
    virtual int Perimeter()=0;
    virtual int Sides()=0;
    virtual char* Name()=0;
};
```

Notice that our CShape class has no implementation, and that each virtual function is followed by =0. This is what we call an abstract class (or interface), because it can't actually be instantiated. Just like a shape is an abstract concept, and we need to be more specific by specifying that our shape is a square or a circle etc. We must inherit from this class, and provide overrides for each virtual abstract function. We do this is so that we can then declare a CShape pointer, which can point to any class type that derives from CShape, whether it be a square, circle or rectangle.

An interface or abstract class declaration defines a contract between the user of the object and the object. The object must implement all of the members in the interface, and the user can only interact with the object via the methods in the interface.

```cpp
class CRectangle: public CShape
{
    protected:
        CRectangle()
        {
            m_nWidth=0;
            m_nLength=0;
        };
    public:
        CRectangle(int nWidth, int nLength)
        {
            m_nWidth=nWidth;
            m_nLength=nLength;
        }
        ~CRectangle(){};
        int Width()
        {
            return m_nWidth;
        }
        int Length()
        {
            return m_nLength;
        }
        int Area()
        {
            return Width() * Length();
        }
        int Perimeter()
        {
            return (2*Width() + 2*Length());
        }
```

```
        int Sides()
        {
                return 4;
        }
        virtual char* Name()
        {
                return "rectangle";
        }

        protected:
        int m_nWidth;
        int m_nLength;
};
```

You'll notice that the implementation is inline; that is, implemented in the declaration itself. This is okay if the body of each member function is very small, typically one or two lines. Also, it is okay to declare short member functions inline, if you don't mind the user of the class seeing the implementation. Remember that normally the classs declaration and implementation are separated, and only the class declaration distributed as a source file. You'll also notice there are two constructors, a private one and a public one. The public one requires two parameters. To instantiate a CRectangle object, we must supply the width and length of the quadrilateral shape. The private one still gets called by the runtime, but the public one must be called when the object is instantiated.

```
void main()
{
    CRectangle myRectangle(50,100);
    int nArea=myRectangle.Area();
    int nPerimeter=myRectangle.Perimeter();
    int nSides=myRectangle.Sides();
    int nLength=myRectangle.Length();
    int nWidth=myRectangle.Width();
    cout << "My Rectangle has length " << nLength << " and width "
        << nWidth << " and a perimeter of " << nPerimeter << "
        units and its area is " << nArea << " square units. It
        has " << nSides << " sides" << endl;
    return 0;
}


Now consider another inherited class:

class CSquare : public CRectangle
{
    private:
        CSquare (){};
    public:
```

```
             CSquare (int nSide)
             {
                     m_nWidth=nSide;
                     m_nLength=nSide;
             };
             ~CSquare (){};
             char* Name()
             {
                     return "square";
             }
};

void main2()
{
     CSquare mySquare(500);
     int nArea=mySquare.Area();
     int nPerimeter=mySquare.Perimeter();
     cout << "My square has side length " << mySquare.Length() << ",
             perimeter " << nPerimeter << " units and area " << mySquare.
             Area() << " units squared." << endl;
}
```

Our CSquare constructor need only take a single argument specifying the side length, since a square has four equal sides. We only need override the public constructor and Name method, the Area and Perimeter member functions are identical.

```
#define pi 3.141592
class CCircle : public CShape
{
private:
     CCircle (){};
public:
     CCircle (int nRadius)
     {
             m_nRadius=nRadius;
     }
     ~CCircle ();
     int Sides()
     {
             return 1;
     }
     int Area()
     {
             return pi * m_nRadius*m_nRadius;
     }
```

```
        int Perimeter()
        {
                return 2*pi*m_nRadius;
        }
        char* Name()
        {
                return "circle";
        }
private:
        int m_nRadius;
};
```

The clever thing about inheritance is that we can now write a function, which only knows about the bass class and pass it a pointer to the base class as folllows:

```
void DescribeShape(CShape* pShape)
{
        /* check the passed in pointer to ensure it is valid, if it is
        zero you'll get an error! */
        if (pShape==0)
                return; // nothing to do, no shape passed to us
        cout << "This is a " << pShape->Name() << endl; /* This prints
                "this is a xxxx" */
        cout << "It's area is " << pShape->Area() << " square units."
        << endl;
        cout << "It's perimeter is" << pShape->Perimeter() << " units."
        << endl;
}

void main3()
{
        CShape* pShape1=new CRectangle(500,1000);
        CShape* pShape2 =new CSquare(1000);
        CShape* pShape3=new CCircle(700);
        DescribeShape(pShape1);
        DescribeShape(pShape2);
        DescribeShape(pShape3);
        delete pShape1;
        delete pShape2;
        delete pShape3;
}
```

Main 3 declares three pointers to CShape objects and creates an instantiation of each. The first is instantiated as a CRectangle, the second as a CSquare and the third as a CCircle. Since all three shapes inherit from our base class, CShape, as long as we only call CShape methods (i.e., methods declared in the base), The three shapes are interchangeable. The output from the above main3 would thus describe each of the three shapes in turn.

Note, the "->" to call a method on the CShape object pointer. Note also the use of the keywords new and delete. Remember how we discussed object lifetime? The new operator creates a new object on the heap, and the delete keyword destroys the object. All our variable declarations prior to this example have been declared on the stack. We'll discuss this further in Lesson 18. For now, you only need to know that if you create an instance of an object using new, you must also call delete to destroy it, because you need to free the memory you used to create the object. You do not need to do this, if declaring variables on the stack. Of course you couldn't do what we want without using the heap, since we want a pointer that can point to any CShape object, without knowing the particular shape we're going to instantiate at the time we declare the pointer.

The CShape object is said to be polymorphic. Polymorphism is the property of having the same interface, but doing different things. The method used to describe our CShape object can describe a square, a rectangle, a circle, etc., but uses the same interface to do so. The CShape can be queried for the number of its sides, its perimeter, its area and its name.

Just as you can override (or overload) methods in a class that inherits from a base class, you can overload operators such as the + - / * etc. For example, you could overload the + operator for a class representing strings, in order to concatenate (join) two strings together and return the resultant string. We will not go into anymore detail about overloading operators in this book, but mention this in passing. One must be very careful when overloading operators to ensure that one only does so, if it would make working with the class more logical and natural. In our example, it is quite natural to think of adding string1 to string2 and getting a resultant string containing the contents of both string1 and string2.

Also note that in our example, our CShape class definition was abstract, i.e., had no implementation. Usually we call an abstract class an interface, and use the "I" rather than the "C" prefix, i.e., we could have called our interface IShape rather than CShape. This would indicate that the shape class is abstract and has no implementation. You will be familiar with the "I" prefix from the IPhone, IPad, etc. This "I" prefix originally came from the notion of an interface, but has been used by marketing departments to capitalize upon the "me" culture.

Activity:

1. What is a base class?

2. What does declaring a member function virtual allow you to do?

3. What does it mean to overload or override a member function in an inherited class?

4. Why would you choose to override a class member in an inherited class?

5. What is an abstract base class (or interface)?

6. a.   What does the "new" C++ operator do?

    b.   What does the "delete" C++ operator do?

7. What does the "->" operator mean?

8. Describe in your own words the reason why we might want a function that takes a pointer to a base class object. (Hint: polymorphic objects).

9. Which methods does a base class pointer allow you to call for any derived class objects?

10. What do you think would happen if a class directly inherited from multiple objects?

Lesson 16

Multiple Inheritance

Vocabulary:

Multiple Inheritance

Memory Verse:

Hebrews 6:12, "That ye be not slothful, but followers of them who through faith and patience inherit the promises."

I asked in the last lesson what you thought would happen if a class inherited from multiple classes. The answer is multiple inheritance. Consider the following:

```
class CSiren
{
    public:
    CSiren();
    ~CSiren();
    Play();
    Stop();
};
```

The Implementation of CSiren is hidden since it is not relevant.

```
class CLightAndSiren : public CSuperLamp, public CSiren
{
    public:
    CLightAndSiren ();
    ~CLightAndSiren ();
};

void main()
{
    CLightAndSiren ls;
```

```
ls.Play(); // start the siren
ls.FlashMode(30); /* flash the lamp for 30 seconds while the siren
is playing */
ls.Stop(); // stop the siren when the lamp stops flashing.
}
```

This class inherits from both CSuperLamp and CSiren. It adds no extra functionality. All we need to do is declare the constructor, which in this case also does nothing but serve as a means of instantiation. This class uses multiple inheritance and inherits all public and protected members of both the CSuperLamp class and CSiren class. This also includes the public and protected members of CLamp which CSuperLamp inherits from.

You can see that multiple inheritance is very powerful. It serves as the mechanism for building large interrelated systems.

Activity:

1. What is the purpose of multiple inheritance?

2. Write an override for the OnOffButton method that starts the siren when the lamp switches on, and stops the siren when the lamp switches off.

Review of Lessons 14 through 16

1. What is an object?

2. What is inheritance?

3. What is multiple inheritance?

4. What does it mean to override a class member?

5. What modifier do you need to mark class members with in order to override them?

6. a. What are the three visibility designations of class members? (Hint: p_____,
   pr_____, p__v____.)

   b. What do each of the three visibility designations mean?

7. What is an abstract base class or interface?

8. Why can't an abstract class be instantiated?

9. What is a base class?

10. What is the purpose of inheritance?

11. What does it mean to declare the implementation of a class member inline?

12. When is it okay to declare the implementation of a class member inline? (Hint: there are actually two answers.)

13. What is the purpose of declaring multiple constructors for an object? (Hint: think of the different kinds of information that might be required when instantiating an object.)

14. a. In what order do constructors get called by the runtime system for an object that inherits from other objects, which in turn inherit from yet other objects?

b. In what order do destructors get called by the runtime system for an object that inherits from other objects, which in turn inherit from yet other objects?

15. When multiple objects inherit from a base class such as the CRectangle, CCircle and CSquare classs examples, the objects are said to be poly_____.

16. What is the purpose of passing a pointer to a base class into a function? (Hint: think of the shape example.)

The Heap and the Stack

Vocabulary:

heap, stack, allocation, deallocation, local variables, global variables, Member Variable, memory leak, push, pop, Instruction Pointer, Stack Pointer, Stack Overflow.

Memory Verse:

Proverbs 4:7, "Wisdom is the principal thing; therefore get wisdom: and with all thy getting get understanding."

In Lesson 15, we introduced you to the heap and the stack without saying much about what they were. This lesson will elaborate on these terms, as well as give a brief overview of the other terms in the vocabulary list.

The Stack

The stack is a small amount of memory set aside for keeping track of memory addresses and local variables for the function currently be executed. When a procedure calls a function, the address of the instruction after the calling instruction is stored on the stack, before execution transfers to the called function. The parameters that need to be passed to the called function also get put on the stack (from right to left, i.e., reverse declaration order). The stack is like a stack of papers. What is placed on the stack first is last to be removed.

Local variables are variables declared inside a function.

For example consider the following:

```
void main()
{
    myFunc(5);
}
```

```
void myFunc(int n)
{
    int j=2;
...
}
```

The machine code stored in main memory for this might look something like:

Contents of memory representing our pseudo machine code fragment.				
Label	Address (Hexadecimal)	Assembly Code Instruction	Machine Code Instruction	Comment
Start:	0000	Push 000A;	0100000a	/* push the address labelled by ContinueLabel onto the stack. */
	0004	Push 5;	01000005	/* push the value 5 onto the stack, which is the parameter we want to pass to MyFunc. */
	0008	Jump MyFunc;	02001000	/* Transfer execution to the address labelled MyFunc. */
ContinueLabel:	000A	…	…	/* other instructions to be executed on return from MyFunc. */
…	…	…	…	/* Other code */
End:	0fff…	brk	00000000	/* End of execution */
MyFunc:	1000	Store 2, F008	0302F008	/* Assignment of the value 2 to the variable j on the stack */
	…	…	…	/* other instructions in MyFunc */
MyFuncEnd:	1FFF	Ret;	FFFF0000	/* pops parameters (in this case 5) off stack, copies return address 000a to Instruction Pointer so that next instruction executed is after the call to MyFunc. */
…	…	…	…	/* other code or data */

The stack would look like:

Contents of the stack at the beginning of execution of the function MyFunc.		
Address (Hexadecimal)	Value at address (Hexadecimal)	Comment
F000	000A	/* Return address of MyFunc. */
F004	0005	/* value of actual parameter n passed into MyFunc */
F008	0002	/* value of local variable j used inside MyFunc */

In the two above tables, you'll notice that the addresses increment by four. This is because each memory address can hold one byte (8 bits). However, in our pseudo assembly code program, an instruction and its operands are always 32 bits wide. In real life, machine code instructions may vary in the number of bytes they occupy, depending on the operands and addressing mode of the instruction. On a 32 bit machine, instructions and their operands are typically a minimum of 32 bits. Assembly code or Machine code is beyond the scope of this book. The above example simply serves to demonstrate how a human readable language may be compiled into its machine code representation, and how that might look in memory if you were to view the raw bytes.

The stack thus contains any parameters or local variables and the return addresses for when a subroutine returns control to its caller. The special register inside the CPU used for pointing to addresses on the stack is called the Stack Pointer, SP. The register used for pointing to the address of the next instruction to be executed is the Instruction Pointer or IP.

When an address is placed on the stack, it is said to be pushed onto the stack. the SP register will point to the address of the stack where the item just pushed occurs. When an item is removed from the stack, it is said to be popped off the stack. SP is simply adjusted to point to the next address on the stack. When the SP reaches the end of the memory set aside for the stack, it wraps around to the start of the stack again. When this occurs, it is called a stack overflow, and can cause some very nasty and hard to find errors.

The main memory is also known as the heap. Thus, a variable may be declared on the stack or on the heap. You can usually recognize this by whether explicit memory allocation was used to instantiate an object or not. If no new keyword (or equivalent) is used to allocate memory on the heap, then the variable is placed on the stack. The stack is faster to access, but is limited in size. Typically only variables of a few to a few hundred bytes are stored on the stack. Anything larger, including object instantiations, are generally stored on the heap. It is not necessary to free or deallocate variables stored on the stack, because the stack is automatically managed by the runtime system each time a function is called or exited.

Note that even though memory may be allocated on the heap, the variable used to refer to that memory is often still stored on the stack. This is important, because if the variable used to point to the heap goes out of scope, there will be no way of knowing the address of the memory allocated on the heap, thus it won't be able to be deallocated.

For example:

```
void main()
{
    int x; // x is stored on the stack.
    int* px=new int; /* px points to space on the heap allocated to
    hold an int. */
}
```

When main exits, px goes out of scope. Unless main returns this value to another calling function, there will be no way of deallocating the memory to which px points.

Remember, most numeric data and short strings and characters are typically placed on the stack. Larger items such as object instantiations and large strings are allocated on the heap. When allocating on the heap it is imperative to also free the memory allocated when it is no longer needed or you will leak resources. This is called a memory leak. Note that variables stored on the stack are only available during the execution of the function in which they are declared. This is known as the scope of the variable (see Lesson 11). In the example above, myFunc declares a local variable called j. This variable is only available inside myFunc. Any code running outside of myFunc can't access this variable. In fact, since it is stored on the stack, as soon as myFunc exits and the stack's contents updated to reflect the next function and its parameters and local variables, there is no guarantee that j will even be there. When a variable is no longer available like this, it is said to go out of scope.

Variables declared on the heap are available outside the function in which they are declared, so long as that memory has not been deallocated or freed by a call to delete. However, though as pointed out, the address of the allocated memory must still be stored in a pointer, which itself is usually stored on the stack.

Example:

```
int* badFunc()
{
    int x=5;
    return &x
}
```

```
void test()
{
    int* px=badFunc();
}
```

The badFunc function returns the address of x. Since the scope of x is only valid for instructions running inside badFunc, the test function will be accessing a variable that will go out of scope as soon as badFunc exits, which means the test function will not yield predictable results.

Now consider:

```
int* goodfunc()
{
    int* px =new int;
    *px=5;
    return px;
}
void test2()
{
    int* p=goodFunc;
    delete p;
}
```

Test2 can access the integer declared inside goodFunc, since it is declared on the heap, and thus doesn't go out of scope when the goodfunc function returns. The test2 function has to free the memory allocated inside goodfunc, otherwise a memory leak would occur. Since GoodFunc returns the address of the pointer pointing to the allocated memory, test2 can free this memory.

A Global Variable is a variable declared at the outermost level of a program and is thus available to all functions running in that program. Typically, global variables are still stored on the stack. The use of Global Variables is discouraged, since complex programs using them are often hard to maintain, because one never knows who, what or when some function may modify the variable. Object oriented programs often use member variables. These are variables global to an object, but not global to the entire program (see Lesson 12).

Note that languages such as Visual Basic and CSharp do all of the memory management, but C++ leaves this up to the programmer. C++ is far more flexible allowing the programmer to manage memory allocation and deallocation, but with flexibility comes responsibility. Many program errors arise from memory leaks or other kinds of memory issues, as we'll discuss in Lesson 33.

Activity:

1. What is the stack used for?

2. What is the heap used for?

3. What is the difference between the heap and the stack?

4. Who is responsible for allocation and deallocation of heap memory?

5. What manages the stack and when?

6. What is the advantage of storing variables on the stack?

7. What is the advantage of storing variables on the heap?

8. What happens if you forget to deallocate memory allocated on the heap?

9. What is the name of the register used for keeping track of items pushed onto or popped off the stack?

10. What is the name of the register used for keeping track of the address containing the next instruction to be executed?

11. What is a stack overflow?

Lesson 19

Introduction to Binary

Vocabulary:

Binary, bit, nibble, byte, word, dword, qword, bitwise operators, and, or, not, xor, bit shift.

Memory Verse:

Ecclesiastes 4:9, "Two are better than one; because they have a good reward for their labour."

Binary is the name of the number system native to a computer. We humans work in decimal, presumably because we were created with ten fingers (digits). Computers, on the other hand, work in Binary, which only has two digits, 0 and 1. This is because inside a computer's memory and CPU, transistors are used to store the data. Because a transistor only has two states, on and off, a single transistor can only hold a single binary digit. By combining many transistors, more data can be stored. Eight transistors can be used together to hold a binary number, which can represent a decimal number from 0 to 255. Numbers are thus expressed as powers of two, rather than powers of ten. For example, consider the following numbers and their representations. Remember that anything to the power of zero is one, 10^0=1, 2^0=1, 1000^0=1:

	As Powers Of 10	As Powers Of 2	Binary
1	10^0	2^0	1
2	2x10^0	2^1	10
3	3x10^0	2^1 +2^0	11
4	4x10^0	2^2	100
5	5x10^0	2^2 +2^0	101
6	6x10^0	2^2 +2^1	110

Continued

	As Powers Of 10	As Powers Of 2	Binary
7	7x10^0	2^2 +2^1 +2^0	111
8	8x10^0	2^3	1000
9	9x10^0	2^3 +2^0	1001
10	10^1	2^3 +2^1	1010
100	10^2	2^6 +2^5 +2^2	1100100
128	10^2 +2x10^1 +8x10^0	2^7	10000000
256	2x10^2 +5x10^1 +6x10^0	2^8	100000000
512	5x10^2 +10^1 +2x10^0	2^9	1000000000
1024	10^3 +2x10^1 +4x10^0	2^10	10000000000
65535	6x10^4 +5x10^3 +5x10^2 +3x10^1 +5x10^0	2^15 +2^14 +2^13 +... +2^0	1111111111111111

Number of binary Digits	Is Called A
1	Bit
4	Nibble
8	Byte
16	Word
32	Double word or dword
64	Quadruple word or qword

Note: In terms of the CPU, a Word contains the number of bits that its largest register can hold. On a 32-bit CPU, this makes a Word 32-bits, and on a 64-bit CPU, a Word is 64-bits. When programming on Windows, however, a Word is always defined as 16-bits, hence the above table.

To calculate the binary representation of a decimal number, do the following steps:

1. Break the number down into a sum of powers of 2. E.g. 5 = 2^2 +0x2^1 +2^0.

2. For each non-zero multiple of a power of 2, write a 1 and for each zero multiple write a 0. Thus, 5=101 binary.

To convert from binary back to decimal, for each 1 add the power of 2 represented by the column in which the 1 is positioned, working from right to left. For example: 00011010 = 2^1 +2^3 +2^4 =26. (Remember the right most digit is 2^0=1.)

Note that we usually include leading zeros up to multiples of eight bits. Thus, if a binary representation has 6 digits, we will add two leading zeros to make it 8 digits long. If the binary representation is 13 bits, we add three leading zeros to make it 16 bits long. This just makes things easier to line up, and keeps columns neat when working with long binary strings. It also helps us picture the memory layout of the computer, which works with bytes, words, dwords and qwords. We usually only deal with nibbles when shifting bits or working with bitwise operators.

Bitwise operators are special mathematical symbols that allow us to compare and combine two binary numbers. The bitwise Or operator will return a 1, if either of the two binary numbers being ored have a 1 in that bit position. For example:

x=00000001

y=00000010

Now, x has the value 1 and y the value 2. If we perform a bitwise Or : x|y, the result is 00000011 i.e. the decimal value 3.

Similarly, the bitwise And operator returns a 1, if both bit positions in the two numbers being Anded is 1, otherwise it will return 0. The And operator is used to give a result containing all bits, which are switched on in the numbers being Anded and 0 for bits whichare not.

In our prior example, x&y will be 0, since comparing the two numbers 00000001 and 00000010, no bit positions contain a 1 in both numbers.

If however x=00000001 and y=00000011

then x&y will be equal to 00000001, since this bit is on in both numbers.

Here's another example:

a=10101010

b=11001100

a&b will be equal to 10001000 or 136.

To work out the result of a bitwise operator, line up the binary numbers one on top of the other, and then compare them. If the operator is Or, for each bit position, if there is a 1 in either number, put a 1 in the result. If both numbers contain a 0 in the same bit position, put a 0 in the result. If the operator is And, only put a 1 in the result, if there is a 1 in the same bit position of both numbers. Otherwise put a 0.

The Not operator flips the bits in a number. For example:

x=00000001

Not x (written ~x) will be 11111110. I.e. the Not operator flips each bit to its opposite value.

Finally, the Exclusive Or operator puts a 1 in the result, if there is a 1 in either of the numbers in the same bit position, but puts a 0 in the result, if the same bit position is 1 in both numbers. For example:

x=11000000

y=01100000

x^ will be 10100000

Bitwise operators should not be confused with logical operators used for combining conditions used in If statements. Bitwise operators do a bit comparison of numbers, whereas logical operators are used to combine the results of subexpressions.

To clarify, if (a || b) means that the If statement will evaluate to true if either condition a is true or condition b is true. Whereas if (a|b) will do a bitwise comparison of the two numbers a and b, and if the bitwise comparison is non-zero, then the If statement would evaluate to true.

Back in Lesson 10 we mentioned that the << and >> operators used for stream insertion and extraction were actually bit shift operators, which had been overloaded for streams because of the similarity in concept. We'll now briefly discuss what these operators do.

Consider the binary number 4: 00000100

The << operator shifts the bits in the operand to the left, effectively multiplying the number by a power of 2. For example, 4<<2 would take the number 4 and shift the bits left by two bits, so 00000100 becomes 00010000, i.e., we multiplied 4 by 2 to the power of 2, or 4. 4 multiplied by 4 is 16.

Similarly, 4>>2 moves the bits right by two bits, effectively dividing by 2 twice. Thus, 4>>2 would be 00000001, i.e., 4 divided by 4 equals 1.

When you shift bits left or right, the number is padded with zeros. You need to be careful when shifting bits that you don't inadvertently shift them too far and obtain an unexpected result.

Consider the following example:

```
BYTE b=128;
BYTE b2=b<<1;
```

What do you think b2 would be equal to?

Be careful! A byte is represented by only 8 bits. Since 128 is 10000000 in binary, shifting left by 1 will cause the result to be 0, not 256. To avoid this, make sure your variable type is large enough to hold the result. The following would work:

```
BYTE b=128;
int n=b<<1;
```

The result in n would be 256 as expected, because n is an integer that is usually represented by 32 bits.

Using the shift operators is typically much faster than asking the CPU to do the calculation using other math operators, because bit shifts are a simpler operation and native to the CPU.

Activity:

1. Write out the powers of 2 from 0 to 256 ($2^0=1$, $2^1=2$, $2^2=4$, $2^3=8$, ...)

2. Convert the following decimal numbers to binary:

    a. 4   b. 12   c. 16   d. 33   e. 65

    f. 127   g. 255   h. 256   i. 30   j. 75

3. Convert the following binary numbers back to decimal:

    a. 00000011   b. 00000111   c. 00001111   d. 00110011   e. 01010101

    f. 10000000   g. 11110000   h. 11000011   i. 00111100   j. 11111111

4. Calculate the following results:

    a. 10000001 & 11001110

    b. 10101010 | 01010101 (Remember | is the bitwise Or operator.)

    c. ~00110011 (Remember ~ is the Not operator.)

    d. 10001111^01111111 (Remember ^ is the XOR operator.)

5. What is the difference between bitwise and logical operators?

6. Calculate 8<<3 (assuming an 8-bit variable).

7. Calculate 128>>4 (assuming an 8-bit variable).

Introduction to Hexadecimal

Vocabulary:

Hexadecimal (or hex)

Memory Verses:

Jeremiah 9:23-24, "Thus saith the LORD, Let not the wise [man] glory in his wisdom, neither let the mighty [man] glory in his might, let not the rich [man] glory in his riches: But let him that glorieth glory in this, that he understandeth and knoweth me, that I am the LORD which exercise lovingkindness, judgment, and righteousness, in the earth: for in these things I delight, saith the LORD."

Hexadecimal, or simply hex, is another number system used in programming. This system uses base 16 rather than base 10; it has 16 digits rather than 10. The digits of this system are 0 through 9, and then a through f. Numbers are thus expressed as powers of 16, rather than powers of ten. Hex is used, because each nibble (four bits) of a binary number can be represented by a single hexadecimal digit, making memory dumps (display of memory content) more compact. For example, consider the following numbers and their representations (Remember that anything to the power of zero is one, $10^0=1$, $16^0=1$, $1000^0=1$.):

Decimal	Hex
0-9	0-9
10	A
11	B
12	C
13	D
14	E

Continued

Decimal	Hex
15	F
16	10
17	11
18	12
19	13
20	14
21	15
22	16
23	17
24	18
25	19
26	2A
27	2B
28	2C
29	2D
30	2E
31	2F
32	20
64	40
128	80
256	100
512	200
1024	400
4096	1000
16384	4000
32768	8000
65535	FFFF
65536	10000
131072	20000

Number of Hex Digits	Is Called A
1	Nibble
2	Byte
4	Word
8	Double word or dword
16	Quadruple word or qword

Note: In terms of the CPU, a Word contains the number of bits that its largest register can hold. On a 32-bit CPU, this makes a Word 32-bits, and on a 64-bit CPU a Word is 64-bits. When programming on Windows, however, a Word is always defined as 16-bits, hence the above table.

Converting between hex and decimal is not as straightforward as converting between decimal and binary, because not many people learn their 16 times tables. It is, however, very useful to remember your 16 times tables, if you are likely to be a programmer by profession.

To calculate the decimal representation of a hex number, starting from the rightmost column, convert the digit to its decimal representation, and then multiply by its power of 16. For example:

$ff = 15 \times 16^0 + 15 \times 16^1 = 255$ decimal.

To calculate the Hex representation of a decimal number, do the following steps:

1. Break the number down into a sum of multiples of powers of 16. E.g. $65 = 4 \times 16^1 + 16^0 = 41$ hex.

Note that we usually include leading zeros, so that the hex number is an even number of digits, usually 2, 4 or 8 digits. Thus, if a Hex representation has 3 digits, we will add one leading zero to make it 4 digits long. If the Hex representation is 7 digits, we add one leading zero to make it 8 hex digits long. This just makes things easier to line up and keeps columns neat when working with long Hex strings. It also helps us picture the memory layout of the computer, which works with bytes, words, dwords and qwords. We usually only deal with nibbles when shifting bits or working with bitwise operators, as we saw in Lesson 19.

Since decimal and hex numbers may be confused if not containing an Alpha character, there are several ways of denoting that a number is to be interpreted as hex. One such way is to precede the number with 0X. Thus, 0x10 is the hex number 10, which is 16 decimal. We can also put an H after the number, e.g. 10H =16 decimal.

Activity:

1. Write out the 16 Hexadecimal digits: 0, 1, ...

2. Learn your 16 times tables by writing them out.

3. Convert the following decimal numbers to hex:

    a. 4   b. 12   c. 16   d. 33   e. 65

    f. 127   g. 255   h. 256   i. 30   j. 75

4. Convert the following Hex numbers back to decimal:

    a. A   b. 10   c. c0   d. ff   e. 100

    f. 20   g. a0   h. 80   i. ff00   j. ffff

Review of Chapters 18 to 20

1. What is the stack used for?

2. What is the heap used for?

3. What is the difference between the heap and the stack?

4. Who is responsible for allocation and deallocation of heap memory?

5. What manages the stack and when?

6. What is the advantage of storing variables on the stack?

7. What is the advantage of storing variables on the heap?

8. What happens if you forget to deallocate memory allocated on the heap?

9. What is the name of the register used for keeping track of items pushed onto or popped off the stack?

10. What is the name of the register used for keeping track of the address containing the next instruction to be executed?

11. What is a stack overflow?

12. Write out the powers of 2 from 0 to 256 ($2^0=1$, $2^1=2$, $2^2=4$, $2^3=8$, ...)

13. Convert the following decimal numbers to binary:

    a. 7   b. 15   c. 16   d. 31   e. 82

    f. 127   g. 128   h. 254   i. 256   j. 192

14. Convert the following binary numbers back to decimal:

    a. 00000010 b. 00001011 c. 01001111 d. 01100110

    e. 10101010 f. 10001000 g. 11110001 h. 11100111 i. 00111100

    j. 11111111

15. Convert the following decimal numbers to hex:

    a. 10   b. 12   c. 16   d. 33   e. 65

    f. 127   g. 255   h. 256   i. 30   j. 75

16. Convert the following hex numbers back to decimal:

    a. A   b. B   c. c0   d. D1   e. 100

    f. 20   g. a0   h. 80   i. ff   j. ABCD

17. How many digits do the following binary terms have:

    a. bit   b. Nibble c. Byte d. Word

    e. DWORD   f. QWORD

18. Why is binary used instead of decimal inside a computer's CPU?

19. How many bits can a single hex digit represent?

20. Why is hexadecimal used instead of binary when displaying memory dumps?

Data Structures 1 - Stack

Vocabulary:

Data Structure, Stack

Memory Verse:

Mark 9:35, "And he sat down, and called the twelve, and saith unto them, If any man desire to be first, the same shall be last of all, and servant of all."

A data structure is a structure made up of intrinsic or basic data types used for representing more complex and abstract concepts. Common data structures include the Stack, Queue, Linked List, Doubly Linked List, Tree and Map. In this lesson we'll first look at the stack.

A stack is similar to a physical stack of papers; the first item pushed onto the stack is the last item removed from the stack. This is known as LIFO access, last in, first out. Stacks are very useful when the state of a program needs to be maintained and a prior state needs to be remembered. You have already been introduced to one use of a stack in Lesson 18. Here is a simple implementation of a stack using an array. This stack holds integers and can hold a maximum of 1000 items.

```
#include "stdafx.h"
#include <iostream>
using namespace std;
// define a constant to be used to represent the maximum stack size
#define MAX_STACK_SIZE 1000
class CSimpleIntStack
{
    public:
    CSimpleIntStack();
    ~CSimpleIntStack();
    void Push(int nVal); // push a value onto the stack
    int Pop(); // pop a value off the stack
```

```cpp
    int Top(); /* return the top element of the stack without popping
    it off. */
    private:
    int m_nStackPointer;
    int m_nItems[MAX_STACK_SIZE];
};

CSimpleIntStack::CSimpleIntStack()
{
    m_nStackPointer=0; // point to the first item
}

CSimpleIntStack::~CSimpleIntStack()
{
    // destructor doesn't do anything.
}

void CSimpleIntStack::Push(int nVal)
{
    // push a value onto the stack
    if (m_nStackPointer < MAX_STACK_SIZE)/* see if there is any more
    room in the stack */
    {// there is so store the value
        m_nItems[m_nStackPointer]=nVal; /* place nVal in the int
        array */
        m_nStackPointer++; /* increment the stack pointer to point
        to the next available slot. */
        m_nItems[m_nStackPointer]=0; /* initialize the new empty
        position in case there used to be something in it. */
    }
}

int CSimpleIntStack::Pop()
{
    // pop a value off the stack
    if (m_nStackPointer ==0)
    return 0; // nothing pushed onto the stack yet.
    /* need to decrement first because a push would have incremented
    the stack pointer to point to a new empty slot */
    m_nStackPointer--; /* decrement the stack pointer to point to
    the item last pushed. */
    return m_nItems[m_nStackPointer]; /* return the item at the top
    of the stack */
}
```

```
int CSimpleIntStack::Top()
{
    if (m_nStackPointer==0)
        return 0; // nothing pushed onto the stack yet
    // return the top element of the stack without popping it off.
    return m_nItems[m_nStackPointer-1]; /* just return the last item
    pushed */
}
```

This implementation is very simple and has virtually no error handling. It also only handles integers. We'll look at how to make more generic data structures when we introduce templates in Lesson 30.

Here's a test function to try it out:

```
int main(int argc, char* argv[])
{
  CSimpleIntStack s; // create an int stack.
  for (int n=1; n <=100; n++)
  {
      s.Push(n); // push the first 100 integers onto the stack.
  }
  // now pop them off and print them in the order they are popped.
  for (int n=1; n <=100; n++)
  {
      int nVal=s.Pop();
      cout << "n= " << n << ", nVal=" << nVal << endl;
  }

      return 0;
}
```

The output would be:

n=1, nVal=100

n=2, nVal=99

...

n=100, nVal=1

Activity:

1. What is a stack and why is it used?

2. What are the limitations of our stack implementation?

3. How might we modify this class to detect an error condition, such as a push or pop failing?

4. What is the difference between the Top and Pop members?

5. How would you make this stack able to hold 5000 rather than 1000 integers?

Data Structures 2 - Queue

Vocabulary:

queue

Memory Verse:

Psalms 119:133, "Order my steps in thy word: and let not any iniquity have dominion over me."

The queue is like a queue of people; the first person on the queue is the first person served. This is also known as FIFO access, first in, first out.

We could implement a simple int queue as follows:

```
#include "stdafx.h"
#include <iostream>
using namespace std;

/* define a constant representing the maximum number of items which
maybe queued */
#define MAX_QUEUE_SIZE 1000
class CSimpleIntQueue
{
    public:
    CSimpleIntQueue();
    ~CSimpleIntQueue();
    bool Enqueue(int nVal); // add an int to the queue
    int Dequeue(); // remove the first item from the queue
    int Front(); /* examine the first item in the queue without
    removing it. */
    int Back() ; /* examine the last item in the queue without
    removing it. */
    int Count(); // obtain the number of items in the queue
```

```cpp
private:
    int m_nNextPos;
    int m_nItems[MAX_QUEUE_SIZE];
};

CSimpleIntQueue::CSimpleIntQueue()
{
    m_nNextPos=0; // queue is empty
}

CSimpleIntQueue::~CSimpleIntQueue()
{
    // destructor doesn't need to do anything
}

bool CSimpleIntQueue::Enqueue(int nVal)
{
    // add an int to the queue
    if (m_nNextPos >=MAX_QUEUE_SIZE)
        return false; // nothing can be added
    m_nItems[m_nNextPos]=nVal;
    m_nNextPos++; /* points to the next available queue position and
    maintains the number of items in the queue */
    return true; // item was enqueued okay.
}
int CSimpleIntQueue::Dequeue()
{
    if (m_nNextPos==0)
        return 0; // nothing in the queue yet
    // otherwise there are still items in the queue
    int nFirstItemValue=m_nItems[0]; /* save the first item in the
    array to return it. */
    /* now move all of the subsequent items toward the front of the
    queue */
    for (int n=0; n < m_nNextPos ;n++)
    {
        m_nItems[n]=m_nItems[n+1]; // move each item left by one
    }
    m_nNextPos--; /* decrement the pointer to the next available
    spot by one */
    //since we've moved all items toward the start of the array.
    m_nItems[m_nNextPos]=0; // clear the end of the queue
    return nFirstItemValue;
}

int CSimpleIntQueue::Front()
```

```
{
    // examine the first item in the queue without removing it.
    return m_nItems[0];
}

int CSimpleIntQueue::Back()
{
    if (m_nNextPos ==0)
        return 0; // nothing in the queue
    // examine the last item in the queue without removing it.
    return m_nItems[m_nNextPos-1]; // remember m_nNextPos is pointing
    to the next available empty slot
}

int CSimpleIntQueue::Count()
{
    /* Since the queue array starts at index 0, m_nNextPos will
coincidentally equal the number of items in the queue. */
    return m_nNextPos;
}

int main(int argc, char* argv[])
{
    CSimpleIntQueue theQueue;
    for (int n=0; n < 20; n++)
    {
        theQueue.Enqueue(n);
    }
    int nCount=theQueue.Count();
    for (int j=1; j <= nCount; j++)
    {
        int nFirstItem=theQueue.Dequeue();
        int nLeft=theQueue.Count();
        cout << "Item " << j << " is " << nFirstItem << " after
        dequeuing only " << nLeft << " items left." << endl;
    }
    return 0;
}
```

Output:

Item 1 is 1, after dequeuing only 19 items left

Item 2 is 2, after dequeuing only 18 items left

Item 3 is 3, after dequeuing only 17 items left

...

Item 20 is 20, after dequeuing only 0 items left

Activity:

1. What is the difference between a Stack and a Queue in terms of the order in which items are removed from each data structure?

2. When is a Stack useful?

3. When is a Queue useful?

4. What are the limitations of our Queue implementation? (Hint: think of the data type, maximum items, performance and memory usage of our implementation of this data structure.)

5. Describe what the following code block in the Dequeue method does and why it is needed.

```
for (int n=0; n < m_nNextPos ;n++)
{
        m_nItems[n]=m_nItems[n+1]; // move each item left by one
}
```

Data Structures 3 - Linked List

Vocabulary:

Linked List, Doubly Linked List

Memory Verse:

Ecclesiastes 12:1, "Remember now thy Creator in the days of thy youth, while the evil days come not, nor the years draw nigh, when thou shalt say, I have no pleasure in them;"

In our last two lessons, we implemented a Stack and Queue using an array. One of the questions asked about the limitations of our implementation of these data structures. One of the limitations was that our implementations used an array of fixed size, which meant that not only was the Stack and Queue limited to 1000 integers, the memory for 1000 integers had to be allocated, even if the Stack or Queue didn't use the 1000 slots. One solution to this problem is the Linked List data structure.

The Linked List data structure is implemented as a linked set of structures where each structure has a pointer to the next structure in the list. It is imperative that we store (or remember) a pointer to the very first node of our list otherwise the whole list will be inaccessible. Just like life, we must *remember our Creator* lest we lose our reference and purpose. Each structure is allocated only if it is required, thus the memory usage is restricted to the number of elements actually required. Also, the maximum number of elements is only limited by physical memory on the computer, and not on the fixed array size declared by the programmer. We will thus implement a Queue using a Linked List rather than a static array. Note the more complex class definition below:

```
#include "stdafx.h"
#include <iostream>
using namespace std;

class CLinkedListQueue
{
```

```
    public:
    CLinkedListQueue();
    virtual ~CLinkedListQueue();
    bool Enqueue(int nVal);
    int Count();
    int Front();
    int Back();
    int Dequeue();

    private:

    typedef struct sListElement
    {
            int nVal; // the value in the link
            sListElement* pNextElement; // a pointer to the next link
    };
    sListElement* m_pFirst; // pointer to first element
    sListElement* m_pLast; // pointer to last element
    int m_nCount; // number of links.
};

CLinkedListQueue:: CLinkedListQueue()
{
    m_pFirst=0;
    m_pLast=0;
    m_nCount=0;
}

CLinkedListQueue::~ CLinkedListQueue()
{// deallocate the memory we allocated for each link
    sListElement* pTemp=m_pFirst;
    sListElement* pNext=0;
    while (pTemp)
    {
            pNext=pTemp->pNextElement; /* so we know where the next
            element is in memory. */
            delete pTemp; // deallocate the memory pointed to by pTemp;
            pTemp=pNext; // now set pTemp to the next element location
    }
    m_pFirst=0;
    m_pLast=0;
}

bool CLinkedListQueue::Enqueue(int nVal)
{// allocate a new link on the heap pointed to by pNew.
    sListElement* pNew=new sListElement;
    pNew->nVal=nVal; // set the new link's value
```

```
    pNew->pNextElement=0; /* there is no link after this one yet so
    set its next ptr to 0 */
    if (m_pLast!=0)// its not the first link
        m_pLast->pNextElement=pNew; /* set the prior last link's
        next ptr to point to the new element we just allocated. */
    m_pLast=pNew; // now make m_pLast point to the newly created link
    if (m_pFirst==0)// this must be the first link
        m_pFirst=pNew; /* so m_pFirst points to the first link
        allocated. */
    m_nCount++; // we've just added a link so increment the counter.
    return true;
}

int CLinkedListQueue::Count()
{
    return m_nCount;
}

int CLinkedListQueue::Front()
{
    if (m_pFirst)
        return m_pFirst->nVal;
    else
        return 0;
}

int CLinkedListQueue::Back()
{
    if (m_pLast)
        return m_pLast->nVal;
    else
        return 0;
}

int CLinkedListQueue::Dequeue()
{
    if (m_pFirst)
    {
        int nVal=m_pFirst->nVal;
        sListElement* pNext=m_pFirst->pNextElement; /* save it
        since we're about to deallocate m_pFirst's memory. */
        if (m_pFirst==m_pLast)
            m_pLast=pNext;
        delete m_pFirst;
        m_pFirst=pNext; /* now m_pFirst points to the next item in
        the queue. */
```

```
            m_nCount--; // one less item in the queue
            return nVal; // the value we saved before deleting.
        }
        else
            return 0; // nothing in the queue
    }


    int main(int argc, char* argv[])
    {
        CLinkedListQueue theQueue;
        for (int n=1; n <=20; n++)
        {
            theQueue.Enqueue(n);
        }
        int nCount=theQueue.Count();
        for (int j=1; j <= nCount; j++)
        {
            int nFirstItem=theQueue.Dequeue();
            int nLeft=theQueue.Count();
            cout << "Item " << j << " is " << nFirstItem << " after
            dequeuing only " << nLeft << " items left." << endl;
        }
        return 0;
    }
```

Note the typedef keyword in the class definition. This says that the sListElement is a new type whose definition is described by the struct containing an int and a pointer to another sListElement. The typedef keyword is specific to C++, but other languages often have similar mechanisms for creating new types or synonyms for existing types.

Activity:

1. You'll notice in the above class that we are careful, for instance, in the destructor, and also in dequeue to save the address of the pointer to the next link before deleting the current link. Why do you think we must do this? Hint: if we did not do this, how would we access the next link in the chain?

2. Why must we set m_pFirst and m_pLast to 0 in the constructor?

3. How could we make this class better? Hint: If the user calls Front or Back, how do they know that 0 is a valid queue entry or if it is an error, because the queue is empty?

4. Why do you think we need to maintain both m_pFirst and m_pLast? Hint: if we only had m_pFirst, how would we enqueue a new item?

5. In Dequeue, why do we need to save a copy of nVal and return it, rather than the actual value in the link?

6. What does the destructor of the class do?

7. What would happen if in Dequeue we did not check to see if m_pLast was pointing to the same memory as m_pFirst before deallocating the memory pointed to by m_pFirst?

8. In our vocabulary we mentioned a doubly linked list. We have not defined this yet but what do you think a doubly linked list is? Hint: A single-linked list as in this lesson makes each link point to its next link in the chain.

Data Structures 4 - Doubly Linked List

Vocabulary:

Doubly Linked List.

Memory Verse:

Isaiah 46:9-10, "Remember the former things of old: for I am God, and there is none else; I am God, and there is none like me, Declaring the end from the beginning, and from ancient times the things that are not yet done, saying, My counsel shall stand, and I will do all my pleasure:"

We asked in the prior lesson what you thought a doubly linked list was. If you said a list in which each element has a pointer to both its next and prior link, you'd be correct. Just as God knows the *end from the beginning,* maintaining links to both the prior and next list node allows backward and forward traversal to search the list in either direction.

There are multiple reasons why we might want to implement a list in this way. The primary reason for using a doubly linked list instead of an array is because a doubly linked list is very efficient when inserting items into the middle of the list. A doubly linked list should be used instead of a singly linked list when you need to traverse the list in reverse, i.e., you need to be able to get from one item to the prior item in the list, in order to insert a new element between two existing ones. An array does not suffer from such traversal limitations, and is very efficient to access items anywhere in the list. If you need to frequently insert items into the middle of an array, however, it can be very inefficient, since you need to move the rest of the items to make room, and sometimes reallocate the array to make more room than was originally allocated. The disadvantage of linked lists is that unless you maintain a pointer to the last element accessed, in order to access an element you need to traverse the list from the first element, following the links until you find the element you're looking for.

Advantages of Arrays	Disadvantages of Arrays	Advantages of Linked Lists	Disadvantages of Linked Lists
Fast to access any element	Inefficient to insert elements into the middle	Efficient to insert elements into the middle	Must traverse the linked list to find the item you want to access
Good for fixed number of elements.	Inefficient when number of elements dynamically changes.	Efficient when number of elements dynamically changes	Memory can become fragmented

Study the following class definition of a doubly linked list:

```
#include "stdafx.h"
#include <iostream>
using namespace std;
class CDoublyLinkedList
{
    public:
    CDoublyLinkedList();
    virtual ~CDoublyLinkedList();
    bool Append(int nVal);
    bool InsertBefore(int nIndex, int nVal);
    bool DeleteItem(int nIndex);
    int Count();
    int GetAt(int nIndex);
    bool SetAt(int nIndex, int nVal);

    private:
    typedef struct sDoublyLinkedListItem
    {
        int nVal;
        sDoublyLinkedListItem* pNext;
        sDoublyLinkedListItem* pPrev;
    };
    sDoublyLinkedListItem* m_pHead;
    sDoublyLinkedListItem* m_pTail;
    int m_nCount;
};

CDoublyLinkedList::CDoublyLinkedList()
{
    m_pHead=0;
    m_pTail=0;
```

```
        m_nCount=0;
}

CDoublyLinkedList::~CDoublyLinkedList()
{
      sDoublyLinkedListItem* pTemp=m_pHead;
      while (pTemp)
      {
            sDoublyLinkedListItem* pNext=pTemp->pNext;
            delete pTemp;
            pTemp=pNext;
      }
      m_pHead=0;
      m_pTail=0;
      m_nCount=0;
}

bool CDoublyLinkedList::Append(int nVal)
{
      sDoublyLinkedListItem* pNew=new sDoublyLinkedListItem;
      pNew->nVal=nVal;
      pNew->pNext=NULL;
      pNew->pPrev=m_pTail;
      if (!m_pHead)
            m_pHead=pNew;
      if (m_pTail)
      {
      m_pTail->pNext=pNew;
            m_pTail=pNew;
      }
      else
            m_pTail=pNew;
      m_nCount++;
      return true;
}

bool CDoublyLinkedList::InsertBefore(int nIndex, int nVal)
{
      if (m_pHead==0)
            return Append(nVal);
      int nThisIndex=0;
      sDoublyLinkedListItem* pCurrent=m_pHead;
      while (pCurrent && nThisIndex < nIndex)
      {
            pCurrent=pCurrent->pNext;
            nThisIndex++;
      }
```

```
        if (!pCurrent)
                return false;
        // create a new item
        sDoublyLinkedListItem* pNew=new sDoublyLinkedListItem;
        pNew->nVal=nVal;
        pNew->pPrev=pCurrent->pPrev;
        pNew->pNext=pCurrent;
        if (pCurrent->pPrev)
                pCurrent->pPrev->pNext=pNew;
        pCurrent->pPrev=pNew;
        if (m_pHead==pCurrent)
                m_pHead=pNew;
        if (m_pTail==0)
        m_pTail=pNew;
        m_nCount++;
        return true;
}


bool CDoublyLinkedList::DeleteItem(int nIndex)
{
        int nThisIndex=0;
        sDoublyLinkedListItem* pCurrent=m_pHead;
        while (pCurrent && nThisIndex < nIndex)
        {
                pCurrent=pCurrent->pNext;
                nThisIndex++;
        }
        if (!pCurrent)
                return false;
        sDoublyLinkedListItem *pPrev=pCurrent->pPrev;
        sDoublyLinkedListItem* pNext=pCurrent->pNext;
        if (pPrev)
                pPrev->pNext=pNext;
        if (pNext)
                pNext->pPrev=pPrev;
        if (m_pHead==pCurrent)
        {
                m_pHead=pNext;
        }
        if (m_pTail==pCurrent)
                m_pTail=pNext;
        delete pCurrent;
        m_nCount--;
        return true;
}
```

```
int CDoublyLinkedList::Count()
{
    return m_nCount;
}

int CDoublyLinkedList::GetAt(int nIndex)
{
int nThisIndex=0;
    sDoublyLinkedListItem* pCurrent=m_pHead;
    while (pCurrent && nThisIndex < nIndex)
    {
        pCurrent=pCurrent->pNext;
        nThisIndex++;
    }
    if (!pCurrent)
        return 0;
    return pCurrent->nVal;
}

bool CDoublyLinkedList::SetAt(int nIndex, int nVal)
{
    int nThisIndex=0;
    sDoublyLinkedListItem* pCurrent=m_pHead;
    while (pCurrent && nThisIndex < nIndex)
    {
        pCurrent=pCurrent->pNext;
        nThisIndex++;
    }
    if (!pCurrent)
        return false;
    pCurrent->nVal=nVal;
    return true;
}

int main(int argc, char* argv[])
{
    CDoublyLinkedList dl;
    for (int n=2; n < 10; n++)
    {
        dl.Append(n);
    }
    dl.InsertBefore(0, 0);
    dl.InsertBefore(1, 1);
    int nCount=dl.Count();
    for (int j=0; j < nCount; j++)
    {
```

```
                int nVal=dl.GetAt(j);
                cout << "j is " << j << " value is " << nVal << endl;
        }
        dl.DeleteItem(1);
        dl.DeleteItem(2);
        dl.DeleteItem(3);
        dl.DeleteItem(4);
        nCount=dl.Count();
        for (int k=0; k < nCount; k++)
        {
                int nVal=dl.GetAt(k);
                cout << "k is " << k << " value is " << nVal << endl;
        }

        return 0;
}
```

Activity:

1. What advantages can you think of for using a doubly linked list? (Hint: think of what operations are more efficient when using a doubly linked list as compared to an array.)

2. What disadvantages can you think of for using a doubly linked list? (Hint: think of the operations that are more efficient when using an array as compared to a doubly linked list.)

3. What does the following code in several methods of our doubly linked list class do?

```
int nThisIndex=0;
sDoublyLinkedListItem* pCurrent=m_pHead;
while (pCurrent && nThisIndex < nIndex)
{
        pCurrent=pCurrent->pNext;
        nThisIndex++;
}
```

4. Annotate the below code with comments explaining what each line does:

```
pNew->pPrev=pCurrent->pPrev;
pNew->pNext=pCurrent;
pCurrent->pPrev=pNew;
if (pCurrent->pPrev)
        pCurrent->pPrev->pNext=pNew;

sDoublyLinkedListItem *pPrev=pCurrent->pPrev;
```

```
sDoublyLinkedListItem* pNext=pCurrent->pNext;
if (pPrev)
    pPrev->pNext=pNext;
if (pNext)
    pNext->pPrev=pPrev;
delete pCurrent;
```

5. How could we have improved this class?

6. Looking at the above test code in Main, there are four DeleteItem calls. Which values do you think get deleted and why?

Lesson 26

Data Structures 5 – Tree

Vocabulary:

Tree, root, leaf, recursive, recursion.

Memory Verse:

Proverbs 11:30, "The fruit of the righteous is a tree of life; and he that winneth souls is wise."

A tree is a data structure that implements a tree of items. Starting at the root, the root may contain two or more branches to other items (or nodes), which in turn contain branches to more nodes etc. The starting node is the root and any node with no further branches is called a leaf node. A tree where every node has exactly two or less branches is called a Binary tree.

Here is a simple binary tree class. Firstly we define the node class from which the tree is constructed.

```
#include "stdafx.h"
#include <iostream>
using namespace std;

class cBinaryTreeNode
{
    public:
    cBinaryTreeNode();
    ~cBinaryTreeNode();
    cBinaryTreeNode* GetLeftBranch();
    cBinaryTreeNode* GetRightBranch();
    int GetNodeValue();
    void SetNodeValue(int nVal);
    void SetLeftBranch(cBinaryTreeNode* pNode);
    void SetRightBranch(cBinaryTreeNode* pNode);
```

```cpp
    cBinaryTreeNode* GetParent();
    void SetParent(cBinaryTreeNode* pNode);

    private:
    cBinaryTreeNode* m_pLeft;
    cBinaryTreeNode* m_pRight;
    cBinaryTreeNode* m_pParent;
    int m_nVal;
};

cBinaryTreeNode::cBinaryTreeNode()
{
    m_nVal=0;
    m_pLeft=0;
    m_pRight=0;
    m_pParent=0;
}

cBinaryTreeNode::~cBinaryTreeNode()
{
/* delete the left and right branch so they in turn delete their
branches. Note we do not need to delete our parent, it will be deleted
when its parent is deleted. */
    if (m_pLeft)
            delete m_pLeft;
    m_pLeft=0;
    if (m_pRight)
            delete m_pRight;
    m_pRight=0;
}

cBinaryTreeNode* cBinaryTreeNode::GetLeftBranch()
{
    return m_pLeft;
}

cBinaryTreeNode* cBinaryTreeNode::GetRightBranch()
{
    return m_pRight;
}

int cBinaryTreeNode::GetNodeValue()
{
    return m_nVal;
}
```

```
void cBinaryTreeNode::SetNodeValue(int nVal)
{
    m_nVal=nVal;
}


void cBinaryTreeNode::SetLeftBranch(cBinaryTreeNode* pNode)
{
    pNode->SetParent(this); /* The special keyword "this" refers to
    the object instance itself. Thus calling pNode->SetParent(this);
    will cause the instance of the object (whose method is currently
    being executed) to become the parent of pNode. */
    if (m_pLeft)//test if there is an existing left branch
        delete m_pLeft; /* if so, delete it and assign the pointer
        to point to the new node */
    m_pLeft=pNode;
}


void cBinaryTreeNode::SetRightBranch(cBinaryTreeNode* pNode)
{
    pNode->SetParent(this);
    if (m_pRight)//test if there is an existing right branch
        delete m_pRight; /* if so, delete it and assign the pointer
        to point to the new node */
    m_pRight=pNode;
}


cBinaryTreeNode* cBinaryTreeNode::GetParent()
{
    return m_pParent;
}


void cBinaryTreeNode::SetParent(cBinaryTreeNode* pNode)
{
    m_pParent=pNode;
}
```

To use this binary tree, our main function must create each node and call that node's methods and functions to add nodes and set the node value. Here is a sample.

```
void AddBranches(cBinaryTreeNode* pRoot, int nRootVal, int nDepth,
int nMaxDepth)
{// first create the root.
    if (pRoot==NULL)
        return; // nothing to do, no root passed to us.
    if (nDepth > nMaxDepth)
```

```
        return; // otherwise we won't stop!
        pRoot->SetNodeValue(nRootVal);
        cBinaryTreeNode* pLeft =new cBinaryTreeNode;
        cBinaryTreeNode* pRight =new cBinaryTreeNode;
        nDepth++;
        pRoot->SetLeftBranch(pLeft);
        pRoot->SetRightBranch(pRight);
        AddBranches(pLeft, nRootVal+1, nDepth, nMaxDepth);
        AddBranches(pRight, nRootVal+2, nDepth, nMaxDepth);
}

void PrintOutTree(cBinaryTreeNode* pNode, int nLevel)
{
        if (pNode==0)
                return;
        cout << "Level " << nLevel << " value " << pNode->GetNodeValue()
<< endl; /* print
        out the tree level and the node value. */
        nLevel++;
        PrintOutTree(pNode->GetLeftBranch(), nLevel);
        PrintOutTree(pNode->GetRightBranch(), nLevel);
}

int main(int argc, char* argv[])
{
        cBinaryTreeNode* pRoot=new cBinaryTreeNode;
        AddBranches(pRoot, 0, 0, 10);
        PrintOutTree(pRoot,0);
        delete pRoot;
}
```

Our Main procedure creates a root, and calls a special function AdBranches to add the branches to the root. This AddBranches function, however, is recursive; it calls itself on each of the left and right branches that it creates. You'll notice that one of its parameters is the depth of the tree, i.e., the number of levels of branches from the root, another of its parameters is the maximum depth. If we don't have a stopping condition, this recursive function would run until we got a stack overflow. The PrintOutTree function is also called recursively, but will stop when it runs out of tree nodes. Study these functions until you understand how they work before proceeding.

Recursion is a very powerful way of writing programs, and lends itself well to tree building and traversal, but you must be very careful your recursive function has a guaranteed stopping condition, or you'll quickly run out of memory!

Activity:

1. a.   What is a tree data structure?

    b.   What is a leaf?

    c.   What is a root?

2. What does recursion mean?

3. Why do you need a stopping condition in a recursive function?

4. Write the stopping condition from the AddBranches function.

5. What does the AddBranches function do? To describe, add comments to each line below:

```
void AddBranches(cBinaryTreeNode* pRoot, int nRootVal, int nDepth,
int nMaxDepth)
{// first create the root.
     if (pRoot==NULL)
             return; // nothing to do, no root passed to us.
     if (nDepth > nMaxDepth)
             return; // otherwise we won't stop!
     pRoot->SetNodeValue(nRootVal);
     cBinaryTreeNode* pLeft =new cBinaryTreeNode;
     cBinaryTreeNode* pRight =new cBinaryTreeNode;
     nDepth++;
     pRoot->SetLeftBranch(pLeft);
     pRoot->SetRightBranch(pRight);
     AddBranches(pLeft, nRootVal+1, nDepth, nMaxDepth);
     AddBranches(pRight, nRootVal+2, nDepth, nMaxDepth);
}
```

6. Once the tree is created with any number of nodes, explain how deleting the root frees all of the other nodes. (Hint: look at the CBinaryTreeNode destructor.)

7. Why do you think each node has a pointer to its parent node?

8. Rather than passing the depth as a parameter to the AddBranches function, how could we modify the tree to keep track of a node's depth? Write down the necessary changes to any existing cBinaryTreeNode functions.

9. For what application might a Binary Tree be most useful?

Data Structures 6 - Hash, Map

Vocabulary:

Hash Map

Memory Verse:

Proverbs 21:21, "He that followeth after righteousness and mercy findeth life, righteousness, and honour."

A hash or map is a data structure that maps unique keys to records in such a way that the key lookup is almost instant. Rather than having to search, the key is generated via applying an algorithm to a string value and then using that key as an index in the hash or map to find the required record. A Hash map (or Hash Table) is most suitted to situations where the speed of data lookup is critical but where efficient memory usage is less important.

Some disadvantages of a Hash Table include: memory requirements for the Hash Table are typically large, the hashing algorithm is complex to implement and understand, and a Hash Map can't be iterated sequentially since the key used for retrieval of values must be known beforehand.

Because a hash function can generate a very large range of values, hash maps are usually implemented using a sparse array; a special data structure that acts like an array, but which is actually an array of arrays where each element is only allocated if needed. You can think of this as an array of pointers to buckets, and each bucket with so many slots. From the hash value, we calculate which bucket the value falls in and the slot in that bucket. If the bucket hasn't yet been alocated, allocate it first, and then allocate the memory pointed to by the slot. The next time a hash falls in that bucket, the bucket is already allocated, so we only need to allocate the slot in that bucket. If the slot is already filled, deallocate (free) it, and replace it with the new content.

Study the below code carefully:

```cpp
#include "stdafx.h"
#include <wtypes.h>
#include <climits>
#define MAX_ENTRIES ULONG_MAX
#define NUM_SLOTS_PER_BUCKET 16384
#define NUM_BUCKETS (MAX_ENTRIES/NUM_SLOTS_PER_BUCKET)


class cHashTable
{
    public:
    cHashTable();
    ~cHashTable();
    /* Note that LPCSTR is a typedef for a constant string pointer,
    i.e. const char* */
    void Add(LPCSTR lpszKey, LPCSTR lpszValue);
    bool Lookup(LPCSTR lpszKey, LPSTR lpszValue, size_t nMax);

    private:
    ULONG Hash(LPCSTR lpszKey);
    void GetBucketAndSlot(ULONG hash, UINT &bucket, UINT &slot);
    typedef LPSTR HashTableBucketEntry; // single bucket entry
    typedef HashTableBucketEntry* HashTableBucketEntryPtr; /* pointer
    to array of entries, i.e. pointer to bucket. */
    HashTableBucketEntryPtr* m_pTable;
};


ULONG cHashTable::Hash(LPCSTR szKey)
{// Uses the djb2 algorithm (k=33) By Dan Bernstein comp.lang.c.
    unsigned long hash = 5381;
    int c;

    while (c = *szKey++)
        hash = ((hash << 5) + hash) + c; /* hash * 33 + c */
    return hash;
}

void cHashTable::GetBucketAndSlot(ULONG hash, UINT &bucket, UINT &slot)
{
    bucket=hash/NUM_SLOTS_PER_BUCKET;
    slot=hash%NUM_SLOTS_PER_BUCKET; /* calculates the remainder of
    hash/NUM_SLOTS_PER_BUCKET */
}
```

```
cHashTable::cHashTable()
{
     /* create the table since the hash function can return any legal
     unsigned long, the table must be large enough to hold that many
     entries. Because this would be a huge waste of memory unless
     full, and because there is a physical size limit on the maximum
     allocation of any single variable, we break this up into buck-
     ets. We only actually allocate the bucket space if we need to,
     otherwise the table simply contains an NULL pointer. */
     m_pTable =new HashTableBucketEntryPtr[NUM_BUCKETS];
     memset(m_pTable, 0, NUM_BUCKETS*sizeof(HashTableBucketEntryPtr));
}


cHashTable::~cHashTable()
{
// delete all strings allocated in any allocated buckets
     for (UINT n=0; n < NUM_BUCKETS; n++)
     {
          if (m_pTable[n]!=0)/* check this bucket for allocated
          strings */
          {
               for (UINT j=0; j < NUM_SLOTS_PER_BUCKET; j++)
               {
                    if (m_pTable[n][j]!=0)
                    delete[] m_pTable[n][j];
                    m_pTable[n][j]=0; // clear the slot.
               }
               delete[] m_pTable[n]; /* delete the bucket pointed
               to by this table entry. */
               m_pTable[n]=0; // clear the bucket pointer
          }
     }
     delete[] m_pTable; /* delete the memory allocated for the table
     itself */
}

void cHashTable::Add(LPCSTR lpszKey, LPCSTR lpszValue)
{
     if (!lpszKey || !lpszValue || !*lpszKey || !*lpszValue)
          return; // nothing to do.
     ULONG hash=Hash(lpszKey);
     UINT bucket=0;
     UINT slot=0;
     GetBucketAndSlot(hash, bucket, slot);
     // first check if a bucket exists, if not, create a new one.
     if (m_pTable[bucket]==0)
```

```
        {
                m_pTable[bucket]=new HashTableBucketEntry[NUM_SLOTS_PER_
                BUCKET];
                // ensure all the slots in the bucket are clear
                memset(m_pTable[bucket],0, NUM_SLOTS_PER_BUCKET*sizeof
                (HashTableBucketEntry));
        }
        /* first check if the bucket slot is free, if not, we need to
        free it or we'll cause a memory leak. */
        if (m_pTable[bucket][slot]!=0)
                delete[] m_pTable[bucket][slot];
        size_t nLen=strlen(lpszValue);
        m_pTable[bucket][slot]=new char[nLen+1];
        strcpy(m_pTable[bucket][slot],lpszValue); /* copy the value from
        the parameter to the newly allocated table entry. */
}


bool cHashTable::Lookup(LPCSTR lpszKey, LPSTR lpszValue, size_t nMax)
{
        if (!lpszKey || !*lpszKey || !lpszValue || nMax < 1)
                return false; // can't do anything.
        ULONG hash=Hash(lpszKey); /* create the hash from the string
        passed in. */
        UINT bucket=0;
        UINT slot=0;
        GetBucketAndSlot(hash, bucket, slot);
        if (m_pTable[bucket]==0)
                return false; // Can't check slot since no bucket allocated.
        if (m_pTable[bucket][slot]!=0)
        {// we've found it.
                // copy it to the buffer provided.
                // use nMax to ensure we don't overrun the buffer passed
                // to us.
                strncpy(lpszValue,m_pTable[bucket][slot],nMax);
                return true;
        }
        return false; // can't find the key in our table.
}


#define MAX_STRLEN 255
int main(int argc, char* argv[])
{
        cHashTable htbl;
        htbl.Add("Joseph", "My favorite verse is Joshua 22:5.");
        htbl.Add("Caleb", "My favorite verse is Psalm 90:12.");
```

```
htbl.Add("Gideon", "My favorite verse is Proverbs 6:6.");

// Now try looking up the values.
char szBuf[MAX_STRLEN]="\0";
const char szKey[]="Joseph";
htbl.Lookup(szKey, szBuf, MAX_STRLEN);
// printf is another function to print formatted data to screen.
printf("Looking up key %s, found value %s", szKey, szBuf);

return 0;
}
```

Activity:

1. What is the main advantage of a Hash Map over a regular array?

2. What are some disadvantages of a Hash Map?

3. Why would you use a Hash Map over other data structures?

4. What is a Hashing function?

5. Why do we use buckets rather than just allocating the entire array for holding data?

Review of Lessons 22 through 27

1. What is a stack and why is it used?

2. What is a queue and why is it used?

3. What is the difference between a Stack and a Queue?

4. What is a linked list and why would you use one?

5. What is a doubly linked list and why would you use one?

6. Why would you use a regular array over a doubly linked list?

7. Annotate the below two code fragments with comments, explaining what each line does:

```
pNew->pPrev=pCurrent->pPrev;
pNew->pNext=pCurrent;
pCurrent->pPrev=pNew;
if (pCurrent->pPrev)
    pCurrent->pPrev->pNext=pNew;

sDoublyLinkedListItem *pPrev=pCurrent->pPrev;
sDoublyLinkedListItem* pNext=pCurrent->pNext;
if (pPrev)
    pPrev->pNext=pNext;
if (pNext)
    pNext->pPrev=pPrev;
delete pCurrent;
```

8. a. What is a tree data structure?

   b. What is a leaf?

   c. What is a root?

9. What does recursion mean?

10. Why do you need a stopping condition in a recursive function?

11. For what application might a Binary Tree be most useful?

12. What is the main advantage of a Hash Map over a regular array?

13. What are some disadvantages of a Hash Map?

14. Why would you use a Hash Map over other data structures?

15. What is a Hashing function?

Sort and Search Algorithms

Vocabulary:

sort, Bubble Sort, Quicksort, Linear Search, Binary Search

Memory Verse:

Deuteronomy 32:7, "Remember the days of old, consider the years of many generations: ask thy father, and he will shew thee; thy elders, and they will tell thee."

Now that we've introduced lots of basic building blocks, its time to discuss real problem solutions. One goal of programming has been to avoid where possible the issue of re-inventing the wheel. To this end, good solutions to many common tasks have been well-defined. Just as mother or grand mother has her true and tried recipies, there are some true and tried methods (or algorithms) for solving programming tasks that are useful to know about, so you don't have to figure them out on your own. Indeed many compilers today come with large, standard libraries of commonly used algorithms, objects and functions. In this lesson we'll discuss some of these algorithms, because even though such libraries exist, it is good to know how some of these common algorithms work and when to choose one over another.

Sorting:

Sorting is one of the most frequent tasks performed by programs (along with searching). There are many such sorting algorithms such as Bubble Sort, Selection Sort, Merge Sort, Heap Sort, and other variants. For small numbers of items, the Bubble sort may suffice. It is easy to understand but is the slowest of all of the cited algorithms. We shall first introduce you to the Bubble sort for its simplicity.

```
// Bubble Sort Function for ascending Order
#include "stdafx.h"
#include <iostream>
#include <windows.h>
```

```cpp
using namespace std;

void BubbleSort(int arr[], size_t nElements)
{
    int i, j;
    bool bSwappedElements=true; // set flag to true to start first pass
    int nTemp; // holding variable
    for(i = 0; (i < nElements) && bSwappedElements==true; i++)
    {
        bSwappedElements=false; // set to true when we do a swap
        for (j=0; j < (nElements-1); j++)
        {
            if (arr[j+1] < arr[j])
            {
                nTemp= arr[j]; // swap elements
                arr[j] = arr[j+1];
                arr[j+1] = nTemp;
                bSwappedElements=true; // indicates a swap
            }
        }
    }
}

int main(int argc, char* argv[])
{
    int a[20]; //declare an array of integers
    srand(GetTickCount()); // init the random number generator.
    cout << "Unsorted: ";
    for (int n=0; n < 20; n++)
    {/* generate a random number between 0 and 100, store in array
        at index n. */
        a[n]=rand()%100;
        cout << a[n] << ", "; // display it
    }
    cout << endl;
    BubbleSort(a,20); // sort it
    cout << "Sorted: ";
    for (int n=0; n < 20; n++)
    {/* generate a random number between 0 and 100, store in array
        at index n. */
        cout << a[n] << ", "; // display it
    }

    return 0;
}
```

The Bubble Sort algorithm is impractically slow for thousands of items. One of the most efficient sorting algorithms is called the Quick Sort algorithm. Quick-Sort uses a divide-and-conquer strategy. First, the sequence to be sorted A is divided into two partitions, such that all elements of the first partition B are less than or equal to all elements of the second Partition (divide). Then, the two partitions are sorted separately using the same recursive application (conquer). Recombination of the two partitions yields the sorted sequence (combine).

```
int Partition( int arr[], int nLeft, int nRight)
{
     int nVal =arr[nLeft];
     int nLeftMargin= nLeft-1;
     int nRightMargin= nRight+1;

     /*The movement of the pointers is handled in a loop. The loop
     terminates with a return to the caller when the left and right
     pointers cross.

       Inside the outer while loop, there are two do … while loops.
     The first do … while moves the right margin pointer leftwards
     until it finds a value less than or equal to val. The second do
     … while loop moves the left margin pointer rightwards, stopping
     when it finds a value greater than or equal to val.
       If the left and right margin pointers have crossed, function
     Partition() should return the position of the right margin
     pointer. Otherwise, a pair of misplaced values have been found;
     these should be exchanged to get low values on the left and high
     values on the right. Then the search for misplaced values can
     resume.
     */
     while(true)
     {
          do nRightMargin--; while (arr[nRightMargin] > nVal);
          do nLeftMargin++; while( arr[nLeftMargin] < nVal);

          if(nLeftMargin < nRightMargin)
          {
               int nSwap= arr[nRightMargin];
               arr[nRightMargin] = arr[nLeftMargin];
               arr[nLeftMargin] = nSwap;
               }
          else
               return nRightMargin;
     }
}
```

```
void Quicksort( int arr[], int nLeft, int nRight)
{
    if(nLeft < nRight)
    {
        int nSplitIndex= Partition(arr,nLeft, nRight);
        Quicksort(arr, nLeft, nSplitIndex);
        Quicksort(arr, nSplitIndex+1, nRight);
    }
}

int main(int argc, char* argv[])
{
    int a[20]; //declare an array of integers
    srand(GetTickCount()); // init the random number generator.
    cout << "Unsorted:";
    for (int n=0; n < 20; n++)
    {/* generate a random number between 0 and 100, store in array
        at index n. */
        a[n]=rand()%100;
        cout << a[n] << ","; // display it
    }
    cout << endl;
    Quicksort(a,0,19); // sort it
    cout << "Sorted:";
    for (int n=0; n < 20; n++)
    {
        cout << a[n] << ","; // display it
    }

    return 0;
}
```

Searching:

Searching is the process of locating an item amongst a collection of data. If the data is not sorted first, every item of data must be checked to find the matching item. If, however, the data is sorted, or is stored in a Hash Table, it can be found extremely rapidly.

Here is a simple function to search an array of integers for an item and to return the index of the item in the array. This is called a Linear Search, and does not require that the array be sorted. For small data sets, or where searches are infrequent, a Linear Search may be quite adequate.

```
int GetIndexOf(int nValue, int arr[], int nArraySize)
{/* Searches nArraySize elements of an array to find nVal and returns
     its index */
for (int i=0; i < nArraySize; i++)
     {
            if (arr[i]==nValue) return i; // we found it.
     }
     return -1; // not found.
}
```

If, however, we had thousands or millions of items and needed to do many searches, this would be very slow. It would be much better if our array was sorted. Then we wouldn't have to search through every item, but simply check halfway points to see if the element we were looking for was greater or less than that point. This is known as a Binary Search, and is much faster than searching through an unsorted array. We will now look at the Binary Search algorithm for finding data in a sorted array.

This version is written as a recursive function for simplicity. What we do is look at the half-way value, if the value we want is greater than the value at the half-way value, we search the top half of the list by looking at its half-way value. If the value we are looking for is less than the half-way value, we search the first half of the list by finding its haf-way value, etc. We stop when we have a single element left that matches or we have nothing left to split.

```
#include "stdafx.h"
#include <iostream>
#include <windows.h>
using namespace std;

int BinarySearch(int nVal, int arr[], int nMin, int nMax)
{// stopping condition
    if (nMin > nMax)
          return -1; // nothing left to search, return -1 as error
    int nHalf=(nMin+nMax)/2;
    if (nVal==arr[nHalf])
          return nHalf;
    else if (nVal < arr[nHalf])
          return BinarySearch(nVal, arr, nMin,nHalf-1);
    else if (nVal > arr[nHalf])
          return BinarySearch(nVal, arr, nHalf+1,nMax);
    else
          return -1;
}
```

Here's the test program which uses the Quicksort function we declared earlier to ensure the array is already sorted:

```
int main(int argc, char* argv[])
{
    int a[20]; //declare an array of integers
    srand(GetTickCount()); // init the random number generator.
    cout << "Unsorted:";
    for (int n=0; n < 20; n++)
    {/* generate a random number between 0 and 100, store in array
        at index n. */
        a[n]=rand()%100;
        cout << a[n] << ","; // display it
    }
    cout << endl;
    Quicksort(a,0,19); // sort it
    cout << "Sorted:";
    for (int n=0; n < 20; n++)
    {
        cout << a[n] << ","; // display it
    }
    cout << endl;
    int nVal=0;
    cout << "Enter a value to search for:";
    cin >> nVal;
    cout << endl;
    int nIndex=BinarySearch(nVal, a, 0, 19);
    if (nIndex ==-1)
        cout << "The number" << nVal << "was not in the array." <<
        endl;
    else
        cout << "Using Binary Search, the index of " << nVal <<
        "is" << nIndex << endl;

    return 0;
}
```

Sorting can also be acomplished using a binary tree, but this is getting beyond the scope of this introduction.

Activity:

1. What is the difference between the Bubble Sort and the Quick Sort algorithms?

2. Can you explain why the bubble Sort algorithm is much slower than the Quick Sort algorithm?

3. Why is it better to sort data before attempting to search for an item?

4. Can you think of an instance where sorting may not be necessary before searching for an item?

5. a. Using a Linear Search, in an array of 1,000,000 elements, in a worst case scenario, how many elements would need to be tested to find a match?

    b. Using Binary Search, in an array of 1,000,000 elements, at most, how many elements need to be tested to find a match?

6. How many steps would it take to find the number 7, if using a Binary Search on the numbers 1 through 10?

7. If you had millions of items to search, you might end up with a stack overflow using a recursive Binary Search. Rewrite the Quick Sort algorithm without recursion. (Hint: use a loop.)

A Brief Look at Templates

Vocabulary:

template, template argument

Memory Verse

Titus 2:7-8, "In all things shewing thyself a pattern of good works: in doctrine shewing uncorruptness, gravity, sincerity, Sound speech, that cannot be condemned; that he that is of the contrary part may be ashamed, having no evil thing to say of you."

A Template is a pattern. Consider writing a class to implement a Binary Tree, but where the type of the data stored in each node was unknown. The pattern is the tree, and the parameter to the pattern is the type of the node. C++ has a powerful way of declaring templates to do exactly this. Below is our tree class from Lesson 26 with the data of the node being templated:

```cpp
// BinaryTree.cpp : Defines the entry point for the console application.
//

#include "stdafx.h"
#include <iostream>
using namespace std;

template <typename t>
class cBinaryTreeNode
{
    public:
    cBinaryTreeNode();
    ~cBinaryTreeNode();
    cBinaryTreeNode* GetLeftBranch();
    cBinaryTreeNode* GetRightBranch();

    t* GetNodeData();
```

```
      void SetNodeData(t val);
      void SetLeftBranch(cBinaryTreeNode* pNode);
      void SetRightBranch(cBinaryTreeNode* pNode);
      cBinaryTreeNode* GetParent();
      void SetParent(cBinaryTreeNode* pNode);

      private:
      cBinaryTreeNode* m_pLeft;
      cBinaryTreeNode* m_pRight;
      cBinaryTreeNode* m_pParent;
      t m_Val;
};

template <typename t>
cBinaryTreeNode<t>::cBinaryTreeNode()
{
      _pLeft=0;
      m_pRight=0;
      m_pParent=0;
}

template <typename t>
cBinaryTreeNode<t>::~cBinaryTreeNode()
{
/* delete the left and right branch so they in turn delete their
branches. Note we do not need to delete our parent, it will be deleted
when its parent is deleted. */
      if (m_pLeft)
            delete m_pLeft;
      m_pLeft=0;
      if (m_pRight)
            delete m_pRight;
      m_pRight=0;
}

template <typename t>
cBinaryTreeNode<t>* cBinaryTreeNode<t>::GetLeftBranch()
{
      return m_pLeft;
}

template <typename t>
cBinaryTreeNode<t>* cBinaryTreeNode<t>::GetRightBranch()
{
      return m_pRight;
}
```

```
template <typename t>
t* cBinaryTreeNode<t>::GetNodeData()
{
    return &m_Val;
}

template <typename t>
void cBinaryTreeNode<t>::SetNodeData(t val)
{
    m_Val=val;
}

template <typename t>
void cBinaryTreeNode<t>::SetLeftBranch(cBinaryTreeNode* pNode)
{
    pNode->SetParent(this);
    if (m_pLeft)//test if there is an existing left branch
        delete m_pLeft; /* if so, delete it and assign the pointer
        to point to the new node */
    m_pLeft=pNode;
}

template <typename t>
void cBinaryTreeNode<t>::SetRightBranch(cBinaryTreeNode* pNode)
{
    pNode->SetParent(this);
    if (m_pRight)//test if there is an existing right branch
        delete m_pRight; /* if so, delete it and assign the pointer
        to point to the new node */
    m_pRight=pNode;
}

template <typename t>
cBinaryTreeNode<t>* cBinaryTreeNode<t>::GetParent()
{
    return m_pParent;
}
```

To use this class, whenever we declare a variable of cBinaryTreeNode, we also need to declare the type of the node to use with the class using <> around the type.

In our example above, to declare the root, we'd declare it as:

```
cBinaryTreeNode<string>* pRoot=new cBinaryTreeNode<string>;
```

to declare a tree of strings. The parameter in the <> is called the template argument. The string class is declared as part of the standard C++ library that comes with Microsoft

Visual Studio. This class includes methods and memory management for handling strings, and is much simpler to use than the primitive character array introduced in Lesson 9.

As another example, in the standard template library, there is a data structure declared for handling all of the functions associated with arrays. The class is called vector. The templated parameter of this class allows the programmer to tell the compiler what kind of element should be stored in the array. For example, we could define a vector of strings as follows:

```
#include <string>
#include <vector>
#include <iostream>
using namespace std;

vector<string> myStringVector;

myStringVector.push_back("Joseph");
myStringVector.push_back("K");
myStringVector.push_back("Stephen");

int nItems=myStringVector.size();
for (int n=0; n < nItems; n++)
{
    cout << "item " n << " is " << myStringVector[n] << endl;
}
```

This is much simpler than all of the necessary code to do the same thing using intrinsic data types introduced in Lesson 9.

You may ask, "Why didn't you just introduce me to the standard library first?" The reason is simple; you need to understand the basics, and how the basics can be built up to make larger building blocks, which on the surface are easier to use, but internally are implemented using simple intrinsic types. At some point you will need to write code using the intrinsic data types to build up your own libraries of functions and classes for more complex solutions.

Activity:

1. What is a template?

2. What is the main reason for using templates?

3. What is a template argument?

4. Assuming a templated array class, CArray, declare a CArray of floats.

5. Using the Microsoft Visual Studio documentation or the Internet, familiarize yourself with the C++ Standard Template Library STL. (Specifically consider the vector, string and map container classes.)

Debugging 1 – Syntax Error, Logic Error, Runtime Error

Vocabulary:

syntax error, logic error, runtime error, Buffer Overrun, Buffer Underrun, Stack corruption, exception.

Memory Verse:

1 Corinthians 4:2, "Moreover it is required in stewards, that a man be found faithful."

There are three kinds of errors that you will face whilst programming. Each has its own techniques to track down and fix. The easiest errors by far to find and fix are syntax errors.

Syntax errors are grammatical errors in the code, such as missing or extra punctuation symbols; mistyped keywords, variable names or function names; references to variables which are out of scope; passing the wrong number or wrong type of parameters to functions, etc. Most of the time, the compiler will tell you exactly where in your program such errors occur, and usually a close examination of the line or surrounding lines will yield the source of the errors.

Logic errors, on the other hand, are not so easy to find and fix. These are errors in your actual algorithm. Once you've found and fixed all of the errors flagged by your compiler, and your program actually runs, you next have to determine why your program is not doing exactly what you thought it should do. We'll cover some logic error debugging techniques in the next lesson on debugging. However, modern compilers allow you to see the value of variables and step through your code line by line making it relatively easy to debug, even the toughest of logic errors.

Runtime errors are any errors that occur when the user is running your program and it malfunctions. You have probably seen that blue screen presented by Windows to tell you that your program has performed an illegal operation and is being shut down, just before you were going to save your day's work! When programming then, you must always put yourself in the position of the user when designing how the program should be used, i.e., its User Interface, but also be meticulous in testing and debugging to minimize the opportunity for such runtime errors that cause your users to lose important information.

The most difficult of all runtime errors to find and fix are caused by buffer overruns, underruns or stack corruption. These kinds of errors are very difficult to track down, because often your program will simply quit and disappear from memory, or behave nicely for a while, and then without warning begin to malfunction. Since the programmer is usually not present to see the customer's computer crash, and even if they were, since the version of the program is typically the release and not the debug version, no debugging information would be provided at the time of the crash to aid in resolving the fault.

Such runtime errors are also often not predictably repeatable, since the fault causing the crash depends on a very specific sequence of events to cause the memory to become corrupt in just the right manner to cause the crash. Only the most experienced programmers can deal with such nasty errors. Good programming techniques are the best defence against these kinds of errors. Using higher level languages such as Visual C# or Visual Basic also reduces these kinds of errors, since most of the memory management is handled by the runtime system.

One of the reasons I chose to teach C++ rather than C#, however, is to make you think more about memory management and resource usage. One drawback to higher level languages is that programmers can easily become sloppy, because the responsibility for making good design choices is masked by the language's resource management. Making the programmer responsible for resource management forces them to think carefully about the design of their program.

A **buffer overrun** is when you write to memory beyond the boundary you intended, and overwrite instructions that when later executed cause unpredictable results. A **buffer underrun** is where you write to memory before the start of a variable's allocated space, and again overwrite instructions that when executed later cause your program to malfunction. **Stack corruption** is yet another variant of corrupting the memory on the stack (see Lesson 18), causing variables or return addresses to become invalid. We'll deal with some examples of buffer over/underruns and stack corruption in the next lesson.

Exception Handlers.

An exception handler is a wrapper around a piece of code, which in the event of an error, gets executed. Exception handling should be used with caution, because it can often mask errors that should be found and fixed. It is, however, a useful technique in certain circumstances when errors of a certain kind are anticipated, and you want to continue gracefully without your program crashing. Such uses may be in the area of network communication or interprocess communication, where there may be errors that are beyond your control, such as a broken cable hindering communication or a resource conflict.

We will not go into exception handling in any further detail in this book, but I want to make you aware of this technique, if you ever need to use it.

It goes without saying that the earlier you find and fix errors while programming, the easier it is to do so and the more stable your program. In the business world, it is also cheaper the earlier you find and fix problems. Software is rarely bug free, however, and some errors will remain long after a program is in the shops and the programmer moved on to other tasks. Testing, therefore, is paramount!

I mentioned above that one of the best defences against error is the use of good programming techniques. We shall discuss some of these techniques in the next lesson.

Activity:

1. What are the three kinds of errors which may arise while programming? Describe each kind, when they occur and the difficulty in resolving them.

2. Why is it better to catch errors earlier in development than later?

3. Look carefully at the below C++ code:

    a. How many syntax errors can you find?

    b. How many logic errors can you find?

    c. What will the return result of this function always be and why?

    ```
    bool TodayIsHotter (
    {
        bool bRes=true;
        int x=GetTemperatureToday();
        int y=GetTemperatureYesterday();
        return bRes || x > y;
    }
    ```

4. Look carefully at the below C++ code:

    a. How many syntax errors can you find?

    b. How many logic errors can you find?

c. What will the return result of the function be and why?

```
bool CalcSumOfFirstTenInts())
{
    int nCounter=1;
    int nRunningTotal=0;
    while (nCounter <= 10)
    {
            nRunningTotal=nRunningTotal+nCounter;
    }
    return nRunningTotal;

}
```

5. Look very carefully at the below sample code and identify the logic error:

```
int x=0;
while (x < 10);
{
    x++;
}
```

Lesson 32

Debugging 2 - Range Checking and Pointer Validation

Vocabulary:

range checking, subscript out of range, bounds checking, pointer validation, null pointer reference.

Memory Verse:

Acts 17:26, "And hath made of one blood all nations of men for to dwell on all the face of the earth, and hath determined the times before appointed, and the bounds of their habitation;"

Range and Bounds Checking

While computers will always follow the instructions you feed them, humans, who are inherently sinful, will not. If you accidentally make a loop iterate too many times and write data beyond the end of a buffer, the computer will follow your erroneous instruction, overwriting some other program instructions or data resulting in unexpected and unpredictable behaviour at some time in the future.

If you try to access an array element beyond the end of the allocated array, you will also cause unpredictable behaviour. This is known as a bounds or subscript error. If you try writing to an element of an array which is out of bounds, i.e., the subscript is beyond the legal range, you'll corrupt memory belonging to other data or instructions, and cause your program to malfunction. Always be careful to check array access code, especially within loops, to ensure you do not cause out of bounds or array subscript errors.

Even if you code your program correctly, when a program asks your user to enter a valid date, for example, you must not assume that the user will do so. A good rule of thumb is to always expect the worst and program to avoid it. You must always add logic to validate data entered by the user, to ensure it is in the expected range and format. If your program expects a number between 0 and 100, you must check that the user did not enter alphabetic or other unexpected characters, a negative number or a number greater than 100. If you ask for a date, check that it is in the required format. If a string, ensure that the user entered some text and that the text is the expected length. The user entering text too large for the buffer you allocated to hold will cause a buffer overrun, if you do not specify the correct buffer size. Always check the user's input.

If you write a function that will be used by others (or even yourself at a later date), never assume they'll pass the correct parameters. Always check the parameters passed to see if pointers are non-zero, ints or other numeric arguments are within the legal ranges, and strings are not empty if you don't expect them to be.

Consider the following example:

```cpp
#include "stdafx.h"
#include <iostream>
#include <string>
#include <vector>
using namespace std;

int main(int argc, char* argv[])
{
    vector<string> myVerses;
    cout << "Enter 5 of your favorite verse references: " << endl;
    int nCounter=1;
    char szVerse[256]="\0";
    while (nCounter <=5)
    {
        cout << "Enter verse reference " << nCounter << ": ";
        cin.getline(szVerse,50);
        cout << endl;
        myVerses.push_back(szVerse);
        nCounter++;
    }
    cout << "Enter a number between 1 and 5: ";
    int nIndex=0;
    cin >> nIndex;
    // Remember when accessing the array, use 0-based, not 1-based
    // so minus one.
    cout << "The verse at index " << nIndex << " is " <<
    myVerses[nIndex-1] << endl;

    return 0;
}
```

If you run this test from the examples from our website (see Appendix 6), you'll notice that if you enter a number out of range, the program will throw an exception, i.e., generate a runtime error. The exception is thrown by the vector class but if it did not have an exception handler, the program would simply malfunction, and most likely display garbage or crash. We could avoid this by adding range checking in a loop as follows:

```cpp
int main(int argc, char* argv[])
{
    vector<string> myVerses;
    cout << "Enter 5 of your favorite verse references: " << endl;
    int nCounter=1;
    char szVerse[256]="\0";
    while (nCounter <=5)
    {
        cout << "Enter verse reference " << nCounter << ": ";
        cin.getline(szVerse,50);
        cout << endl;
        myVerses.push_back(szVerse);
        nCounter++;
    }
    int nIndex=0;
    do
    {
        cout << "Enter a number between 1 and 5: ";
        cin >> nIndex;
    } while (nIndex < 1 || nIndex > 5);
    // Remember when accessing the array, use 0-based, not 1-based
    // so minus one.
    cout << "The verse at index " << nIndex << " is " <<
    myVerses[nIndex-1] << endl;

    return 0;
}
```

Now, if the user enters a number out of range, the program will simply ask them again for a number between 1 and 5. The loop exits once the user enters a number within the appropriate range.

Pointer Validation

Back in Lesson 9 we introduced the pointer. We also said that it was both powerful but dangerous! It is dangerous for several reasons: you must ensure that what it points to is valid; you must ensure that when you've finished with what it points to, you free the memory used by the object; when multiple pointers point to the same object, you must manage the lifetime of the object using reference counting (beyond the scope of this book), etc. Rule number one with pointers is to initialize them to 0 when not pointing to a valid object, and then always check their validity before using them. For example:

```
MyClass* p;
```

P is a pointer to a myClass object, but it has not been initialized. It could literally point to anything anywhere in the computer's memory. Calling a method via p such as

```
p->doSomething();
```

would most likely cause the program to crash or hang.

```
MyClass* p=0;
```

Calling p->DoSomething(); now would cause an exception to be thrown. Since p is a NULL pointer.

Both of the above examples are interesting, because whilst you should check if a pointer is not NULL, i.e. 0, you can't assume that just because it isn't NULL, it points to something valid. You must ensure that you carefully manage what the pointer points to, and when it no longer points to anything valid, set it to 0 and always test it to be not NULL before using it.

A correct example:

```
MyClass* p=0;
    /*
    ...
    Some other code which is not listed which may or may not set p
    to a valid object.
    */
    if (p) // test if p is not null.
    p->DoSomething(); /* safe, we test p and it is null so we don't
    execute the methodcall.
    */
```

Here's another example:

```
myClass* p=new myClass;
```

Now, p points to an instantiation of myClass, a valid object.

If we test p, i.e., check the value of p, it would be pointing to the memory where myClass has been instantiated.

If we now delete (or free) the memory pointed to by p:

```
delete p;
```

p still points to the same memory, but deleting what p pointed to would invalidate the object, and thus you could not safely call methods on p such as p->DoSomething();

If you delete p, you should set it to 0 immediately, so there is no chance of calling it and referring to possibly invalid memory.

```
delete p;
p=0;
```

Before using p next, test it.

```
If (p==0)
      return FALSE;
```

Stack Corruption

Consider the following simple example of a couple of variables declared on the stack:

```
char szName[7]="Joseph";
int nLimit=7;
```

If you then had a loop that stored characters to szName, which looped from 0 to 7 instead of 6, and used the nLimit variable declared after the string as a loop counter, you may very well cause your loop to malfunction. By writing past the end of your string buffer, you would potentially change the value of nLimit, which in turn would make your loop execute an unpredictable number of times. This is because the string and int variables most likely share contiguous stack memory, so writing beyond the end of the string would change the value of nLimit unintentionally. This is called stack corruption. Now imagine that rather than the value of nLimit following the string, a return address of a function was stored on the stack. You'd overwrite that address, and thus a function call would not return to its proper address, and likely cause the processor to execute some meaningless data at some arbitrary address, which the processor would errantly interpret as instructions. At best you'd get some malfunction in your program, at worst you'd get a crash that would be very hard to debug.

Activity:

1. Describe three kinds of range or bounds checking one should be careful to perform while developing software.

2. In the following code snip, add a comment showing any invalid bounds errors, and add the appropriate bounds or range checks instead:

```
// put alphabet into szTemp
char szTemp[26]="\0";
for (int nIdx=1; nIdx <=26; nIdx++)
```

```
    {
        szTemp[nIdx]=64+nIdx;
    }
```

3. In the following code snip, add comments wherever an inappropriate pointer operation is performed.

```
CLamp* pLamp=0;
CLamp* pLamp2;
CLamp* pLamp3=0;
pLamp=new cLamp;
pLamp->OnOffButton();
delete pLamp;
pLamp->OnOffButton();
if (pLamp2)
pLamp2->OnOffButton();
    pLamp3->OnOffButton;
```

4. In the following function, add appropriate parameter checking.

```
int RemainderFromDivision(int nDividend, int nDivisor)
{
  int nQuotient=nDivisor/nDividend; // integer division will round
  int nMaxMultiples=nQuotient*nDividend;
  int nRemainder=nDivisor-nMaxMultiples;
  return nRemainder;
}
```

Debugging 3 - Dangling Reference, Memory Leak, Null Pointer Error

Vocabulary:

Dangling reference, Memory Leak, Null Pointer error,

Memory Verse:

Proverbs 18:9, "He also that is slothful in his work is brother to him that is a great waster."

Three related issues that you must look out for during programming with pointers are the dangling reference, memory leak and NULL pointer error. We've briefly touched on some of these issues previously, but we'll look in more depth at these issues in this lesson.

A **dangling reference** is where a pointer points to an object that has been deleted, and thus points at invalid memory. Calling methods on that object pointer will thus cause unpredictable results or a program crash.

A **Memory leak** is caused when all references to an object are destroyed, but the object itself is not deleted. For example, a linked list pointer may have been changed to point to a subsequent node in the list without the node to which it used to point being deallocated. This means that the memory used by the node will still be allocated and thus unavailable to your program, and there will be no way of freeing that memory since no pointer refers to that memory in order to deallocate it.

Here's an example:
```
CLamp* p=new CLamp; /* instantiate p to point to a new instance of
CLamp. */
p=0; // Memory Leak!
```

We didn't deallocate p first so memory is still allocated on the heap for the CLamp object, but was assigned to 0, which means that p no longer points to the allocated memory on the heap. This causes a memory leak, since the memory is stil allocated but is no longer referenced by p. Since it is no longer referenced by p, and there is no other pointer variable pointing to our memory that was allocated, we can't deallocate it either. This memory is thus no longer available to our program, and is called a memory leak. It remains unavailable until our program exits at which time the Operating System reclaims all memory allocated by our program.

A Null Pointer error is where a pointer's value has been inadvertently set to 0 when it was expected to still point at a valid object. Calls on that pointer will thus cause your program to crash with an invalid memory reference, typically manifesting in one of those notorious blue screen errors.

Consider our previous example:

```
CLamp* p=new CLamp; /* instantiate p to point to a new instance of
CLamp. */
p=0; // Memory Leak!
p->DoSomething(); // woops, p is null!
```

Activity:

1. Add comments in the below code wherever a memory leak, dangling reference or null pointer error would occur:

```
CLamp* p=new CLamp();
p->OnOffButton();
int nBrightness=0;
while (nBrightness < 10)
{
    p->SetBrightness(nBrightness++);
    wait(20);
}
p=new CLampAndSiren();
p->OnOffButton();
wait(30);

CLamp* pLampArray[5];
for (int n=0; n < 5; n++)
{
    pLampArray[n]=new CLamp();
}

for (int j=0; j <=5; j++)
```

```
    {
        pLampArray[j]->OnOffButton();
        wait(5);
        pLampArray[j]->OnOffButton();
    }
    for (int k=0; k < 5; k++)
    {
        pLampArray[k]=0;
            delete pLampArray[k];
    }
```

Review of Lessons 31 through 33

1. Define the following terms and give an example of each:

   a.   Syntax error,

   b.   Logic error,

   c.   Runtime error,

   d.   Buffer Overrun,

   e.   Buffer Underrun,

   f.   Stack corruption,

   g.   Exception,

   h.   Range checking,

   i.   Subscript validation (or bounds checking),

   j.   Pointer validation,

   k.   Null pointer error,

   l.   Dangling reference,

   m.   Memory Leak,

2. Add comments to the below code fragments to mark any syntax errors:

   a.

```
if GetPassword())
   RunProgram()
else
   PrintError();
```

160

b.

```
if (NetworkReady()))
    SendData();
```

c.

```
int main(int argc, char* argv)
(
    for (int n=0; n < argc; n++)
    {
        cout << "Parameter " << n << "=" << argv[n] << endl;
    }
    return 0
)
```

3. Add comments to the following code snippets to show any logic errors:

a.

```
while (n < 10);
{
    cout << "n=" << n << endl;
}
```

b.

```
int aEvenNumbers[10];
int nEven=2;
for (int n=0; n <=10; n++)
{
    aEvenNumbers[n]=nEven;
    nEven*=2;
}
```

c.

```
int max(int a, int b)
{
    if (a > b);
        return a;
    else
        return b;
}

void test()
{
    cout << "Enter two numbers: ";
```

```
        cin >>a >> b;
        cout << "The maximum of " << a << " and " << b " is " <<
        max(a, b) << endl;
        return 0;
}
```

4. Mark any memory leaks, null pointer errors, dangling references or other possible pointer related issues in the below code fragments:

   a.

```
CLamp* p=new CLamp;
pLamp->OnOffButton();
pLamp=0;
```

   b.

```
CLamp* pLamp=new CLamp;
pLamp->OnOffButton();
delete pLamp;
if (pLamp->IsOn())
        pLamp->OnOffButton();
pLamp=0;
```

   c.

```
void Describe(cShape* pShape)
{
        if (pShape==0)
                return;
        cout << "The shape is a " << pShape->Name() << endl;
}

void test()
{
        CShape* pShape1;
        CShape* pShape2=new CRectangle(50,100);
        Describe(pShape1);
        Describe(pShape2);
}
```

Lesson 35

Compiler Directives

Vocabulary:

directive, symbol, substitution

Memory Verse:

1 Peter 3:18, "For Christ also hath once suffered for sins, the just for the unjust, that he might bring us to God, being put to death in the flesh, but quickened by the Spirit:"

We've already introduced the #include syntax in an earlier lesson to include the contents of another file into this file at the point of the #include directive. In this lesson, we will learn more about compiler directives before letting you loose on a real life program.

Have you noticed text near the top of some source files of the form #define symbol definition?

This is known as a compiler directive, similar to the #include statement, which we've already learned about. The #define directive allows you to define a named symbol in place of a literal value. The literal is substituted for the symbol prior to compilation.

For example:

```
#define PI 3.142
```

Anywhere in your code where the symbol PI was written, the compiler would replace it with the literal value 3.142 before compilation. The scope of this substitution is from the point in the file where it is declared to the end of the file, and in any file that includes this file.

Using symbol replacement is very useful when you want to be able to change a value used throughout your program. You can simply define the symbol and its literal value, and then refer to the symbol throughout your code. If you need to change the value of the symbol, you only need to change it in one place. There are preferred ways of doing

163

such replacement in C++, such as through the use of constant variable declarations, but this method is still extremely popular and is found in almost all code you'll find in the real world.

Not only can you define symbols for literal values, but you can actually define what are known as macros which allow you to substitute a pattern for actual code. Consider the following:

```
#define MAX(a,b) ((a)>(b))?(a):(b)
```

The ? is a special ternary if operator that says if the expression to its left is true, return the expression immediately after it, otherwise return the expression after the colon. (Ternary, three parameters.) In the above macro, if a is greater than b then a is returned, otherwise b is returned. This operator can be used in normal functions.

This is equivalent to the following function

```
bool max(int a, int b)
{
    if (a>b)
        return a;
    else
        return b;
}
```

The difference between writing a macro and a function is that macros are actually expanded in the code such that what they define replaces the instance of the macro symbol. In our above example, any text of the form MAX(expr1,expr2) in your source code would be replaced literally by the expression ((expr1)>(expr2))?(expr1):(expr2) before the compiler actually compiles your code. You must be very careful with macros, because of the literal substitution which takes place. Macros are not type safe, which means that if you write code like max("hello", 5) in your source code, the macro will be replaced, but you'll get a strange compilation error that might be hard to trace. Use macros with caution.

As pointed out earlier, variable names, function names and macro names are arbitrary, though they should be carefully chosen to reflect their purpose. You can tell the difference between a variable and function name by the parentheses following a function name.

Telling the difference between a function and macro name, however, is not as easy. To aid with this, there is a widely used convention that is well accepted in the programming community. Function names are usually written using mixed upper and lower case letters, where the first letter of each word in the variable name is uppercase (known as camel cased), whereas macro names are usually written using uppercase letters separated by underscore characters. For example, MAX() would refer to a macro, whereas Max() would refer to a function name. NTH_ROOT() would refer to a macro, whereas NthRoot() would refer to a function. This is not enforced by the compiler, but is simply a convention to make it easier to identify the difference. If in doubt, find the declaration's implementation.

The #ifdef directive tests the value of a symbol. For example:

```
#ifdef CPLUSPLUS
#include <someheader>
#endif
```

says that if the symbol CPLUSPLUS is defined, include the text of the someheader file in this file right here.

Similarly, #ifndef can be used to check if a symbol has not yet been defined.

```
#ifndef MY_SYMBOL
#define MY_SYMBOL 55
#endif
```

says that if MY_SYMBOL is not defined, define it as 55.

Remember, symbols are only relevant to the compiler during compilation, and are not the same as variables that are used in your program at runtime. Symbols are used to control the compilation of your source code. Note the # before the directive. This distinguishes a compiler directive from a language keyword, i.e., #if is a directive, whereas if is a keyword. Remember, directives control compilation of your code, and keywords control the flow of your code at runtime.

While looking at real life source code you will notice some header files with a wrapper of the form:

```
#ifndef XYZ_H_INCLUDED
#define XYZ_H_INCLUDED
// class definition here
...
#endif // XYZ_H_INCLUDED
```

This is a mechanism for conditionally including this source code, if the symbol XYZ_H_INCLUDED has not yet been defined. If the symbol has been defined, then it means this header is already included and don't do it again. While there is a more modern #pragma directive that can accomplish the same thing (#pragma once), this mechanism is still in lots of source code you'll encounter. You might think it strange that one would need to control if a header is included multiple times in a file. For small projects this is generally not necessary, because you can easily manage a handful of files. In large complex systems with thousands of files, however, many including others that might include others, interdependencies often occur. Including a source file multiple times in a project will generally cause compilation errors, because, as described earlier, the contents of the file being included is literally placed in the file at the point of the #include directive. This means that if you include a file multiple times, you'll get multiple declarations of the same variables, and functions that will lead to compilation errors due to ambiguous code.

Activity:

1. What is the difference between a macro and a function?

2. What is one way of protecting against the contents of a file being included multiple times when several files include common headers, and other files include these files? Example: File a includes file b, file c includes file b, file d includes file a, file c and file e.

3. What is one advantage of using #define to define a symbol to be used in place of a literal value?

4. What is one danger of using #define to define a symbol, rather than using a constant variable declaration?

5. a. Describe a compiler directive that can be used to conditionally include different files, depending on the value of a defined symbol.

    b. Give an example when this might be useful.

Introduction to Windows Applications

Vocabulary:

GUI, message loop, thread, window, form, control, event, framework.

Memory Verse

1 Samuel 16:7, "But the LORD said unto Samuel, Look not on his countenance, or on the height of his stature; because I have refused him: for [the LORD seeth] not as man seeth; for man looketh on the outward appearance, but the LORD looketh on the heart."

The programs in this book so far have been Console applications, which are extremely simple, and are not what you would expect to interact with on a "modern" PC. Now its time to discuss Windows and introduce you to Windows programming.

In the old days, only twenty years ago, computer operators did not use a mouse to click on fancy icons to get their work done, but often worked with commandline programs as demonstrated so far in this curriculum. No doubt the introduction of Microsoft Windows and the Apple Macintosh changed all of that. Today, rather than being presented with a plain looking screen, you are dazzled with graphics, icons, video, sound and animation. Indeed, Microsoft Windows can even run multiple applications and even multiple parts of the same application seemingly simultaneously. Since in the "real" world, you'll most likely be writing applications for Windows or other Graphical User Interface (GUIs), now's the time to introduce some of the concepts behind this somewhat more complex environment. Behind all of that dazzle is lots and lots of plain old code.

When you run a Windows application, you are usually presented with a form or window with a title bar across the top, a menu bar beneath the title bar, a toolbar beneath the menu, a document area (also known as the client area), and a status line. You can activate menu items or toolbar buttons by hovering your mouse over them and clicking a button. You can enter text into a document, and cut and paste text between the document and other applications. How does all of this work?

A typical Windows application is usually multithreaded. This means that two or more parts of the program run seemingly symultaneously. On a single CPU computer, the CPU pre-emptively runs one task for a few milliseconds, then puts that aside and executes the next task for a few milliseconds, etc. On a multicore or multi processor computer, tasks really do run symultaneously. In a Windows application, one thread is usually dedicated to processing all of the window messages for input, such as mouse clicks, keystrokes, etc, while other threads perform video or sound processing, etc. The thread that processes the input executes a tight loop known as a message loop that waits for messages to arrive. It then dispatches the messages to the appropriate message handler, and then waits for more messages. This messaging system is fundamental to Windows aplications.

To make Windows Programming easier, frameworks have been devised that handle all of the behind the scenes messaging, so that you, the programmer, can concentrate more on the actual tasks you want the application to perform. One such framework that has been around for quite some time, and which is used in many Windows applications, is known as MFC, Microsoft Foundation Classes. (See Appendix 4.)

Typically, you'd use the Integrated Development Environment (IDE) to create a form, and then use a visual toolbox to drop controls, such as a menubar, toolbar, edit control, etc., onto the form. The IDE generates a heap of boiler plate code that you then fill in, adding your own functions for making the application do what you want it to do.

For example, say you wanted to write a simple text editor like the Notepad that comes with Windows. You wouldn't want to write the actual text box from scratch. Imagine having to write all of the code to collect characters from the user, handle cursor movement, editing, cut and paste, etc. You don't have to. You can simply drop an Edit Control onto a form, and then add the code to hook up the Edit Control to the menus to load and save your files. In fact, even this can be done by the various Wizards that come with the IDE. (Note: I do not like to use the word Wizard, but it is what the Windows Developers chose to call them. I will refer to them from now on as Boilerplate generators).

Once the boilerplate generator has done its work, you can simply inspect the generic code created for you and add your custom classes and logic.

What the boiler plate code does when you create a window is essentially add a class that draws the window on the screen, and runs a message pump waiting for messages to be posted to that window. Messages are bits of data sent by the operating system to windows with such message loops in order to command an application. For example, when you type a character in an edit, the Operating System (OS) will send a WM_CHAR message to the Window. The Window's message loop will then process that message, and draw the character or otherwise process it. Similarly, when you click the mouse on a menu item, a message is sent to the window hosting the menubar. Its message loop processes the message, and performs the action represented by the menu item.

As mentioned earlier, frameworks such as MFC make writing applications much easier, because they do the bulk of the behind-the-scenes-work to draw the window and add the infrastructure for acting on mouse or keyboard input. The boilerplate generator will add a class and methods for processing all of the necessary events, such as mouse and keyboard input. All you need do is fill in the missing code.

Handlers that are called in response to input are known as events. When you click a mouse on the Save button, for example, a message is sent to that window that calls code to eventually trigger or fire the onClick event for that button. The boilerplate generator might simply add an empty method to your class called save_onclick. You would then add your code to this method to grab the content of the edit control, and write it out to the disk, again making use of the MFC classes or other framework to do so.

MFC has a way of literally hooking up class member variables to User Interface controls. For example, you could hook up the m_bItalic variable in your class to a toolbar press button, so that when you press the Italic toolbar button with your mouse, this variable is changed automatically. This makes programming the User Interface (UI) much easier, because you only need worry about the actual implementation, rather than all of the details of how to process the mouse movement, how to make the button look like it is pressed, etc. This MFC process is called data exchange (which is beyond the scope of this book).

Activity:

Below is part of the header file generated by the IDE for the KJBible project discussed in the next chapter. (Header comments and includes have been removed for brevity.)

```
// KJBible.h : main header file for the KJBIBLE application

class CKJBibleApp : public CWinApp
{
    public:
    CKJBibleApp();

    // Overrides
    // ClassWizard generated virtual function overrides
    //{{AFX_VIRTUAL(CKJBibleApp)
        public:
        virtual BOOL InitInstance();
    //}}AFX_VIRTUAL

    // Implementation
    //{{AFX_MSG(CKJBibleApp)
        afx_msg void OnAppAbout();
```

```
            // NOTE - the ClassWizard will add and remove member
               functions here.
            // DO NOT EDIT what you see in these blocks of generated
               code !
       //}}AFX_MSG
       DECLARE_MESSAGE_MAP()
  };


  /////////////////////////////////////////////////////////////////////
  //////////

  //{{AFX_INSERT_LOCATION}}
  // Microsoft Visual C++ will insert additional declarations immediately
     before the previous line.
```

1. What is the name of the class?

2. Which class does this class inherit from?

3. What are the public methods declared in this class definition (i.e., excluding those inherited by this class)?

4. a. What do you think the line DECLARE_MESSAGE_MAP() does?

    b. Is this a Macro or a function declaration?

    c. How can you tell?

5. Can you identify any event handlers in this class declaration?

6. If there are any event handlers, what command do you think it is implementing?

7. What do you think InitInstance does?

8. Using the Internet or online documentation, find and list the overidable members of the CWinApp MFC class.

9. What methods does the CKJBibleApp class override from its inherited class?

10. What is the main purpose of the CWinApp MFC class?

Studying a Working Program

Memory Verse:

Ecclesiastes 12:12-13, "And further, by these, my son, be admonished: of making many books there is no end; and much study is a weariness of the flesh. Let us hear the conclusion of the whole matter: Fear God, and keep his commandments: for this is the whole duty of man."

This book has only touched on some of the many facits of programming and only on one language. There are literally hundreds of programming languages in use today, and it is an overwhelming task to become proficient in the thousands of libraries available, even for a single language. In the real world, each programmer knows a bit about several languages, and only a bit more about the particular area in which he works every day. Most of the time, we learn on the fly. When we need to perform a task, we do some quick research to find out if someone has already written code to do what we want and packaged it in a library, which we can make use of with our particular compiler and environment. Sometimes, such libraries are distributed freely and other times we must purchase the library and a license to distribute it with our code. There are thus several skills you need to get started doing real programming:

1. Familiarity with the language you will be using,

2. Familiarity with the compiler and development environment you will be using,

3. Good research skills to be able to find out what you need to know when you don't know something,

4. Good problem solving skills,

5. Basic debugging skills as introduced in the prior chapters.

The best way to become good at programming is to study a real system. Download a free compiler from the Internet, such as Microsoft Visual C++ Express, Visual C# Express or Microsoft Visual Basic Express, and then look at the samples and study one carefully until you understand the flow of execution, and have a reasonable understanding of how it works. To access the sample programs discussed in this book, along with several language compilers, go to www.faithfulgenerations.com, and click on the Programming Curriculum link. Once you have compiled the source code using your development environment, begin experimenting. There is no substitute to learning through experience, making mistakes, getting frustrated, and learning to persevere, research, problem solve, debug and test. Start small and build up.

KJBible is one such sample we've included for you to get started. This is a simple King James Bible application written by Ben Graff (Released under the *GNU General Public License*). This program is thus free to copy, modify and distribute, so long as you also distribute the license file and give others access to the source code. The program allows you to view the Holy Bible in four columns, search for words, jump to a particular book and save a bookmark. The program uses MFC, Microsoft Foundation Classes, to create its user interface. As alluded to in the prior activity, MFC's base application class is called CWinApp. MFC applications inherit from this base class to add default implementation for most of the nuts and bolts for creating the main window and running the message loop. You'll notice a method called InitInstance in the KJBible.h and KJBible.cpp files. InitInstance, and its complement, ExitInstance, are used to initialize and clean up your application respectively. In KJBible, only InitInstance has been overridden. ExitInstance defaults to the CWinApp base implementation, which for KJBible is sufficient.

The KJBible program does the following:

1. Creates a window, menu and toolbar,

2. Loads the Bible text of the KingJames from a resource file into a large string,

3. Displays the text in four columns under two headings,

4. Allows you to page up, page down, or arrow through the text by adjusting a pointer into this large string and redisplaying the text from the new position,

5. Demonstrates very simple file IO by allowing the user to save the font, color and bookmark to disk, and to reload them next time you run the program.

While initial inspection might leave you perplexed as to the seemingly unfamiliar notation in many of the source files, I'll try to clarify some of these before you delve into the source and attempt to modify the program.

When you create a project using a tool such as Microsoft Visual Studio, the development environment will create templates for much of the code necessary to draw the windows on your screen, create the mechanism for capturing mouse and keyboard input, and doing many of the common tasks such as handling resizing, fonts, colorization, etc. Generally the tool will create much more code than you actually need, and will place comments where you need to fill in the missing pieces.

Lines such as IMPLEMENT_DYNCREATE(CMainFrame, CFrameWnd) are macros expanded by the MFC system. See Lesson 35 for a brief discussion of symbols and macros. Remember, a macro is a shorthand way of writing code that is expanded by the compiler to generate more complex code. Though this macro looks a bit like a function call, you can tell it is a macro, because the name is uppercase, and there is no semicolon to tell you it is a statement. While functions can have any case characters in their names, there is a convension that is generally accepted, where macros and defined symbols use uppercase and underscore characters, while functions typically use mixed case characters.

MFC is a complex architecture, but even a beginner can quickly follow the flow of a program once they know where to start. There are three basic classes of interest that make up the framework of an MFC application:

1. The CMainFrame class creates the main application window.

2. A class that defines the document type and structure. For KJBible, this class is defined in KJBibleDoc.h and KJBibleDoc.cpp. In the case of KJBible, this does very little.

3. A class which defines how the document is viewed on screen. In the case of KJBible, this is where all of the code of interest is implemented.

Start by looking at the InitInstance method of the KJBibleApp class defined in KJBible.h, and implemented in KJBible.cpp. You'll see how InitInstance shows the main window, and loads the text of the Bible from a resource and sets a string pointer to the text. Don't worry if you don't understand everything; the idea is that you get an overview of what is happening first. As you study the code further, you will begin to fit the puzzle pieces together. When a programmer begins looking at a program written by someone else, they must study it until they have a reasonable understanding of the general flow before they begin to fix problems or add new features. Programming is far more reading, studying and often designing than actual coding. I might spend an entire day researching a problem to find that the solution is a one line code change.

Next, open KJBibleView.h and KJBibleView.cpp. You can begin to study the code that loads and displays the Bible, handles the messages for clicking the various UI components and which reads and writes the user's settings to disk.

Find and study the method called OnDraw. This is the main function responsible for drawing the text onto the window. (OnDraw is declared in KJBibleView.h on line 49, and implemented in KJBibleView.cpp, starting at line 280). When certain UI elements are clicked, messages are sent to the view class that causes the window to be redrawn. This is the heart of the whole program. Toolbar Buttons that move back and forward through the text simply calculate the starting position of the pointer into the Bible text, and ask the view to redraw the text from that pointer's position.

Here are some observations and a quick walk through of the OnDraw method (which is included below):

1. This event handler is called whenever the WM_DRAW window message is sent to this window. The event handler takes a pointer to an object of type CDC, which is a Display Context used to draw text onto. Every window has a display context. It returns no value (hence the void return type). the WM_DRAW message is sent either on demand as part of the message handlers asociated with the toolbar buttons (as we'll see later), or by the Operating System to force a window to update its contents.

2. An int variable, nColumn is declared. It is not assigned a value at the point of declaration, again not good practise!

3. First, the handler creates a font object in order to draw the text. This piece of code is not the best example of clean code, but I have left it as is since the real world contains such coding. Note the line:

```
if ((pOldFont = pDC->SelectObject(&CTempFont)) != NULL)
```

This line contains a side-effect, namely, pOldFont (a pointer to a font object) is assigned to the result of pDC->SelectObject(&CTempFont) as part of the test in the "if" statement. It is a side-effect, because as part of the test whether the SelectFont method succeeds, the result is at the same time assigned to a variable. Side-effects may be clever, but they are difficult to understand. This line might have been better written as two lines:

```
pOldFont = pDC->SelectObject(&CTempFont);
if (pOldFont!=null)
    ...
```

4. The m_bRethink variable is a class member (we can tell from the m_ prefix) and a bool (we can tell from the b prefix). We can deduce that this variable is used to keep track of whether certain calculations need to be re-evaluated or not.

5. GetClientRect(&m_CDrawRect); obtains the client area rectangle used for drawing the Bible text. Again, we can tell that the m_CDrawRect is a member variable. It is declared on line 106 of kjBibleView.h.

6. m_nCeiling = (m_CDrawRect.bottom - 50) / CFontInfo.tmHeight; calculates the value of the window height minus 50 divided by the font height. It stores it in a class member m_nCeiling. If the window height was less than 50, this value would be negative, which wouldn't make sense. The author of this class has assumed (correctly or incorrectly) this will never be the case. I personally would have made sure this value was always valid by correcting it to a minimum value, if it became less than a useful value. This value is used to calculate the number of lines of text that can be drawn in the window. We can tell this, because it divides the client area (minus a top margin used for displaying the book titles) by the average font character height. This is the kind of code that probably should be documented in a comment, but just reading the logic should tell you what I've deduced for you. Remember, I did not write this program and am looking at it as you are, albeit with probably more programming experience.

7. m_nPieceLength = (m_CDrawRect.right / 4) / CFontInfo.tmAveCharWidth; This line calculates the number of characters to be displayed in each row of each of four columns in the window. Again, we can tell this because, first, the client width is divided by 4, and then divided by the average font character width. It is then stored in the member variable m_nPieceLength.

8. A comment tells us why the next line: m_nPieceLength -= (int) (m_nPieceLength * .22); was added, namely to account for a further gap between the columns of 22% of the previously calculated number. Again, this is stored back in the member variable m_nPieceLength.

9. The next line: if (m_nPieceLength > 10 && m_nCeiling > 3) tests to see if we have a column width of at least ten characters and a client height of at least three lines. If this test is true, the program then decides whether to generate the text from the current pointer forward or backward, i.e., to display the next or prior text, or to simply redisplay the text from the same position with the newly calculated client dimensions. (This could be because the window was resized.)

10. Rather than calculating the new text position in this function, two other helper functions are called as appropriate:

```
                    if (m_nCommand == -1)
                            createPrevious();
                    else if (m_nCommand == 1)
                            createForward(true);
                    else
                            createForward(false);
```

Note that if the command is not 1 or -1, createForward(false); just redraws the text from the current pointer within the newly calculated client dimensions. CreateForward takes a bool parameter, which is used to decide whether to redraw from the current position, or whether to advance the pointer to display the next lot of text.

11. Note the m_nCommand = 0; which resets the member variable used to determine the command to execute. This way, if multiple WM_DRAW messages get sent to this window from the Operating System instead of from one of the toolbar buttons, which is supposed to advance or retreat the text, the text will only be redrawn, not advanced or retreated.

12. Next, the two book names are displayed above the four text columns. This is done by first calculating the two rectangles for each of the book titles, and then drawing the text of the two book titles to these two rectangles.

13. Then the four text columns are actually drawn. You can see this from the loop

```
        /*      Display each column */
        for (nColumn = 0; nColumn < 4; nColumn ++)
                displayColumn(nColumn, pDC);
```

14. Finally, if the m_bSaveSettings flag is true, the current font choice and book position is written to disk and the flag cleared.

```
void CKJBibleView::OnDraw(CDC* pDC)
{
    CFont CTempFont, *pOldFont;
    int nColumn;

    if ((CTempFont.CreateFontIndirect(&m_CFont)) != 0)
    {
        if ((pOldFont = pDC->SelectObject(&CTempFont)) != NULL)
        {
                /*
                 *      If the size of the sentance fragments or font
                height needs to be re-computed, then
                 *      re-evaluate and re-create the display columns
                 */
```

```
if (m_bRethink)
{
      TEXTMETRIC CFontInfo;

      m_bRethink = false;
      GetClientRect(&m_CDrawRect);
      pDC->GetTextMetrics(&CFontInfo);
      m_nCeiling = (m_CDrawRect.bottom - 50) /
CFontInfo.tmHeight;
      m_nPieceLength = (m_CDrawRect.right / 4) /
CFontInfo.tmAveCharWidth;

      /*  For the space between the columns, 22% of
the characters will be taken off */
      m_nPieceLength -= (int) (m_nPieceLength * .22);

      if (m_nPieceLength > 10 && m_nCeiling > 3)
      {
          if (m_nCommand == -1)
              createPrevious();
          else if (m_nCommand == 1)
              createForward(true);
          else
              createForward(false);

          m_nCommand = 0;
      }

      /*  Get the book heading and display rect */
      getHeadings();
      m_CBook1.top = m_CDrawRect.top;
      m_CBook1.bottom = m_CDrawRect.top +
CFontInfo.tmHeight;
      m_CBook1.left = m_CDrawRect.left;
      m_CBook1.right = m_CDrawRect.right;

      m_CBook2 = m_CBook1;
      m_CBook2.left += m_CDrawRect.right >> 1;
}

pDC->SetTextColor(m_nColor);

/*    Display each book heading */
pDC->DrawText(m_sHeading1, &m_CBook1, 0);
pDC->DrawText(m_sHeading2, &m_CBook2, 0);
```

```
/*      Display each column */
for (nColumn = 0; nColumn < 4; nColumn ++)
        displayColumn(nColumn, pDC);

pDC->SelectObject(pOldFont);

/*
*       My text formatting is not perfect, and with
        wacky fonts this
*       can lead to a crash. Make sure a successfull
        OnDraw() occurs
*       BEFORE the font settings are saved. If there
        is a crash from
*       the wacky font, this ensures the old font will
        be used at
*       startup next time
*/
if (m_bSaveSettings)
{
        saveSettings();
        m_bSaveSettings = false;
}
        }
    }
}
```

There is much that could be done with this program. You could add a combobox for moving to specific chapters in a book; allow the user to choose the number of columns to display (instead of four); add the ability to link notes with a particular verse, etc. Such suggestions are left as exercises for you to think about and experiment with.

In order to compile this project, you will need Visual Studio or an equivalent integrated development environment. I compiled this using Visual Studio 2010. The .sln and .vcxproj files represent the Solution and Project files for Visual Studio 2010. If you open the project file in the appropriate version of Visual Studio, it will ask you if you want to open the solution instead, go ahead. If you open the project file in a newer version of Visual Studio, you'll need to allow the newer version to convert the project file to the latest project format, and then save this as a new solution. See Appendix 1, if you have difficulty building and running the project.

Once the project is opened, simply compile it from the Build menu. The executable will be placed in a bin\release or bin\debug folder under the directory containing your project. (See Appendix 2 for a discussion of build configurations.) You may also need a supporting dll, msvcr70.dll, to run the executable. This is also included in the dlls folder. Make sure you copy it to the same folder as the executable (.exe) file if you get an error without it. Make sure you always keep a backup of the original files, in case your experiments get you into a mess from which you can't recover.

Remember, God has given each of us intelligence, but we must apply our minds to the task and learn character through perseverance. We will never be the Perfect Programmer, but this book should give you a healthy appreciation of, and invoke worship of, The one and only Perfect Programmer!

Appendix 1

Getting started with the KJBible Project

1. Determine what version of Visual Studio you will be using to compile the project. (If you haven't yet installed Visual Studio, see Appendix 6). Likely you'll be using Visual Studio 2010 or later. If you're using Visual Studio 2010, simply click on the KJBible.sln file from Windows Explorer or open it from the Open Project/Solution menu of Visual Studio.

2. To build the project, choose Build Solution from the Build menu. After a few seconds you should see a message in the Output Window stating the build has succeeded.

3. If using a later version of Visual Studio and opening the solution doesn't seem to work, or if building the project results in errors, you could try clicking the project file rather than the solution file, and allowing Visual Studio to convert your project into a new solution. I did this to convert from the Visual Studio version 6.0 project file to get it to compile in Visual Studio 2010.

4. Once you have successfully built the project, depending on whether you built the Release or Debug version, the executable, KJBible.exe will be located in either a Release or Debug folder under the main project directory. To run the program, copy the KJBible.exe to another folder on your Computer's hard disk where it can be easily located. Next, click on the KJBible.exe file to run it. If you get an error message about a missing DLL, see the next step.

5. Locate the msvcr70.dll file in the dlls folder at the same level as the Release or Debug folder, and copy this file to the same folder you copied the KJBible.exe file to. You should now be able to click on the KJBible.exe file to run the program.

6. Now its time to begin experimenting with modifying the source code to change or add functionality. Whenever you want to test your program, you can simply run it from Visual Studio, or copy the .exe file as in step 4 above.

7. To run it from Visual Studio, just click on Start Debugging from the Debug menu, and the program will be run inside the Integrated Development Environment. You can then see the immediate effects of your changes, find and fix errors and watch how your program executes. It is beyond the scope of this book to discuss Visual Studio as an Integrated Development Environment.

Appendix 2

Build Configurations

I mentioned in Lesson 36 about two possible configurations that your program can be built in, Debug and Release. Release is the configuration you'd use in order to build a small executable for distribution. When building for Release, only what needs to be included in the executable for your program to run is compiled into the code. When building for Debug, however, extra code is compiled into the program, so that if an error occurs more diagnostic information will be available to help debug the error. When running the debug version of the program, a special database file KJBible.pdb will also be generated, which should be placed in the same location as the executable. This way, if a runtime error occurs, the PDB will enable the runtime system to tell you exactly where the error occurred. Remember our discussion of compiler directives? You might see blocks of code such as:

```
#ifdef _DEBUG
...
#endif
```

This block will be compiled if building the Debug configuration, otherwise it will be left out. There is nothing special about configurations; they simply enable you to conditionally compile code based on the presence of compiler directives.

From within Visual Studio, go to the Build menu and choose "Configuration Manager ..." You'll be placed on a Combobox with the names of build configurations. Typically, a project will have at least a Release and Debug configuration. As mentioned earlier, build for Release if you are finished debugging and plan to distribute your program, otherwise build for Debug if you are still in the process of debugging it.

You may notice other configurations such as Static Release. This is where all of the functions from other DLLs are actually copied into the executable, so you don't have to distribute other DLLs (such as MSVCRT70.DLL) with the executable. Remember, depending on the build configuration, the executable may be placed in a bin\release or bin\debug folder under the project folder where you saved the main project file.

Comparing C++ to C#

C# is a relatively new language based on C++ syntax, but offers the ease of memory management found in other languages such as Visual Basic. This means that you never need to worry about deleting objects created on the heap, or about managing the lifetime of objects via manual reference counting. The table below describes some of the main differences between C++ and C#. With a bit of investigation and research, it is quite easy to transition from using C++ to C#. For many applications, C# is much easier to use, because of its memory management and more consistent usage. For example, many functions available in multiple C++ libraries exist as a single implementation in the C# Common Library Runtime (CLR).

C++	C#	Comments
Allows multiple class inheritance.	Allows only inheritance from a single base class.	C# does allow classes to inherit from multiple interfaces.
Programmer is responsible for memory management unless a custom library is obtained to implement memory management.	Has full memory management as part of the language implementation.	
Disallows class member initialization at point of declaration. Note C++ 11 does allow member initialization but since C++ 11 was only formally accepted in 2011, some compilers do not yet support this new feature of the language.	Allows class member initialization at point of declaration.	C# enforces variable initialization before first use.
Semicolon must follow class declaration.	No semicolon required after class declaration.	

Continued

C++	C#	Comments
-> Or . Operators used to access methods of an object, depending on whether the object variable refers to an object on the heap or the stack.	. Operator always used to refer to a subnamespace, object method or property.	e.g. in C++, obj->method or obj.method. in C# always obj.methodName, obj.propName or namespace.subnamespace.subsubnamespace, etc.
Allows global functions.	All functions must belong to a class or struct.	
Static modifier applied to an item at file scope in C++ means that the item is only accessible within that file. At function level scope, the static member maintains state across calls to the containing function.	In C#, static means the item declared as static belongs to the class as opposed to an instance of an object of that class.	In C#, One must refer to a static member, unless the member is within the same scope, qualifying it by its class, e.g. myClass.staticMember.
Allows the use of function pointers, i.e., pointers that point to an instance of a function.	Defines a specific type called a Delegate, which is essentially the same as a function pointer.	
Event handlers for handling common system events or user-defined application events must be manually programmed using system level functions, message loops or custom libraries.	C# Defines a specific type called an Event that allows the runtime to call a user-defined handler to process common system events or user-defined application events.	C# makes it very easy to program event handlers for such things as mouse, keyboard, network or any other system events. Microsoft Visual C++ does offer custom libraries such as MFC to do similar things, but C#'s builtin language support for events is far simpler to program.

Continued

C++	C#	Comments
	C# allows anonymous methods (methods with no name) to be assigned to event handlers.	
Private class members need to manually be wrapped by Accessor methods to hide the internal implementation of the class.	C# offers properties that make it very easy to automatically hide private class members and enforce the use of accessor methods.	

C++:

```
e.g:
class test
{
    private:
    int m_nID;

    public:
    int GetID()
    {
        return m_nID;
    }
    void SetID(int nID)
    {
        m_nID=nID;
    }
}
};
```

C#:

```
e.g:
public class test
{
    private:
    int m_nID=0;

    public:
    int id{
        set{m_nID=value;}
        get{return m_nID;}
    }
}
```

Or the autoimplemented property version:

```
public class test
{
    public int id{set; get;}
}
```

Continued

C++	C#	Comments

Entry point of all C++ applications is the function with signature.
 	
`int main(int argc, char* argv[])`
 	
`{`
 	
`...`
 	
`}`
	Entry point of all C# applications is a static member of a class called Main, which may or may not declare parameters.
	
	e.g:
	
	`public static void Main()`
	
	`{`
	
	`...`
	
	`}`
		Note the case of main and Main in C++ vs C#.

Declaration of arrays: `type_name var_name[];`	Declaration of arrays: `type_name[] var_name;`	Note the [] location in each.
The bool type may be easily cast to other types such as int.	The bool type has no builtin conversion to other types such as int.	In C#, the values of bool are true and false, not 1 and 0.
The long type in C++ is usually 32 bits.	The long type in C# is 64 bits.	
In C++, a struct and class are symantically similar. The only real difference is the default visibility of members. Members of a struct are public by default. Members of a class are private by default.	In C#, structs are value types while classes are reference types, meaning structs are passed by value, whereas classes are passed by reference. Structs are stored on the stack, while class instances are stored on the heap.	
The switch statement allows fall-through from one case statement to the next.	The switch statement disallows fall-through from one case statement to the next.	
To call a base class implementation from a derived class, you must qualify with the base class's name, i.e., myBaseClass->methodName();	To call a base class implementation from a derived class, you must qualify with the base keyword, i.e., base.methodName();	

Continued

C++	C#	Comments

In C++, calling a method through a base class pointer assigned to a derived class instance will only invoke the base class implementation, if the method was not declared virtual. Otherwise, if declared virtual, the derived implementation of the object pointed to will always be called.
 	
For example:
 	
`class CShape`
 	
`{`
 	
`public:`
 	
    `virtual int sides()`
 	
    `{`
 	
        `return 0;`
 	
    `}`
 	
`};`
 	
`class CRectangle : public CShape`
 	
`{`
 	
`public:`
 	
    `virtual int sides()`
 	
    `{`
 	
        `return 4;`
 	
    `}`
 	
`};`
 	
`CShape* p=new CRectangle;`
 	
`int nSides=p->sides()`
 	
would yield 4.
	In C#, calling a method through a base class pointer assigned to a derived class instance will invoke the base class implementation, unless the method in the derived class is declared with the override modifier. The base class method must also be declared with the virtual modifier.
	
	For example:
	
	`public class CShape`
	
	`{`
	
	        `public virtual int sides()`
	
	        `{`
	
	                `return 0;`
	
	        `}`
	
	`}`
	
	`public class CRectangle : CShape`
	
	`{`
	
	        `public override int sides()`
	
	        `{`
	
	                `return 4;`
	
	        `}`
	
	`}`
	
	`CShape* p=new CRectangle;`
	
	`int nSides=p->sides()`
	
	would yield 4.	

Continued

C++	C#	Comments
While iterators have been defined in C++ libraries such as STL, there is no generic keyword for iterating a collection.	C# defines the foreach statement to iterate through a collection of objects using indexers.	An indexer is similar to an STL iterator.
Compiler directives are used to include header files (e.g. #include "header.h").	There are no header files or #include directives in C#:. The using directive is used to reference types in other namespaces, without fully qualifying the type names.	
C++ allows default values for method parameters.	In C#, method parameters cannot have default values assigned. You must use method overloads if you want to acomplish the same effect.	
C++ supports bit fields allowing exact number of bits to be specified for types.	C# does not support bit fields.	
C++ allows macro definition.	C# does not allow macro definition.	
C++ has templates.	C# does not have templates.	

Important C++/C# Libraries and Frameworks

MFC - Microsoft Foundation Classes: a C++ framework providing classes and macros for creating Windows applications. This framework enables the creation and management of multiple document interface and single document interface type applications, employing standard Windows controls, such as edits, buttons, checkboxes, radio buttons, listboxes, toolbars, etc. More information on MFC may be found at http://msdn.microsoft.com/en-us/library/4wcy52ec(v=vs.80).aspx

STL - Standard Template Library: provides a set of C++ container classes, algorithms and iterators basic to programming. Containers include vector, list, deque, set, multiset, map, multimap, hash_set, hash_multiset, hash_map, and hash_multimap. Many useful algorithms are included to operate on these containers, such as for searching, sorting, reversing, etc. Containers and algorithms are templated, so that you can easily define for example a list of strings, etc. More information on STL may be found in Appendix 9 and at http://www.sgi.com/tech/stl/index.html.

WPF - Windows Presentation Foundation: WPF is part of the Microsoft .Net Framework. WPF separates the process of designing the UI from the process of coding the solution. Rather than the developer doing both, the UI can be described using a special markup language like HTML called XML or XAML (Extensible Application Markup Language to be precise). Once the UI has been described by the designers, the coders can simply hook up the behind the scenes code (known as Code Behind), so that the UI does what the designers want. When the application is deployed, it can be made to run as a stand-alone aplication as a traditional Windows application, or it can be made to run in a web browser, allowing the application to be distributed across the Internet. The Code Behind WPF applications maybe written in C# or Visual Basic. (See Appendix 4 for a brief overview of C#).

The categories of controls provided by WPF include:

Buttons: Button and RepeatButton.

Data Display: DataGrid, ListView,and TreeView.

Date Display and Selection: Calendar and DatePicker.

Dialog Boxes: OpenFileDialog, PrintDialog and SaveFileDialog.

Digital Ink: InkCanvas and InkPresenter.

Documents: DocumentViewer, FlowDocumentPageViewer, FlowDocumentReader, FlowDocumentScrollViewer and StickyNoteControl.

Input: TextBox, RichTextBox, and PasswordBox.

Layout: Border, BulletDecorator, Canvas, DockPanel, Expander, Grid, GridView, GridSplitter, GroupBox, Panel, ResizeGrip, Separator, ScrollBar, ScrollViewer, StackPanel, Thumb, Viewbox, VirtualizingStackPanel, Window and WrapPanel.

Media: Image, MediaElement and SoundPlayerAction.

Menus: ContextMenu, Menu and ToolBar.

Navigation: Frame, Hyperlink, Page, NavigationWindow and TabControl.

Selection: CheckBox, ComboBox, ListBox, RadioButton and Slider.

User Information: AccessText, Label, Popup, ProgressBar, StatusBar, TextBlock and ToolTip.

More information on WPF may be found at http://msdn.microsoft.com/en-us/library/ms754130.aspx

There are many other useful third party libraries for C++, C# and many other languages. It can be overwhelming to say the least. You are best off starting with what has been around for a while, since you are likely to find more examples and support for your endeavor. I recommend that you write Windows applications using either MFC and STL, or WPF. Both are immediatley accessible from Visual Studio 2005 or above and both have good documentation.

Appendix 5

Helpful Tips for Good Programming

God's standard is utter perfection! This was clearly demonstrated both in His perfect creation and in His moral excellence outlined in the law given to Moses. As a programmer you will experience lots of frustration as you attempt to come up with the perfect design, and then a bug-free program. Both are very difficult and often impossible to achieve. Good design is certainly extremely important, but as you will soon find out, productivity ultimately gains the money, not eons of time spent in seeking perfection. This just highlights our imperfect and sinful nature and our incredible need for God's saving grace in the Lord Jesus Christ.

As you begin programming, you will soon learn that you will need to strike a balance between good design and a working program. Over the years I've known both extremes, programmers who spend weeks on trying to come up with a perfect design and end up with nothing to show for their work, and at the other extreme, those who sloppily threw a program together that worked, but was riddled with bugs and unmaintainable when the program's functionality needed to be extended. Good design most certainly cannot be underestimated, but in the end you will need to meet financial or time deadlines. In reality, perfect software is rarely achieved, so anything you can do to help those who might have to extend your program or fix bugs in your code in the future will be very helpful indeed.

Here are some helpful tips for good programming:

1. Name variables wisely to ensure the reader understands the variable's purpose and intended use. Avoid one letter names such as X or J, etc., unless the variable participates in a well understood formula, where the variable's name would be readily understood by the user of the formula.

2. Keep variable declaration as close to the place where you first use the variables as possible. Also, declare them in the innermost scope necessary. There was once a convention where variables were all declared at the top of a function. It makes it much easier for someone debugging your code to locate the variable declaration as

near to the place of first use as possible. It also avoids the possibility that the variable won't be accidentally misused or reassigned between the point of declaration and the point you intended to first use the variable. Avoid using global variables that could potentially be changed by a totally unrelated piece of code.

3. Remember to initialize variables before use. Many strange and extremely hard to track down program errors are caused by uninitialized variables. If you do not initialize a variable, it will most likely contain a random value.

    ```
    int nMyAge; // uninitialized, could be 32967

    int nMyAge=40; // correct.
    ```

    To make this point more forcefully, imagine an uninitialized bool variable as follows:

    ```
    bool bAllowProgramToRun;
    ...
    if (BAllowProgramToRun)
        RunMyProcedure();
    else
        ReportError();
    ```

    If you ran this code, sometimes your program would run and sometimes it wouldn't, and you'd have no idea why, especially if the declaration of the bool variable was a long way away from its first use in this "if" statement.

    Remember that in C++ you cannot initialize a class member variable in the class header. You must initialize it in the constructor of the class (see Lesson 12).

4. Write small functions and methods whose task is very specific. Don't try and make a function perform multiple unrelated tasks. Try and keep functions to less than a screen or about 25 lines. If a function or method grows too large, break out some of the logic into a helper function. Large unwieldy methods or functions are hard to debug and easily become unmaintainable. Related to this is keeping the body of loops small. Again, create a helper function called from the body of the loop to achieve this.

5. If a method or function is not intended to change the state of a class, declare it as const so that anyone maintaining the function is warned by the compiler, if they unintentionally add code that modifies the class state (see Lesson 11).

6. Add lots of comments, especially to clarify your logical intention or decision to implement a solution in a particular way.

7. Do not try and optimize your code until you have proven that it needs optimization.

8. Make your classes encapsulate single logical objects. Don't create monolythic classes that represent multiple objects, or that try and do too much.

9. Keep your class interfaces small. Only expose what you have to, and hide any methods that the outside world do not need to know about (by declaring them private).

10. Don't add class methods that you think you might need, but don't actually use. I.e., if you do so, remove the unused methods prior to release. Unused methods just clutter code.

11. Avoid interdependence between classes. When class A depends on class B and Class B depends on class A, this becomes unmaintainable when you must modify one of the classes or the program is extended, causing more and more unintended interdependencies.

12. Avoid nested "if" and "case" statements if you can.

```
if (GetCorrectPassword())
{
    int nChoice=GetUserChoice();
    if (nChoice > 0)
    {
        switch (nChoice)
        {
            case 1:
                DoChoice1();
                break;
            case 2:
                ...
            default:
                break;
        }
    }
}
```

is more clearly expressed as:

```
if (GetCorrectPassword()==false)
    return;
int nChoice=GetUserChoice();
if (nChoice==0)
    return;
switch (nChoice)
{
    case 1:
        DoChoice1();
```

```
        break;
    case 2:
        ...
    default:
        break;
}
```

13. A function should only operate on its parameters and return a value. Do not write functions that cause side-effects. For example, a function should not change the value of a global variable or class member. Functions that cause unanticipated side-effects make debugging a program very difficult.

    Consider the following example:

```
static int sMyValue=0;

int Square(int nValue)
{
    sMyValue++;
    return nValue*nValue;
}
```

    This function looks like it simply squares the parameter passed to it from its name, but on closer inspection we find that it changes the global variable sMyValue. The caller of the function would not expect sMyValue to be changed by a function, which appears to return the square of a number. If the intention was to increment sMyValue as well, in order to count the number of times the Square function was called, it could either be incremented at the point where the function is called (this would be preferred), or another parameter could be passed by reference to the Square function. In the second possibility, the name of the function should be changed too, in order to reflect the double operation. As mentioned, though, incrementing the counter would be better at the point of calling the function in keeping with point 3 above. You might think this example is trivial, but in the case when you only have access to the class header with the function or method signature, and do not know or have access to the function or method's implementation, you'd never know about the side-effect. Remember, it may be someone else maintaining code you write sometime in the distant future when you've long forgotten why you did what you did, and you will likely not even be around to ask.

14. Use parentheses to make the order of precedence of a calculation clear. x+y * z is very different from (x +y) *z, and unless one is very familiar with compiler precedence, it is wise to make your intentions very clear, even if you think the compiler will get it right.

15. Use pre-existing libraries rather than writing your own, you gain the benefit of using well-tested code, as well as avoiding the need to re-invent the wheel. This might seem obvious, but often I've found myself wanting to write code that I'm familiar with, rather than taking the time to find and learn how to use a pre-existing library. For example, use the STL string or the MFC CString class instead of trying to manage string allocation yourself, and risk creating buffer overruns or memory leaks, etc.

16. Use enumerated values or symbolic constants, rather than literal values. It is much easier to change a symbolic constant, rather than have to change every instance of a literal in your program, and risk accidentally changing a literal that should not actually be changed. For example, you may have a literal value 3.5 in your program representing some weighting. You may also have another 3.5 in your program that has no relevance to this weighting, but is used in a calculation. If you wanted to change the weighting constant from 3.5 to 3.8, you (or someone else) might accidentally change the instance of the literal, which had nothing to do with the weighting, especially if they do a global search and replace. Instead, either use a symbolic constant for the weighting or an enumerated value. Remember the #define directive?

```
#define WEIGHTING 3.5
```

or

```
enum
{
    weighting=3.5
};
```

Then use the symbol or enumerated value wherever the weighting is located in your code.

17. Think about the Accessibility of your User Interface. Not everyone who uses your program may be able to use a mouse. Can they operate every control with the keyboard? Do your controls have meaningful prompts? Make sure you use text labels as well as graphical icons to label controls. Screen readers cannot interpret the meaning of graphical icons, but they can read the text of the label to the blind user. Don't just think that accessibility is about disabled users. If an ordinary user can't work out how to use your application within the first few minutes of use without consulting the manual, they probably won't use your program at all, and will look for one that is easier to use.

18. Don't change your code once it is working satisfactorily, unless you have good reason to do so. A seemingly innocuous change has unintentionally caused many a bug. The old adage is worth remembering: If it isn't broken, don't fix it.

19. Treat compiler warnings as errors. Since a program will still compile with warnings, unlike actual syntax errors, programmers often think they can ignore the warnings. A common mistake is to compare a signed variable with an unsigned variable, which will yield a compiler warning about a signed-unsigned mismatch. If a variable is only ever guaranteed to have a known set of safe values, it might not be a problem, but comparing an unsigned variable that you think should be negative with -1 can never be true, and will cause errors that will be hard to trace. Another example is a warning about a potential loss of data when assigning a variable of a larger size to a variable of a smaller size. Consider what would happen if you assigned a 16 bit integer to an 8-bit byte variable. Some of the bits would be lost, resulting in the byte variable not having the expected value. Again, such errors are hard to track down.

20. Test your code! Do not assume that future maintainers of your code know what you assumed about how people would use your code. Test your functions and methods to ensure they cope with invalid parameter values: null pointers, empty strings, unexpected range values, etc. Check that loops always have an exit condition that is guaranteed to be true to avoid infinite loops. If a function is recursive, ensure that it always has an exit condition. Ensure that all code branches of a function return a value. I can't stress it enough, *CHECK YOUR WORK!*

Appendix 6

Downloading and Installing
Accompanying Software

To download the accompanying software:

1. Open your web browser and point it to www.theperfectprogrammer.com.

2. Click on the "Download Software & Samples" link.

3. Save the samples.exe file to a location on your hard disk, which you'll be able to easily find.

4. Once downloaded, click on the samples.exe file. This will run the self extracting archive, and ask you where you want to save its contents.

5. Choose a folder on your hard drive to extract the files to. If the folder doesn't yet exist, create it first.

6. Once extracted, you may explore the folder. (Click on Start, then Run and enter the path to the folder where you saved the contents, i.e., c:\programming, then click Ok).

7. The folder will contain several subfolders.

8. The Software folder will contain free versions of compilers that you may install by running their individual installers.

9. The Examples folder will contain all of the examples in this curriculum, including the KJBible project.

10. Other subfolders may be added by the time you download this archive.

11. To run the Visual C++ Express installer, open the Software folder, then open the C++ folder and finally run the vcsetup.exe file.

12. Follow the prompts and accept default values for all options, unless you understand how to change them and what to change them to.

13. To get started with the Visual Studio Integrated Development Environment (IDE) see Appendix 1. Typically, you can either click on a project's solution file (ending in .sln), or open Visual Studio and use its Open Solution dialog to locate and open any of the example projects.

Appendix 7

Vocabulary Table

	Lesson and Vocabulary
l1	computer, input, output, data, processor, storage, memory, keyboard, monitor, peripheral.
l2	address, random access, sequential access, byte, kilobyte, megabyte, gigabyte, terabyte.
l3	instruction, compiler, machine code, divide and conquer, high level, programming language.
l5	syntax, grammar, statement, execution, sequential, flow, loop, iteration, branch.
l6	do, while, comment, declare, variable, assignment.
l7	if then else, switch, case, default, function, return value, Hungarian Notation, argument, parameter, logical operator, and, or, not.
l9	int, string, array, float, struct, bool, pointer, object, variant, void.
l10	stream, library, include, compiler directive, namespace, token.
l11	Function, Caller, Procedure, subroutine, Return Type, Parameter (or argument), Pass by Value, Pass by Reference, scope, const.
l12	Class, Object, encapsulation, reuse, state, interface, method, member, instantiation.
l14	inheritance, derived, private, protected, public.
l15	virtual member, base class, inline implementation, abstract class, polymorphism.
l16	Multiple Inheritance.
l18	heap, stack, allocation, deallocation, local variables, global variables, Member Variable, memory leak, push, pop, Instruction Pointer, Stack Pointer, Stack Overflow.

199

119	Binary, bit, nibble, byte, word, dword, qword, bitwise operators, and, or, not, xor, bit shift.
120	Hexadecimal (or hex).
122	Data Structure, Stack.
123	queue.
124	Linked List.
125	Doubly Linked List.
126	Tree, root, leaf, recursive, recursion.
127	hash, map.
129	sort, Bubble Sort, Quicksort, Linear Search, Binary Search.
130	template, template argument.
131	syntax error, logic error, runtime error, Buffer Overrun, Buffer Underrun, Stack corruption, exception.
132	range checking, subscript out of range, bounds checking, pointer validation, null pointer reference.
133	Dangling reference, Memory Leak, Null Pointer error.
135	directive, symbol, substitution.
136	GUI, message loop, thread, window, form, control, event, framework.

Caste Hungarian Notation

Hungarian Notation was named after the country of origin of its inventor, Charles Simonyi, a programmer who worked at Xerox PARC circa 1972-1981, and who later became Chief Architect at Microsoft.

While there are many naming conventions in use today, including even many variants of Hungarian notation, we will use what is known as Caste Hungarian notation throughout this curriculum, as it is the convention preferred by the author.

There are many programmers who vehemently disagree with the use of Hungarian Notation, because they argue that in modern programming environments one can simply hover the mouse over a variable to know its type. Many other programmers, however, including myself, think this notation's benefits far outweigh its perceived drawbacks. While long Hungarian looking prefixes obscure code clarity more than they help it, Cast Hungarian Notation is extremely helpful. Consequently, I highly recommend this simplified version of Hungarian notation. In Caste Hungarian, the prefix is used mostly to denote which "caste" of data type a variable falls into (integers, floating points, classes, etc...), rather than trying to represent every single flavour of a basic type.

Variable prefixes are composed of three parts: a scope modifier, a type modifier, and a type prefix (in that order). Scope modifier and type modifier may not apply. Consequently, the overall prefix length is kept reasonable, with the average being around two letters. This system conveys most of the advantages of Hungarian Notation without it's disadvantages. Below is a table of the suggested prefixes:

Type prefix	Meaning	Example
b	boolean	bool bHasEffect;

Type prefix	Meaning	Example
c (or none*)	class	Creature cMonster;
ch	char (used as a char)	char chLetterGrade;
d	double, long double	double dPi;
e	enum	Color eColor;
f	float	float fPercent;
n	short, int, long char (used as an integer)	int nValue;
s	Struct	Rectangle sRect;
str	C++ MFC or STL string	std::string strName;
sz	Null-terminated string (also known as a C style string, see Lesson 9.)	char szName[20];

The following type modifiers are placed prior to the prefix if they apply:

Type modifier	Meaning	Example
A	array on stack	int anValue[10];
P	pointer	int* pnValue;
pa	dynamic array	int* panValue = new int[10];
R	reference	int rnValue;
U	unsigned	unsigned int unValue;

The following scope modifiers are placed before the prefix if they apply:

Scope modifier	Meaning	Example
g_	global variable	int g_nGlobalValue;
m_	member of class	int m_nMemberValue;
s_	static member of class	int s_nValue;

Summary of Most Used C++ Headers

In the following table, the first column indicates the header file to include in your project in order to use the functions or classes listed in the second column. For example, to make use of the Standard Template Library Vector and string classes (briefly introduced in Lesson 30), you'd include the vector and string headers in your project. You would also need to remember to put the "using namespace std" at the top of your implementation file, or qualify each call to a vector operation with the std:: prefix, since the vector and string classes reside in the std namespace.

For example:

```
#include <vector>
#include <string>
using namespace std;

vector<string> myStringVector; // declare a vector of strings
or if you omitted the "using namespace std":

std::vector<string> myStringVector;
```

Input / Output

#include <iostream>	Stream I/O. cout and cin, istream and ostream, endl and other i/o manipulators.
#include <fstream>	File I/O. ifstream and ofstream.
#include <sstream>	I/O to and from strings. istringstream and ostringstream.

C functions

#include <cstring>	C-string (array of chars) functions (strcpy(), strcmp(), strstr(), strchr(), etc.).

#include <cctype>	char functions (isalnum(), isalpha(), isdigit(), islower(), ispunct(),isspace(), isupper(), tolower(), toupper(), etc.)
#include <cstdlib>	abs(), exit(), …
#include <climits>	CHAR_BIT (bits per char), CHAR_MIN, CHAR_MAX, SHRT_MIN, SHRT_MAX, INT_MIN, INT_MAX, LONG_MIN, LONG_MAX, … C++ defines a **numeric_limits** template.
#include <cfloat>	FLT_MIN, FLT_MAX, FLT_DIG, DBL_MIN, DBL_MAX, DBL_DIG, … C++ defines a **numeric_limits** template.

STL (*Standard Template Library*)

#include <string>	String type and functions.
#include <vector>	Fast insertion/deletion at back, random access. Implementation: dynamic array allocation/reallocation.
#include <list>	Fast insertion/deletion everywhere. No direct access. Implementation: doubly linked list.
#include <deque>	Double-ended queue with fast insertion/deletion at front and back, direct access (one-level indirection). Implementation: multiple dynamically allocated blocks.
#include <stack>	**stack** - LIFO access, based on **deque**.
#include <queue>	**queue** (FIFO, based on **deque**) and **priority_queue** (retrieval of highest priority element first, based on **vector**).
#include <map>	**map** and **multimap** classes. Fast lookup based on key yields single/multiple entries. Implementation: balanced binary tree.
#include <set>	**set** and **multiset** containing single/multiple values. Fast lookup. Implementation: balanced binary tree.
#include <algorithm>	Many algorithms for working with containers.

To determine the correct syntax of any function in any library, you could load the header file into Visual Studio and study it, or you can use an Internet search engine such as google to search for the library and function. For example, if you wanted to find out the syntax of the strcpy function to copy one C style character string to another, (not the STL string of Lesson 30, but the intrinsic type introduced in Lesson 9), you'd enter something like "C++ strcpy" into the Google search engine (without the quotes). One of the first search results would be the C++ strcpy reference. Clicking on this link would bring you to a page that would explain the function's usage, show you the syntax and tell you the header to include in your project. Visual Studio also has online help of its own that can be loaded from the Visual Studio installation disks.

Any information on making use of Windows libraries which are part of the operating system may be found in the Windows Software Development Kit (SDK). This can be downloaded from the Internet or from the Visual Studio installation disks.

C++ Built-in Keywords and Operators

C++ Built-in Keywords

Keyword	Description
asm	assembly language, code is not portable across CPU types
auto	optional local declaration
bool	basic declaration of type Boolean
break	used to exit loop or switch
case	choice in a switch
catch	catch block that handles a thrown exception
char	basic declaration of a type character
class	start a class definition
const	prefix declaration meaning variable can not be changed
const_cast	remove 'const' property
continue	go to bottom of loop
default	optional last case of a switch
delete	free space created by 'new' (do not use 'free')
do	executable statement, do-while loop
double	basic declaration double precision floating point
dynamic_cast	cast a pointer type if legal, else return null
else	executable statement, part of "if" structure
enum	basic declaration of enumeration type
explicit	restricts constructors to not allow automatic type conversion
export	precedes a template that can be used by other files
extern	prefix declaration meaning variable is defined externally
FALSE	value of type bool
float	basic declaration of floating point
for	executable statement, for loop

friend	a function or class which can access the internal implementation of another class without using inheritance
goto	jump within function to a label
if	executable statement
inline	expand the code rather than call it
int	basic declaration of integer
long	prefix declaration applying to many types
long int	example of a type that is a long integer
long un-signed int	example of sequence of reserved words
mutable	override const member functions in classes
namespace	a scope for declarations and function prototypes
new	get storage, free storage later with 'delete' (do not use malloc)
operator	followed by an operator symbol, can define overloaded functions
private	the declarations after this are not visible outside the class
protected	the declarations after this are for classes that inherit this class
public	the declarations after this are visible outside the class
register	prefix declaration meaning keep variable in register
reinter-pret_cast	converts a type into another type (i.e., int to pointer)
return	executable statement with or without a value
short	prefix declaration applying to many types
signed	prefix declaration applying to some types
sizeof	operator applying to variables and types, gives size in bytes
static	prefix declaration to make local variable static
static_cast	a normal cast with no run time checking
struct	declaration of a structure, like a record
switch	executable statement for cases
template	defines template class or function
this	the class object itself
throw	throw an exception
TRUE	value of type bool
try	try block that precedes a catch block
typedef	creates a new type name for an existing type
typeid	function for getting the type of a typename
typename	specifies the following name is a type
union	declaration of variables that are in the same memory locations

unsigned	prefix declaration applying to some types
using	makes an entity in a namespace directly visible
using namespace	make the namespace visible (in scope)
virtual	this method is hidden if overloaded by a derived class
void	declaration of a typeless variable or no formal parameters
volatile	prefix declaration meaning the variable can be changed at any time
wchar_t	basic declaration for type wide character (internationalization)
while	executable statement, while loop or do-while loop

C++ Built-in Operators

Operator	Description/Example
::	scope resolution for class, namespace, etc.
( )	grouping parenthesis, function call
[ ]	array indexing, also [ ][ ], etc.
->	selector, structure pointer employee->wage = 7.50 ;
.	select structure element employee.wage = 7.50 ;
sizeof	size in bytes, sizeof a or sizeof (int)
typedef	defining a type
++	increment, pre or post to a variable
--	decrement, pre or post to a variable
!	relational not, complement, ! a yields true or false
~	bitwise not, ones complement, ~ a
+	unary plus, + a
-	unary minus, - a
(type)	a cast, explicit type conversion, (float) i, (*fun)(a,b), (int *)x
new	allocate storage
delete	deallocate storage
*	indirect, the value of a pointer, * p is value at pointer p address
&	the memory address, & b is the memory address of variable b
.*	pointer to member operator, to class (same as ->)
->*	pointer to member operator, to class pointer
*	multiply, a * b
/	divide, a / b
%	modulo, a % b (Returns the remainder of a divided by b.)
+	add, a + b

-	subtract, a - b
<<	shift left or insert, left operand is shifted left by right operand bits
>>	shift right or extract, left operand is shifted right by right operand bits
<	less than, result is true or false, a < b
<=	less than or equal, result is true or false, a <= b
>	greater than, result is true or false, a > b
>=	greater than or equal, result is true or false, a >= b
==	equal, result is true or false, a == b
!=	not equal, result is true or false, a != b
&	bitwise and, a & b
^	bitwise exclusive or, a ^ b (A or b but not both.)
|	bitwise or, a | b
&&	Logical and, result is true or false, a < b && c >= d (Both conditions must be true.)
||	Logical or, result is true or false, a < b || c >= d (Either condition must be true.)
?	exp1 ? exp2 : exp3 result is exp2 if exp1 != 0, else result is exp3
:	see above
=	Assignment: x=5 assigns the value 5 to the variable x.
+=	add and assign: x+=5 takes what is in x, adds 5 to it and places result back in x. This is equivalent to x=x + 5.
-=	subtract and assign: x-=5 takes what is in x, subtracts 5 from it and places result back in x. This is equivalent to x=x - 5.
*=	multiply and assign: x*=5 takes what is in x, multiplies it by 5 and places result back in x. This is equivalent to x=x * 5.
/=	divide and assign: x/=5 takes what is in x, divides it by 5 and places result back in x. This is equivalent to x=x / 5.
%=	modulo and assign: x%=5 takes what is in x, divides it by 5, obtains the remainder, and places result back in x. This is equivalent to x=x % 5.
<<=	shift left and assign: x<<=5 takes what is in x, shifts it left by 5 bits and places result back in x. This is equivalent to x=x << 5.
>>=	shift right and assign: x>>=5 takes what is in x, shifts it right by 5 bits and places result back in x. This is equivalent to x=x>>5.
&=	bitwise "and" and assign: x&=y takes what is in x, performs a bitwise and operation with the value in y, and places result back in x. This is equivalent to x=x & y.

^=	bitwise exclusive or and assign: x^=y takes what is in x, performs a bitwise exclusive "or" operation with the value in y, and places result back in x. This is equivalent to x=x ^ y.	
|=	bitwise or and assign: x|=y takes what is in x, performs a bitwise "or" operation with the value in y, and places result back in x. This is equivalent to x=x | y.	
,	separator as in (y=x,z=++x)	

A clarification:

I mentioned that the "&" operator was used for both bitwise "and", as well as when passing variables by reference instead of value, i.e., when passing the address of a variable rather than what is stored in the variable. Similarly, "*" is used to multiply two numbers as well as dereference a pointer, i.e., to obtain the value of what the pointer points to rather than the address stored in the pointer. How then do you tell the difference?

You can tell that "&" means "address of" when you see it used with a right hand operand that is a variable and a left hand operand of a type, or where there is no left hand operand at all. For example:

```
void p(int& x); /* passing an integer variable, x, by
reference. */

j= &x; // store the address of x in j.

int a =b&c; /* Perform bitwise "and" b and c and store result
in a. */

x=*p; /* obtain the value pointed to by the pointer p
(dereference p) and store in x. */

int x=y * z; // multiply y and z and store in x;
```

Note on C++ 11

Please note that C++ 11 was formally ratified in 2011. This revision of C++ adds many new features to the language, which make it both more powerful and easier to use. As time goes on, more compilers will fully support the new language features. Below, I've outlined just a handful of the new features, which make the language easier to use from the introductory perspective presented in this book.

auto — deduction of a type from an initializer

Consider

```
auto x = 7;
```

Here x will have the type int, because that's the type of its initializer. In general, we can write

```
auto x = expression;
```

and the type of x will be the type of the value computed from "expression."

The use of auto to deduce the type of a variable from its initializer is obviously most useful when that type is either hard to know exactly or hard to write.

Initializer lists

Consider

```
vector<double> v = { 1, 2, 3.456, 99.99 };

list<pair<string,string>> languages = {

    {"Nygaard","Simula"}, {"Richards","BCPL"}, {"Ritchie","C"}

};
```

Initializer lists allow a uniform method of initializing all variable types at their point of declaration. Previously this method of initialization only worked for some data types such as arrays.

In-class member initializers

C++ 11 allows class member variables to be initialized at the point of their declaration. Previously, this could only be done at the time of construction for non-static members. For example:

```
class CLamp

{

public:

...

Private:

    int m_nBrightness = 5; /* initialization now allowed here in
C++ 11 */

};
```

nullptr — a null pointer literal

nullptr is a literal denoting the null pointer; it is not an integer:

```
char* p = nullptr;

int* q = nullptr;
```

Move Semantics

Traditionally, if you wanted to copy the value of a variable to another variable, we'd have to copy its contents from one place in memory pointed to by the first variable to the new memory location pointed to by the second. For large objects (such as strings of millions of characters), this could be expensive. C++ 11 introduces move semantics, rather than copy semantics, so that when assigning one variable to another in the context of transferring ownership, where the variable on the right hand side of the assignment operator is about to be destroyed anyway, the resources pointed to by the right hand operand are transferred, or moved, to the left hand operand without copying the data. Think of this as like passing an object such as a book from one person to the next. Only one person has a copy of the book. Compare this to the old copy semantics, which would be like one person photocopying the other person's book, then, destroying the other person's copy. This is done via a Move constructor (beyond the scope of this book).

For more information about C++ 11, please visit http://www.stroustrup.com/C++11FAQ.html

A Simple Cell?

Darwin's disciple, Ernst Haeckel, claimed that a cell was a "simple lump" of aluminous combination of carbon.45 It was upon this assumption of simplicity becoming complexity that Darwin's theory of evolution rested. He could not have been more wrong!

Phenominal Complexity. "A bacterium is far more complex than any inanimate system known to man. There is not a laboratory in the world that can compete with the biochemical activity of the smallest living organism."[46]

"A living cell is a marvel of detailed and complex architecture. Seen through a microscope there is an appearance of almost frantic activity. On a deeper level it is known that molecules are being synthesized at an enormous rate. Almost any enzyme catalyzes the synthesis of more than 100 other molecules per second. In ten minutes, a sizeable fraction of total mass of a metabolizing bacterial cell has been synthesized. The information content of a simple cell had been estimated as around 10^{12} bits, comparable to about a hundred million pages of the Encyclopaedia Britannica."[47]

"… Each of those 100 trillion cells functions like a walled city. Power plants generate the cell's energy. Factories produce proteins, vital units of chemical commerce. Complex transportation systems guide specific chemicals from point to point within the cell and beyond. Sentries at the barricades control the export and import markets, and monitor the outside world for signs of danger. Disciplined biological armies stand ready to grapple with invaders. A centralized genetic government maintains order."[48]

ATP. Adenosine Triphosphate (ATP) is the most important energy fuel in all lifeforms. All living things need to make ATP, often called the "energy currency of life."[49] ATP is a molecule with a critical role. Its job is to provide immediately usable energy for cellular machines. ATP-driven protein machines power almost every process occurring inside living cells, including manufacturing DNA, RNA, and proteins, garbage collection, and transporting chemicals into, out of and within cells.[50]

Molecular Motors. Now, let us consider the power-plant which produces this ATP. Life depends on an incredible enzyme called ATP synthase, which is the world's tiniest rotary motor.

The F1-ATPase motor has nine components. F1-ATPase is a flattened sphere about 10 nm across by 8 nm high—so tiny that 10^{17} would fill the volume of a pinhead. This has been shown to spin "like a motor" to produce ATP, a chemical that is the "energy currency" of life. This motor produces an immense torque (turning force) for its size. In the experiment, it rotated a strand of another protein, actin, one hundred times its own length. Also, when driving a heavy load, it probably changes to a lower gear, as any well-designed motor should.[51] The gearing mechanism inside these tiny motors appears to be similar to a meshed gear.[52]

Each cell has not one, but thousands of these ATP Synthase motors rotating at over 9,000 rpm, each cranking out three ATP molecules every revolution. Nearly 100% of the spinning momentum is converted to chemical energy in the form of ATP molecules! Each of the human body's 14 trillion cells performs this reaction about a million times per minute. Over half a body weight of ATP is made and consumed every day![53]

DNA (deoxyribonucleic acid) is a very large string of more than a billion molecules. It is normally referred to as a very long spiraling ladder or helix. In a similar way that we use two digits (1 and 0) as the basis for programming our computers, our cells use four digits for their programming.

With more than one billion molecules and 1/3 (333+ million) of those being the programming molecules, there are more than 122.9637×10^{32} different combinations in just one chromosome. Now multiply that by the 46 chromosomes you have in every cell in your body and you will begin to see how complex this information system is.[54]

The amount of information that could be contained in a pinhead volume of DNA would make a pile of books 500 times higher than from here to the moon![55]

"The complexity of the simplest known type of cell is so great that it is impossible to accept that such an object could have been thrown together suddenly by some kind of freakish, vastly improbable, event. Such an occurrence would be indistinguishable from a miracle."[56]

"O the depth of the riches both of the wisdom and knowledge of God! how unsearchable are his judgments, and his ways past finding out! For who hath known the mind of the Lord? or who hath been his counsellor? Or who hath first given to him, and it shall be recompensed unto him again? For of him, and through him, and to him, [are] all things: to whom [be] glory for ever. Amen" (Romans 11:33-36).

Appendix 12

The Human Brain
(Compiled from http://www.christiananswers.net/q-eden/life-complexity.html)

It has been said that man's three pound brain is the most complex and orderly arrangement of matter in the entire universe![57]

"If a million cortical nerve cells were connected one with another in groups of only two neurons each in all possible combinations, the number of different patterns of interneur-onic connection thus provided would be expressed by 10 to the 2,783,000th. This, of course, is not the actual structure, ... but the illustration may serve to impress upon us the inconceivable complexity of the interconnections of the ninety-two hundred million [9,200,000,000] nerve cells known to exist in the cerebral cortex"[58]

"There are an astonishingly large number of interconnections possible within the brain, far exceeding the estimate of the total number of atoms in the whole visible universe. *There are only 10 to the 70th atoms in the entire observable universe.*"[59]

The design of the human brain is truly awesome and beyond our understanding. Every cubic inch [2.54 centimeters] of the human brain contains at least 100 million nerve cells interconnected by 10 thousand miles of fibers. It is estimated that the total number of nerve cells in the human brain is about 100 billion. Far more complicated than any computer, the human brain is capable of storing and creatively manipulating seemingly infinite amounts of information. Its capabilities and potential stagger the imagination. The more we use it, the better it becomes.

The brain capabilities of even the smallest insects are mind-boggling. The tiny speck of a brain found in a little ant, butterfly or bee enable them not only to see, smell, taste and move, but even to fly with great precision. Butterflies routinely navigate enormous distances. Bees and ants carry on complex social organizations, building projects, and communications. These miniature brains put our computers and avionics to shame, in comparison.

"When one considers that the entire chemical information to construct a man, elephant, frog, or an orchid was compressed into two minuscule reproductive cells [sperm and egg nuclei], one can only be astounded. In addition to this, all the information is available on the genes to repair the body (not only to construct it) when it is injured. If one were to request an engineer to accomplish this feat of information miniaturization, one would be considered fit for the psychiatric clinic."[60]

"The fool hath said in his heart, *There is* no God ..."

—Psalm 14:1

"The fear of the LORD *is* the beginning of wisdom: and the knowledge of the holy *is* understanding."

—Proverbs 9:10

"Hearken unto this, O Job: stand still, and consider the wondrous works of God." (Insert your own name.)

—Job 37:14

"O LORD, how great are thy works! *and* thy thoughts are very deep."

—Psalm 92:5

"Know ye that the LORD he is God: it is he that hath made us, and not we ourselves; we are his people, and the sheep of his pasture."

—Psalm 100:3

"I will praise thee; for I am fearfully *and* wonderfully made: marvellous *are* thy works; and *that* my soul knoweth right well."

—Psalm 139:14

"Know therefore this day, and consider it in thine heart, that the LORD he *is* God in heaven above, and upon the earth beneath: there is none else."

—Deuteronomy 4:39

"Only fear the LORD, and serve him in truth with all your heart: for consider how great *things* he hath done for you."

—1 Samuel 12:24

God's Prior Claim to the TCP Internet Protocol

Memory Verse: Proverbs 6:6-8

"Go to the ant, thou sluggard; consider her ways, and be wise: Which having no guide, overseer, or ruler, Provideth her meat in the summer, and gathereth her food in the harvest."

Biologist Deborah Gordon and computer scientist Balaji Prabhakar of Stanford University have found harvester ants use a system to control the rate of sending out ant foragers that works in the same way internet protocols control data transfer on the Internet. Gordon has been studying harvester ants, Pogonomyrmex barbatus, which forage for seeds, and notes the ants have a system where the rate of sending out foragers corresponds well with the availability of food. Ants leave the nest individually and return when they collect a seed. If the ants return quickly with seeds, then more foragers are sent out. However, if foragers are slow to return, or start returning without seeds, fewer foragers leave the nest.

Prabhakar noted this control system is similar to the way Transmission Control Protocol (TCP) works to control the movement of data over the Internet. When a file is sent from one place to another over the Internet, it is broken up into small sections or packets. When the destination site for the file receives a packet, it sends an acknowledgment to the source. If the acknowledgments arrive quickly back at the source site, this indicates there is enough bandwidth to transmit more, and the source site can increase the rate of sending the packets. If acknowledgments slow down, this indicates congestion and fewer packets are sent. This feedback loop helps avoid congestion on the Internet.

To confirm the similarity of these two control systems, Prabhakar wrote a math formula or algorithm to predict foraging behaviour depending on availability of food, and Gordon conducted experiments with ants that manipulated the rate of forager return. They found the TCP-inspired algorithm almost exactly matched the ant behaviour found in Gordon's experiments. They also found the forager control system matched two other features of

TCP. One is known as "slow start," where a source sends out a large number of packets in order to assess the available bandwidth. In the same way, ants start their foraging by sending out numerous individuals, then increasing or decreasing the "sending out rate" according to the rate of returning foragers. If the ant foragers are prevented from returning to the nest for more than twenty minutes, no more are sent out. This is similar to the "time out" function of TCP. This function occurs when a file source ceases transmission if a data link is broken and no acknowledgements come back. The researchers have nicknamed the ant colony's control system the "Anternet."[62]

Prabhakar suggested the harvester ants evolved this mechanism over millions of years. We *know* that no computer or random chance process wrote the TCP algorithm, and neither did the ant *evolve* it. Just as Internet data transfer protocols work because computer scientists outside the system both created and applied them, so the ants foraging control system shows the same *design evidence* of being applied to the ants by the algorithm's Creator, God. The fact that a computer scientist was needed to write the algorithm, which then was applied experimentally to the ants to achieve the same results they accomplish naturally, proves this beyond any doubt.[63]

The Travelling Salesman Problem
Efficiently Executed by Bees

Memory Verse: Job 12:7

"But ask now the beasts, and *they shall teach thee;* and the fowls of the air, and they shall tell thee" (italics added).

One mind-boggling algorithm that has intrigued many computer scientists for years is the "Travelling Salesman Problem" (TSP). Given a list of nodes in a network, (e.g. cities on a map,) and the distances between them, this algorithm attempts to find the shortest possible route such that each node is visited only once. When there are more than a few nodes, as the number of locations increases, the complexity of the problem increases dramatically!

As a simple example, if there are n cities, then the complexity of solving the TSP using the simplest algorithm is proportional to *n* factorial (n!). For four cities, this is proportional to 4x3x2x1 =24 operations. However for fifty cities, (50x49x48x ... 3x2x1) the complexity jumps up to a value proportional to 3.041e+64 operations. If this were to be performed on a 1 GHz home PC, you'd be waiting for something in the vicinity of $9x10_{46}$ years (nine with forty-six zeros after it)! (Much more optimal solutions have been devised, but they are still limited both in time and number of nodes, and usually need to be run on extremely fast multicore processor super computers.)[64] Using the simplest algorithm, it would take an average 1 GHz home computer about ten hours to solve the TSP for only seventeen cities.[65] Such computations "keep supercomputers busy for days," remarked University of London professor, Lars Chittka.[66] Yet in the wild, bees link *hundreds* of flowers while minimizing travel distance, and find their way home.

Scientists from the University of London, using artificially computer-generated flowers, observed that bees learn to rapidly solve the Travelling Salesman Problem.[67] They are the first non-human species found capable of solving such a complex problem, and can do it for hundreds of flowers. Professor Chittka says that bees are able "to link hundreds of flowers in a way that minimizes travel distance, and then reliably find their way home—not a trivial feat if you have a brain the size of a pinhead!"[68] Using artificial computer-controlled flowers, the researchers found that bees can do this "even if they discover the flowers in a different order."[69] Co-author Dr Mathieu Lihoreau observed that despite the size of the bee's brain, they have "advanced cognitive capacities."[70]

Like many scientists who will not acknowledge God the creator and designer of all, these researchers have not considered the implications of their findings. Surely a problem as complex as the Travelling Salesman algorithm proves that such a process cannot be arrived at through blind pitiless chance.[71] It has taken many scientists great research to program (and not as efficiently as a humble bumble bee), and much more research to develop the computers to execute the algorithm within the confines of digital memory. As the bees demonstrate, it required thoughtful, careful, deliberate design, the design of the master creator, the Almighty God. He alone was not only able to program the algorithm into the brain of the bee, but also design the bee to navigate flowers in the wild using this algorithm over vast geographical distances.

Critics of this research[72] say this report trivializes the work of computer scientists, claiming it is an overstatement to say that bees arbitrarily solved the general TSP. While bees may have a limit to the number of flowers they can solve this problem for, nevertheless, they can do it for hundreds of flowers, which is still phenomenally complex as already demonstrated. Rather than trivializing the work of computer scientists, who clearly are smart people, this reinforces the unequivocal evidence of design of the infinitely wiser God.[73] Truly God hath chosen the foolish things of the world to confound the wise![74]

Conclusion

Now that you have been presented with the overwhelming evidence of design from the "simplest" cell to the human brain, and understand the impossibility and absurdity of a computer programming itself through random chance over time, you might wonder why many scientists will not believe the truth. I can only think of two reasons. First, they are unwilling to come under the authority of God, because they love their sin more than truth. Or, they are deceived by the mountains of rhetoric propagated by the education system in which they were nurtured, which has abandoned the very foundation upon which it was begun—a belief in the almighty God of absolutes who revealed the truth in the Lord Jesus Christ.

"Because that which may be known of God is manifest in them; for God hath shewed it unto them. For the invisible things of him from the creation of the world are clearly seen, being understood by the things that are made, even his eternal power and Godhead; so that they are without excuse: Because that, when they knew God, they glorified him not as God, neither were thankful; but became vain in their imaginations, and their foolish heart was darkened" (Romans 1:19-21).

The truth is, the more we are drawn into sin, the more we are willing to suppress the truth, because we do not want to face up to our accountability to God. As you move in to higher education, and if you attend college away from home, guard your heart! If you fall away from the Lord, it will not be because you lack evidence to believe: it will be because you desire freedom from God's authority. Again I remind you of the wisdom of Solomon who said, "Keep thy heart with all diligence; for out of it [are] the issues of life" (Proverbs 4:23).

Though me without eyes, and my teacher without hands, God has graciously enabled us to independently work in this very rewarding area of software engineering, where every single day, as we grapple with intelligent design and implementation of software, we are constantly confronted by the brilliance of the *Perfect Programmer*. If God has given you all of your physical faculties, how much more may you excel if you apply yourself to this branch of study.

I encourage you to allow the Lord to direct your vocational journey through the wisdom of His Word, through godly parents, through godly mentors and discerning church leaders. We who have a foundation of truth have great potential as software engineers as we apply Christian principles of diligence, patience and perseverance to our research and development of high quality software.

—Joseph Stephen

Answers

Introduction Answers

1. At creation, man was created with perfect knowledge, wisdom and intellect and had no need of computing devices for rapid calculation or data storage.

2. After the fall, as man began to degenerate, his genetic makeup was affected by sin and his memory began to fail. God thus told man to record His Word, in order to preserve it and enable them to pass it from generation to generation without error.

3. If there is no God of absolutes, if all is random as the evolutionists claim, then experimental science would be impossible, because there would be no guarantee that an experiment performed at one point in time would yield the same results as at another point in time. We could rely on no laws of physics, motion, thermodynamics or any other mathematical, logical, chemical or physical law. Even if an experiment yielded the same results many times over, if there were no absolutes, then this would still be insufficient to trust such experiments as being valid or reliable.

4. Logic, love, kindness and faithfulness are all immaterial concepts that cannot be explained in a solely physical universe.

5. Evolution cannot explain such immaterial concepts as logic, love, kindness or faithfulness, because evolution denies the existance of anything immaterial.

6. It is impossible for non-living matter to evolve into living matter, because life itself is immaterial. Even if you could create the raw material necessary to build a lifeless creature, evolution cannot give life to that mixture of chemicals. Also, matter by itself contains no information necessary for reproduction. For something to reproduce itself, it must solve the four problems described by Von Neumann. It must be able:

   a. To store instructions in a memory.

   b. To duplicate these instructions.

   c. To implement a factory to read the instructions from the memory, and create a new instance of the entity using the instructions stored.

d. To manage all these functions via a central controller.

A self-reproducing system must contain the program of its own construction. What Von Neuman proved was that self reproduction requires intelligent design, not just the material from which to construct the new entity, but the controller and instructions to do it—hardware and software, i.e., a programmed computer.

7. A monkey cannot write an intelligent computer program, no matter how long it types. A computer program requires intelligence, just as the design of anything with meaning and purpose. Let's simplify the problem somewhat for ease of calculation. Let's assume the keyboard only has 50 keys, and that we don't care about upper and lowercase. Here's the solution:

Solution taken from http://www.answersingenesis.org/home/area/tools/xnv2n3.asp

Could Monkeys Type the 23rd Psalm?

Let us imagine a special typewriter, 'user-friendly' to apes, with 50 keys, comprised of 26 capital letters, 10 numbers, one space bar, and 13 symbols for punctuation, etc. For the sake of simplicity we shall disregard lower-case letters and settle for typing all to be in capitals, and we shall disregard leap years.

How long would it take an operator, on the average, to correctly type the 23rd Psalm, by randomly striking keys? To obtain the answer, let us first consider the first verse of the Psalm, which reads: 'THE LORD IS MY SHEPHERD, I SHALL NOT WANT.'

According to the Multiplication Rule of the Probability (in simplified form)1 the chance of correctly typing the three designated letters 'THE; from possibilities is 1 in 50 x 50 x 50, which equals 125,000. At a rate of one strike per second, the average time taken to make 125,000 strikes is 34.72 hours.

The chance of randomly typing the eight keys (seven letters and one space) in the right sequence of the two words THE LORD is 1 in 50 x 50 ... eight times (i.e. 50^8). This is 1 chance in 39,062 billion. There are 31,536,000 seconds in a year, so the average time taken in years to make 39,062 billion strikes at the rate of one strike per second would be 1,238,663.7 years.

The time taken on the average to correctly type the whole of verse 1 of the 23rd Psalm, which contains 42 letters, punctuation, and spaces, would be 50^{42} divided by 31,536,000 (seconds in a year), which is 7.2×10^{63} years.

And the time taken on the average to correctly type the whole of the 23rd Psalm, made up of 603 letters, verse numbers, punctuation, and spaces, would be 50^{603} divided by 31,536,000 which is 9.552×10^{1016} years. 2 If the letter 'b' stands for billion (10^9), this could be written as about one bbbbbbbbbbbbbbbbbbbbbbbbbbbbbbbbbbbbbbbbbbbbbbbbbbbbbbbbbbbbbb bbbbbbbbbbbbbbbbbbbbbbbbbbbbbbbbbbbbbbbbbbbbbbbbbbbbbbbbbbbbb years.

By comparison, the evolutionists' age of the earth is (only) 4.6 billion years, and the evolutionists' age of the universe is (only) almost 15 billion years.

Note, we haven't even discussed the monkey typing the right computer programming code to print the 23rd Psalm, but only discussed the probability of it typing the Psalm itself.

References and Endnotes

1. The formula used here, $1/p^r$, is not strictly accurate, but is used for the sake of simplicity in the comparison of time. According to W. Feller, *An Introduction to Probability Theory and Its Application* (3rd Edition, 1957), Vol. 1, pp. 332-324., "Application to the theory of success runs," the formula for the mean time u measured in number of symbols is given by $u = 1-p^r/qpr$ or $u - 1-p^r/qp^r$ where $q = 1-p$. In our case $p = 1/50$, and the whole Psalm $r = 603$. But for practical purposes it hardly differs.

2. If we take the solar year of 365 days, 5 hours, 48 minutes, 46 seconds, or 31,556,926 seconds (from which the concept of leap year is derived), the answer would be 9.546×10^{1016} years (using $1/p^r$ for ease of comparison).

8. Many of the world's greatest scientists believed in the God of the Bible as the creator of everything, and the one who imposed law and order upon His creation.

9. Science is built upon faith.

10. God allowed the printing press to be invented, coinciding with the reformation, to help preserve and disseminate His Word to the common people.

Lesson 1: Answers

Discuss with supervisor.

Lesson 2: Answers

1. Discuss with supervisor.

2. Discuss with supervisor.

3. You will retrieve the wrong book as follows:

   a. If the book was inserted before its correct address, then you will find the book from the prior address at this books address, i.e., inserting the book prior to its original address will move all subsequent books along by one.

   b. If the book was inserted after its correct address, the book following the original will have shifted backward to take the original books place, thus you'll retrieve the following book from the original books location.

   You will not get the right book, but assuming books must move to make way for the insertion, you will be able to tell exactly which book will be found at the old address as seen above.

4. Random access memory means that any address in the computer's memory may be accessed in any order. Sequential memory access means that memory can only be accessed in order from first address to last address, and that all intermediate addresses must be visited in succession. i.e., you can't skip addresses.

Lesson 3: Answers

1. Discuss with supervisor.

2. Discuss with supervisor.

3. We do not usually program a computer in the native language of the CPU, because these instructions are too numerous, and do not correspond easily to the human logic used to describe the overall task being performed. It would be analogous to comparing the overall body function to lift ones hand to perform a hand shake, and the millions of instructions necessary to generate electrical signals that must be sent by the brain to accomplish the hand shake. Also, because of the expense of developing software, we want to write it in a language that is portable across CPU types. If we write a program in the native instructions of a Pentium type processor, it would not run on a RISC type processor. If we, however, write our software in a language such

as C++, we can use a CPU type specific compiler to generate the write machine code for each processor type, thus reducing the cost of developing software for multiple CPU types.

4. A compiler is the tool that translates the human readable code into the machine language understood by the CPU.

5. Divide and Conquer means to break up a task into smaller more manageable tasks, in order to solve a large problem.

6. God first presented the Divide and Conquer concept to the world when he gave Adam a help meet to help him in his dominion mandate, so there could be a division of labour (Gen 2:18-24, 1:28).

Lesson 4: Review Answers

1. A computer is a device that can execute instructions.

2. Memory is the ability to store data and instructions used by the computer. Memory is divided up into locations called addresses.

3. The two kinds of memory are RAM (Random Access Memory) and permanent storage. RAM is memory stored in chips, and is only maintained when power to the computer is on. Examples of permanent storage include printouts, CDROMs, hard disks, floppy disks, USB drives and tape drives.

4. Each memory location is called an address.

5. RAM memory is typically very fast to access, and so is used to store program instructions and data being executed by the computer. Permanent storage is generally much slower to access and is necessary, because if power to the computer's memory fails, you'd lose all of your hard work. permanent storage is used to keep long term copies of data or programs.

6.

   a. A byte is eight bits (1s and 0s), typically a single character.

   b. A kilobyte is one thousand bytes.

   c. A megabyte is one thousand kilobytes.

   d. A gigabyte is one thousand megabytes.

   e. A terabyte is one thousand gigabytes.

7. Data is information used by the computer program that is not part of the instructions of the program. Examples might include the text to be printed to the screen, bytes representing a digital representation of a photo, sound or animation used by your program, etc.

8. The process of getting data into a computer is called input.

9. The process of getting the results out of a computer is called output.

10. The tool used to translate human readable languages to the native computer language is called a compiler.

11. We need to express computer programs in an English-like language, because it better reflects how we think of solving problems. To express the solution to a problem in terms of machine language would be very tedious indeed. It would be analogous to describing every electrical pulse needed to be sent by the brain in order to shake hands, rather than simply issue the command "shake hands."

12. In order to program, one must be able to use a divide and conquer strategy to break up a complex task into simpler tasks, until the simple tasks approximate commands offered by the computer language you are using to solve the problem.

13. Discuss with your supervisor.

14. A programming statement must always have the same meaning.

15. The statement is ambiguous. It could mean that the lion ate from the boy's hand and was very friendly, or, it could mean that the lion bit off the boy's hand and ate it, meaning that the lion was savage.

16. God is a God of order. Order is important in a library, because if books were not in some predictable order, it would take a very long time to locate books. Order is important when programming a computer, because instructions must be given in the order they are to be executed, and data must be stored in order in the memory. Otherwise, the data won't be found, or, the wrong data will be calculated, displayed, played, etc. Also, when computers communicate, they must pass information across a network in a predictable order, otherwise they won't be able to communicate at all.

17. A computer's memory holds instructions and data.

18. mouse, trackball, keyboard, camera, scanner, barcode reader, biometric input pad, touch screen, microphone, hard disk, USB drive, CDROM, DVD, light or pressure sensors, etc.

19. screen (or monitor), printer, speakers, hard disk, USB drive, writeable-CD/DVD, projector, mechanical or robotic arm, etc.

20. God made man in His own image (Gen. 1:26). Man's brain is more powerful than any computer, and in fact even a single cell is superior but similar to a computer as Von Neuman described. A single cell is able to store data. It has a processing controller to copy data and execute instructions, and is thus able to execute its own built-in instructions to reproduce itself.

Lesson 5: Answers

1. To set table for ten, instructions similar to the following are acceptable:

   a. Walk to drawer.

   b. Open drawer.

   c. Take out ten knives.

   d. Take out ten forks.

   e. Shut drawer.

   f. Walk to head of table.

   g. Place fork on table level with left edge of chair perpendicular to edge of table, and with prongs away from table edge.

   h. Place knife on table level with right edge of chair perpendicular to table edge, and with blade facing toward fork.

   i. Move to place to left.

   j. If place contains a knife and fork then go to l.

   k. Go to g.

   l. Walk to cupboard.

   m. Open cupboard.

   n. Take out ten dinner plates.

   o. Shut cupboard.

   p. Walk to head of table.

   q. Place a plate between the fork and knife.

   r. Move to place to left.

   s. If plate already there then go to u.

t. Go to o.

u. Go to dresser.

v. Take vase of flowers.

w. Walk to table.

x. Place vase in middle of table.

y. Walk to head of table.

z. Sit down.

2. Instructions similar to the following are acceptable.

a. Ask user for temperature.

b. If temperature equals 0, then print freezing.

c. If temperature less than 15, then print cold.

d. If temperature less than 27, then print warm.

e. If temperature less than 40, then print hot!

3. Instructions similar to the following are acceptable.

a. Ask user for temperature.

b. If temperature equals 0, then print freezing.

c. If temperature less than 15, then print cold.

d. If temperature less than 27, then print warm.

e. If temperature less than 40, then print hot!

f. Ask user if they want to continue.

g. If yes go to a.

h. Stop.

Lesson 6: Answers

1.

a. Declares an integer variable i and initializes it to 1.

b. Declares another integer variable j and initializes it to 0.

    c. While i is less than or equal to 5, adds i to j and then adds 1 to i. In effect, this code adds up the first five integers, i.e., calculates 1+2+3+4+5.

2.

iteration value of i value of j

1	1	1
2	2	3
3	3	6
4	4	10
5	5	15

    After the code finishes, j will be 15.

3. totalChildren=20

4. In most programming languages, if a single * is used between two numbers or two number variables, (variables containing numbers), the * means multiplication.

5.

    a. 4, 16, after this, 16 * 16 is 256, which is greater than 50, and thus the loop would exit.

    b. The loop would execute twice.

    c. 256.

6. Seven Times Tables:

```
int nCount=1;
int nAnswer=0;
while (nCount <=12)
{
   nAnswer=nCount*7;
   cout << nCount << " times 7 =" << nAnswer << endl;
   nCount=nCount+1;
}
```

7. The first form of the while construct: do {statements} while (condition) is guaranteed to execute the statements in the body of the loop at least once as the test condition is only checked after the statements are executed. The second form of the while loop: while (condition) {statements} may never execute the body of the loop as

the condition is checked beforehand. If the condition is false, the loop body is not executed.

Lesson 7: Answers

1. A function is a named set of instructions to calculate or perform some task that returns (passes back) a result to the caller of the function.

2. This little program presents a menu to the user consisting of four choices:

    Please choose one of the following:

    1. Calculate perimeter.

    2. Calculate area.

    3. Calculate volume.

    4. Exit.

    The program then waits for the user to enter a number from one to four (followed by the Enter key). Based upon the user's selection, one of four actions occur. If the user chooses a number outside this range, an error message is printed, and the user must choose another number. If the user chooses 1, the user is then asked for the width and length. The perimeter is calculated, printed, and then the user returned to the main menu. If the user chooses area, they are asked for the width and length. The area is calculated, printed and the user returned to the first menu. If the user chooses three, they are asked to enter a length, width and height. The volume calculated, printed and then the user returned to the main menu. If the user chooses four, the program exits with a "goodbye" message.

3.

    a. Dividing up a program into smaller functions is called divide and conquer. The most important reason this is done is because it is easier to solve lots of little problems, rather than one very complex one. Thus, we break up a complex problem into smaller, more manageable tasks.

    b. We often break up a complex problem into natural tasks that reflect the way we think of the problem. For example, in our calculator problem, each task of calculating perimeter, area and volume are naturally different tasks, as is printing the menu. this complex problem fits naturally into the four functions written.

    c. A program may be very large, and may require multiple programmers to write the code. The program is thus broken up to share the large task amongst programming resources.

    d. It is much easier to debug (find and resolve problems in) smaller functions than it is to try and figure out what is happening in very long functions.

    e. Often, programs outlive the time a programmer is assigned to that task, as programmers change departments or jobs. Writing smaller, more manageable functions is easier than maintaining the program by new programmers who may be unfamiliar with the history of the code.

    f. It is much easier to test smaller functions, rather than complex ones.

4. The declarations between the parentheses after a function's name are its arguments or parameters.

5. They are used for passing information into a function in order for it to perform its calculations or operations.

6. Formal parameters are the declarations after the function name in the actual function signature. Actual parameters are the actual values passed to the function in any particular call to that function.

7. We could have moved the body of the loop (which iterates until the user has entered a valid choice) into its own separate function called GetUserSelection.

8.

    a. x, y, nAverage, n1, n2, a, b.

    b. average, max, main.

    c. x, y

    d. n1, n2, a, b.

    e. int.

    f. average(5,9) is 7, max(5,9) is 9.

Lesson 8: Review Answers

1.

    a. Each complete instruction and its associated data is called a statement. A statement is made up of keywords, function calls, data and punctuation. A keyword is a word with a specific meaning, which the compiler can translate into machine code instructions. The punctuation helps the compiler to understand each statement by indicating the end of the statement, or clarifying which part of the statement should be translated first. Statements must be unambiguous and follow strict grammatical rules.

b. A branch is where execution of a statement may jump to a new, non-sequential statement based upon a condition. In other words, if some condition is true, execution will follow one path, and if false, execution will follow another path.

c. A loop is a statement or block of statements that is repeated.

The statements themselves are not duplicated. Rather, execution flows from the first statement in the block to the last statement in the block, and then begins again at the start of the block until some exit condition enables execution to break out of the loop. The exit condition may be checked prior to or after the statements of the loop body are executed.

d. Syntax is the grammatical rules that apply to a computer programming language. For example, in C++, every statement must be terminated by a semicolon or the end of a block (right brace).

e. A variable is a named memory location or locations that hold(s) an arbitrary value, which can be changed during the execution of the program. For example, nCounter might be declared as an integer and used to hold the value of a loop counter.

f. Declaration is the introduction of a new variable, function definition or constant to your program. Many programming languages insist that before a variable can be used in your program, it must be declared. The declaration defines the type of the variable (the kind of values it can hold), the name of the variable, and, possibly the initial value of the variable.

g. Assignment is the process of assigning a value to a variable. For example, x=5 assigns the value 5 to the variable x assuming that x has been first declared as an integer.

h. A Data Type is the kind of data that a variable can hold. For example, a variable might be of type string, character, number, boolean, etc.

2.

a. Two branching constructs are the if ... then statement and the switch statement.

b. An if ... then statement is used when there is only two (or a small possible number of) branches,

e.g.

```
if (x > 5) then
      DoSomething();
else
```

```
                DoSomethingElse();
```
or
```
        if (x > 7) then
                DoSomething();
        else
                if (y > 0) then
                        DoSomethingElse();
                else
                        DoYetAnotherThing();
```

A switch statement is used when there are multiple possibilities. For example, x is a variable that holds a number, a switch statement might look like this:

```
        switch (x)
        {
                case 1:
                        DoOption1();
                        break;
                case 2:
                        DoOption2();
                        break;
                case 3:
                        DoOption3();
                        break;
                default: // any other value
                        DoDefaultThing();
                        break;
        }
```

3. A common error when writing loops is to cause an infinite loop by not correctly coding an exit condition, so that the loop is never exited.

4. A program comment is human readable text describing what a program fragment does. A program comment should be used to clarify a program fragment that is otherwise unclear. Program comments should not be used to describe what is already obvious.

5. A function is a named set of instructions that returns the result of the function to the caller.

6. In C++ A function name has a parameter list surrounded by () after the function name, whereas a variable name does not contain () after it. Note that the parameter list may be empty, but the () must still be present.

7. In a function call, the parameters that are being passed to the function are placed within the parentheses. For example, if we want to find the square of a number, we

might call the square function as follows: x=square(5); 5 is passed to the square function and the result of calling square with the value 5 is stored in the variable x, thus, x would equal 25.

8.

   a. The instructions within the function's body are executed, and the final answer passed back to the caller.

   b. The function returns its value to the point where the function call was made. The result is usually stored in a variable for use within the calling code.

9. Functions and variables are given names to identify their purpose in your program.

10.

   a. Hungarian notation is the practise of preceeding the human readable part of a variable name with a letter or few letters, which help describe the type and scope of the variable. For instance, nCounter is a numerical counter, bResult is a boolean result, szName is a string, pObj is a pointer to an object, etc.

   b. This naming convention helps the reader of the program code identify the type and scope of a variable being referred to, without having to look back to where the variable was first declared (which in a large function might be many lines previous).

11.

   a. x, y, nAverage, n1, n2, a, b.

   b. average, max, main.

   c. x, y

   d. n1, n2, a, b.

   e. int.

   f. average(25,17) is 21, max(25,17) is 25.

Lesson 9: Answers

1.

nCounter is an int initialized to 0.

chMiddleInitial is a character initialized to "k."

szFirstName is a string that can hold a maximum of 25 characters, and which is initialized to the value "Joseph." Remember, a string is simply an array of characters.

chWidth is a character left uninitialized.

chLength is a character left uninitialized.

fWidth is a decimal (floating point) value initialized to 2.54.

fHeight is a decimal (floating point) value initialized to 3.17.

arrBookmarks is an array of 50 integers that is left uninitialized.

2. Identify the errors below:

   b. Be careful, while this looks like an error, since a character can be converted to an integer, chMiddleInitial+nCounter will not generate a compiler error. Instead, nResult will hold the value of nCounter plus the ANSI value of chMiddle. In this case the variable chMiddle has the value 'K' and nCounter 0, thus the value stored in nResult will be 117 +0 = 117, as the ANSI value of the letter K is 117. The compiler will always attempt to coerce variables to matching types, if possible. Data types such as int, float, double and char can all be coerced into numeric types, and thus mathematical operations on these types will generally not fail. Other types such as arrays cannot be coerced to numeric types by the compiler without the help of the programmer.

      chMiddleInitial * nCounter;

   c. Error: int nRet=szFirstName+chMiddleInitial; While it is possible to add a character to a string, the result is not a number (or integer), and thus the result can't be stored in a variable declared to be of type int.

   d. While chWidth*chLength looks like it should be erroneous, since you can't multiply two characters, the values in these variables wil be treated as unsigned short integers and the multiplication will thus succeed, and the result stored in the int variable, nResult. Since chWidth and chLength are uninitialized, the result stored in nResult is unpredictable.

3.

   a. pszTemp is a pointer variable that points to the first letter of the string stored in szFirstName, thus, the actual value of pszTemp would be the address of the letter "J."

   b. nResult is an int, thus its value would be 8 since the decimal part of 3.17 * 2.54 would be discarded.

c. float fResult can hold a floating point number, thus its value would be 8.0518, i.e. 2.54 * 3.17.

4. We declared pszTemp as a pointer to the character string szFirstName, which means it starts out pointing at the "J."

   a. Now pszTemp points to 'o'

   b. Now pszTemp points to 's'

   c. Now pszTemp would be pointing immediately after the h at a NULL or 0 character.

   d. pszTemp is now pointing to some arbitrary memory beyond the end of szFirstName. Remember, szFirstName is only allocated 25 characters. We were already pointing at character 7 and 7+30 is 37. Since szFirstName only had 25 characters, this is 12 characters beyond the end of the allocated memory for szFirstName. This is known as a buffer overrun. We do not know what is beyond the end of szFirstName; it could be the memory used by another variable, or it could be program instructions. If we were to read from this address we'd get some unexpected data, and if we wrote to this address we might overwrite some instructions or data, causing our program to crash or malfunction. Note that when you unintentionally write to memory beyond the end of a variable's allocation like this, the program may run fine for a while until execution moves into the overwritten instructions. At that point the program will malfunction, crash or hang. These are the hardest kinds of errors to track down, because their affect is not always seen immediately. Be very careful!

5. Add comments to the following short program to describe what each line does:

```
void MysteryFunction()
{
    int nCounter=9; // nCounter is an integer with the value 9.
    char szFirst[12]="hello world"; /* szFirst is a string whose
value is "hello world". */
    char szSecond[12=""; /* szSecond is a string which can hold upto
12 characters but is initialy empty. */
    for (int nIndex=0; nIndex < 10; nIndex++) /* loop counts from 0
to 10, i.e. over 11 values */
    {
        szSecond[nIndex]=szFirst[nCounter]; // copy in reverse
szFirst to szSecond
        nCounter--; // decrement iCounter
    }
    print(szSecond); // dlrow olleh
}
```

To clarify, on the first iteration, copy the character at position 10 of the first string to position 0 of the second string, then increment nIndex and decrement nCounter. On the second iteration, copy the character from position 9 of szFirst to position 1 of szSecond. The incrementing of nIndex and decrementing of nCounter continue until nIndex reaches position 11, and nCounter reaches position 0. Thus the final result is that hello world will be copied backward into szSecond.

6.

    a. An array is a collection of the same data type that may be accessed by an index.

    b. An array can be recognized by the [] after the variable name. Usually this contains the size or number of elements in the array.

7. You must access the values of an array by referring to the array via an index from the start of the array, i.e., a[0] for the first element, a[1] for the second, a[n] for the nth element.

8.

```
int arrInts[50];
for (int nIndex=0; nIndex <50; nIndex++)
{
    arrInts[nIndex]=nIndex;
}
```

9. If you try to read from memory beyond the end of the array, you will obtain unexpected results. If you try to write to memory beyond the end of the array, you will most likely cause your program to crash, because you will be overwriting other program instructions or corrupting other program data stored in the memory at those addresses. For example, in our above question, a[50] would refer to memory beyond the end of the array, since the array memory goes from a[0] to a[49].

10.

Advantages:

Arrays are simple to declare and easy to use.

The array datatype is very fast to access, because the items are stored in a sequential range of memory addresses, and can be accessed by simply adjusting an index into the array.

Disadvantages:

The memory for the array must be allocated at the time you declare it, which means you need to know how many items are going to be stored in the array.

Memory may be wasted, because you allocate more than you need.

If you need to insert items into the middle of an array, you will need to move the existing items to make room for the inserted items, which can be slow. Because the array is a consecutive range of memory addresses, you may need to reallocate the array somewhere else in memory to make room for the inserted items, if you run out of space in the allocated range.

Lesson 10: Answers

1.

   a. stdafx.h and iostream.

   b. 254 (The 255th is a NULL character marking the end of the string.)

   c. First, the length of szName is obtained (from the strlen function) and stored in nLen, which is a synonym for unsigned int. Then the content of szName is copied into szNameInReverse in reverse order.

   d. The abs function takes the absolute value of a number. This means that if a number is negative, it drops the negative sign and makes it positive. If two ages are subtracted and the result is minus, the abs function simply drops the minus. This is so we can report the difference in age as a positive number of years, regardless of the order in which the two ages are entered.

   e. 2 arguments.

   f.

```cpp
// Include standard header file
#include "stdafx.h"
// Include header for handling input and output
#include <iostream>
// Avoid having to prefix all functions in the std (standard)
// namespace with std::
using namespace std;
// Main procedure taking two parameters supplied by command line.
// returns an int.
int main(int argc, char* argv[])
{// Asks user to enter name
    cout << "Hello, plese enter your name: ";
    // declare array of 255 characters (string) to hold name.
    // initialize to empty string.
    char szName[255]="\0";
```

```cpp
// ditto for another name.
char szTheirName[255]="\0";
//Wait for user to type their name and press Enter.
cin >> szName;
// Print hello followed by their name and ask them how old they
// are.
cout << "Hello " << szName << " how old are you? ";
// declare int to hold user's age and initialize to 0.
int nAge=0;
// Wait for user to type their age and press Enter.
cin >> nAge;
// Show a message telling the user's name and how old they are.
cout << szName << " is " << nAge << " years old." << endl;
// Ask user if they have a sibling.
cout << "Do you have a sibling (y/n)? ";
/* declare a char variable to hold a single character response
and initialize to NULL. */
char ch=0;
/* declare an int variable to hold their sibling or friend's
age and init to 0. */
int nTheirAge=0;
// Wait for the user to type their age and press Enter.
cin >>ch;
// Test if ch is 'y' or 'n'
if (ch=='y')
{// ask user for age of their sibling.
    cout << "How old is your oldest or youngest sibling? ";
}
else// no siblings, ask for age of friend.
    cout << "Enter the age of a friend or relative then: ";
// Wait for user to type age of sib or friend and press Enter.
cin >> nTheirAge;
// Ask user for sib or friend's name.
cout << "What is their name? ";
// Wait for user to type name and press Enter.
cin >> szTheirName;
/* Test the age of the sib or friend and print an appropriate
message. */
switch (nTheirAge)
{
    case 0:
        cout << "Newborn: Children are a blessing from the
        Lord (Ps 127:3-5" << endl;
        break;
```

```
        case 2:
             cout << "Toddlers are very cute! The Lord Jesus
             carried young children in His arms (Mark 9:36)."
             << endl;
             break;
        case 3:
             cout << "Samuel was probably between 3 and 5 when he
             was taken to Eli to serve the Lord (1 Sam 1:24)."
             << endl;
             break;
        case 12:
             cout << "The Lord Jesus was a responsible 12 year old
             and was known for his growth in wisdom, He is our
             example (Luke 2:42-52)." << endl;
             break;
        default:
             cout << "So teach us to number our days and apply our
             hearts unto wisdom (Psalm 90:12)." << endl;
             break;
}
// Test who is older and print an appropriate message.
if (nAge > nTheirAge)
     cout << "Remember, " << szName << " to disciple " <<
          szTheirName << " by setting a good example 1 Tim
          4:12." << endl;
else
     cout << "Even though you're younger than " << szTheirName
          << ", you can be
          a good example to them (1 Tim 4:12)." << endl;
/* calc absolute difference between ages and print a message
telling the number of years difference. */
cout << "There are " << abs(nTheirAge-nAge) << " years
difference between " << szName << " and " << szTheirName << "."
<< endl;
// print combined ages.
cout << "Your combined age is " << nAge+nTheirAge << endl;
// Declare char array of 255 (string) to hold name in reverse.
// init to empty string.
char szNameInReverse[255]="\0";
/* obtain length of string (actual characters, may be less than
255). */
size_t nLen=strlen(szName);
/* Loop through szName string and copy chars in reverse to
string just declared above. */
for (size_t n=0; n < nLen; n++)
```

```
        {
                szNameInReverse[n]=szName[nLen-n-1];
        }
        // Display the name in reverse.
        cout << "Your name backward is " << szNameInReverse << endl;
        /* Main returns 0 to tell Operating System that program exited
        with no errors. */
        return 0;
}
```

2. A file stream allows you to read and write to files on disk. It does this by associating a disk file with a stream object from which you can insert or extract data. See the fstream library for more information.

3. You must open a file stream before reading or writing data to the stream.

4. You must close a file stream once you've finished reading or writing data.

5. A string stream is used for inserting or extracting multiple pieces of data into or out of a string object. It is useful when you want to format variables of different types, and then wish to display or write the string to a file.

Lesson 11: Answers

1. The value stored in x is still 10, because the parameter is passed by value; the value stored in x is copied to the formal parameter of the Triple function, and thus inside the triple function. Any changes made to the parameter do not affect memory outside the function.

2. x will be 30, since the result of calling the Triple function is stored in x, overwriting its original value. To clarify, the value of x is originally 10. It is passed by value to the Triple function, i.e., copied to the formal parameter k. The Triple function multiplies k by 3 and stores the result in k. The Triple function then returns the value of k, which is 30 to the calling code, but the calling code now stores that value in the x variable, overwriting the 10, which was originally stored in x.

3. The value stored in x will be 8, because the MySpecialFunc function's formal parameter z is declared to be pass-by-reference, which means that the memory address of the actual parameter x is copied to the formal parameter z, not the value. The actual parameter passed to MySpecialFunc is x, which is initialized to the value 3. MySpecialFunc thus directly refers to the memory of the x variable in the calling function. When it does its calculation, z=z+5, z points to the memory of x, which contains the value 3. The value 5 is added to 3, and then stored back in the memory pointed to by z, which is the same memory named by x.

4. The value in x after calling YourSpecialFunc will be 5. This is because regardless of what happens inside YourSpecialFunc, the value 5 is returned to the caller, which is stored in the x variable, overwriting whatever was previously stored in x. Actually, what would happen is that the memory address of x is copied to the formal parameter z, as z is declared to be pass-by-reference. The calculation z=z+9 would take the value in z, which is 3, add 9 to it and store it back in z (which refers to the memory pointed to by x). thus, immediatley prior to returning, x would contain the value 12. However, since the function returns the value 5, and the caller stores the function's result in x, 12 will be immediately overwritten again by the return result of 5.

5. x will contain the value 51. The formal parameter to AnotherFunc is pass-by-reference, which means the address of the actual parameter x will be copied to z. Inside AnotherFunc, the contents of the memory pointed to by z, which is 7, will be multiplied by itself, (49), and 2 added to it (51), and then stored back in z. The value of z is returned to the caller. The caller stores the return result in the y variable thus. The x variable will still contain 51, because of the body of AnotherFunc directly accessing x by reference through z.

6. The YourSpecialFunc function in question 4 is the worst design because the calculation inside the function is ignored and the number 5 is just returned. The calculation is literally thrown away and thus redundant.

7. A variable's scope is the block of code in which it is accessible.

8. 27, undefined, 3, 2. At the first print statement, the x immediately above it is within the same block, and thus has scope. At the second print statement, there is no x in scope because the {} mark the code block, and within the code block containing that second print statement there is no x declared. At the third print statement, the x (=3) declared in the same block is printed, because it overrides the x declared at the block immediately enclosing this block. At the final print statement, the x(=2) within the same block is printed, because the x (=3) is no longer in scope as its block was closed off by a }.

9. A function returns a value to the caller, whereas a procedure does not.

10. The return type of a function is the type of the result of the function, i.e., the type of variable, which must be declared to hold the result of the function.

11. A formal parameter is the declaration of a variable within the function signature. An actual parameter is the value actually passed to that function when the calling code calls (makes use of) that function.

12. You should only use pass-by-reference when the memory required for the parameter you need to pass to a function is large, i.e., when you need to pass a string to a function. If simply passing numbers, pass-by-value is the preferred method.

13. To avoid a function unintentionally modifying a variable passed by reference, declare the formal parameter and the function to be const in the function signature.

Lesson 12: Answers

1. An object is an encapsulation of related methods, functions and variables which logically describe a single concept.

2. Some of the advantages to Object Oriented programming include:

    a. In the real world we think in terms of objects. Being able to describe the solution to a problem in terms of the interaction between objects more naturally fits the way we think about the world around us, making it easier to describe and declare solutions to real world problems.

    b. Object Oriented programming lends itself to the reuse of code, because it gives us a mechanism for describing and enforcing the use of an object through its interface, while hiding the detail of how that object actually works. This makes building large systems easier, because objects written by different sources can be linked together through their interfaces without the user of those objects knowing anything about how the objects were written.

    c. Collections of related objects can be distributed as a library further contributing to code reuse.

    d. Debugging of code becomes easier, since well tested objects can be distributed, rather than a programmer having to write code from scratch.

    e. Because the user must interact with an object via its interface and cannot access the object's implementation directly, the implementation can be later updated without adversely affecting code using the object.

3. The user of the object interacts with the object via its interface.

4. The user of the object is typically not permitted to know how the object was implemented, so that they do not make assumptions about the internal code that might later be updated, and thereby render their code inoperable.

5. An object is typically distributed as a header file containing the interface, and a compiled object file or library containing the compiled implementation.

6. An object's declaration is its definition. It's implementation is the code that makes the object do what its definition declares, when an instance of it is instantiated (or created). Its instantiation is its actual creation and usage. An example might be the design of a house on paper, compared to its actual construction from that same design.

7.

   a. The constructor of the object is a special method that initializes the object ready for use.

   b. The constructor is called when the object is instantiated.

   c. The constructor is called implicitly by the runtime system, or explicitly by the user of the object in the case of a public constructor requiring parameters.

8.

   a. The destructor of the object frees resources used by the object.

   b. It is called when the object is destroyed.

   c. The runtime system calls the destructor i.e., the user of the object doesn't directly call it.

9. The life-time of an object is the scope of the object. This is the time in which the instantiation of the object is valid.

10. Procedural programming is the method of programming where the solution is described in terms of procedures and functions that interact with each other. Object Oriented programming is the method of describing solutions in terms of the interaction of objects.

Lesson 13: Review Answers

1. Variables must be declared to be of a particular data type to ensure that they are used appropriately throughout the program code. For example, if a variable is of type int, it cannot be used to hold a string. Attempting to do so will yield a compiler error when you attempt to compile the code.

2.

   a. Passing a variable by value means that the value of the actual parameter is copied to the formal parameter when a function is called, and thus the memory of the original actual parameter is not modified. The formal parameter maybe modified inside the function body without the memory referred to by the actual parameter being affected.

b. Passing a variable by reference passes the address of the actual parameter into the formal parameter when a function is called. Modifying the content of the formal parameter inside the function body also modifies the memory of the actual parameter outside the function.

c. Passing a parameter by value is preferred when the size of the parameter is small, i.e., passing a number into a function. Passing a parameter by reference is preferred when the size of the parameter is large, i.e., passing a string or object into a function.

d. You need to be careful when passing a variable by reference into a function, so that the function doesn't unintentionally modify the actual parameter.

e. You should declare the formal parameter to be const and the function to be const, so that if the function unintentionally modifies the value of the parameter, the compiler will issue a warning.

3. Consider the two declarations below:

```
int n=5;
int* pn=n;
```

a. A pointer to a variable of a given type does not hold a value of that type, but the memory address where the value of that type is stored. A variable of the same type is a named memory address, which holds the actual value of that type.

b. pn holds the address where an integer is stored.

c. *pn holds the integer value 5 as pn points to the memory address of the variable n.

d. arrInts is an array which can hold 100 integers.

e.

```
int nCountByTwo=2;
for (int n=0; n < 100; n++)
{
    arrInts[n]=nCountByTwo;
    nCountByTwo=nCountByTwo+2; // increment by two each time.
}
```

f. If in the above loop you allowed n to reach 100 rather than stopping at 99, you'd write to memory outside the array and possibly overwrite other program instructions or data, causing your program to malfunction.

4. What are some of the main advantages of object oriented programming?

   a. In the real world, we think in terms of objects. Being able to describe the solution to a problem in terms of the interaction between objects more naturally fits the way we think about the world around us, making it easier to describe and declare solutions to real world problems.

   b. Object Oriented programming lends itself to the reuse of code, because it gives us a mechanism for describing and enforcing the use of an object through its interface, while hiding the detail of how that object actually works. This makes building large systems easier, because objects written by different sources can be linked together through their interfaces without the user of those objects knowing anything about how the objects were written.

   c. Collections of related objects can be distributed as a library further contributing to code reuse.

   d. Debugging of code becomes easier, since well tested objects can be distributed rather than having to write code from scratch.

   e. Because the user must interact with an object via its interface and cannot access the object's implementation directly, the implementation can be later updated without adversely affecting users of the object.

5.

   a. We separate an object's class definition from its implementation, because we distribute the interface as a human readable file, whereas we distrubute the object's implementation as a compiled object file or library.

   b. We want to enforce a strict usage of the object via its interface and avoid the user making any assumptions about the way the object was implemented.

   c. The implementation of the class is typically distributed as a compiled object file or library.

6. Consider the following class definition:

```
class cTalkingBible
{
    public:
    cTalkingBible();
    ~cTalkingBible();
    void Play();
    void Stop();
    void NextBook();
```

```
            void PriorBook();
            void NextChapter();
            void PriorChapter();
            void NextVerse();
            void PriorVerse();

            private:
            LoadText();
            int m_nCurrentBook;
            int m_nCurrentChapter;
            int m_nCurrentVerse;
            bool m_bIsPlaying;
};
```

a. The public members are:

```
    cTalkingBible();
    ~cTalkingBible();
    void Play();
    void Stop();
    void NextBook();
    void PriorBook();
    void NextChapter();
    void PriorChapter();
    void NextVerse();
    void PriorVerse();
```

b. The private members are:

```
    LoadText();
    int m_nCurrentBook;
    int m_nCurrentChapter;
    int m_nCurrentVerse;
    bool m_bIsPlaying;
```

c. Any user of the object can access the public members.

d. Only the actual implementation of the object can access the private members, i.e., they are private to the internals of the object.

e.

m_nCurrentBook is a cclass member variable, which holds an int, and looks like it would be used to store the book number of the book being read by the talking Bible.

m_nCurrentChapter is a cclass member variable, which holds an int, and looks like it would be used to store the chapter number of the book being read by the talking Bible.

m_nCurrentVerse is a cclass member variable that holds an int, and looks like it would be used to store the verse number of the chapter being read by the talking Bible.

m_bIsPlaying is a cclass member variable that holds a boolean value, and looks like it would be used to store whether the talking Bible is currently playing text or is paused.

7. An object's declaration is its definition. It's implementation is the code that makes the object do what its definition declares, when an instance of it is instantiated (or created). Its instantiation is its actual usage. For example, a house plan is analogous to the class declaration, whereas the bricks and mortar of the built house is the instantiation of the implementation.

8.

   a. An object's constructor initializes the object during instantiation.

   b. An object's destructor cleans up or frees resources used by the instantiation of the object.

   c. The runtime calls the constructor and destructor when the object is instantiated and destroyed. The user may call the constructor to instantiate an object whose constructor requires parameters in order to instantiate the object.

9. An object's life-time is the scope of the object's validity, i.e., the time in which its instantiation is valid.

10. Class members may be:

   a. Public - the user of the object can access the member.

   b. Private - only the implementation of the object can access the member.

   c. Protected - only the object implementation or objects that inherit from this object can access these members. (We haven't dealt with inheritance yet.)

Lesson 14: Answers

1. Inheritance is the ability of one class object definition to inherit members from another class object definition.

2.

   a. Public - the user of the object can access the member.

   b. Private - only the implementation of the object can access the member.

   c. Protected - only the object implementation or objects that inherit from this object can access these members.

3. The main advantage of inheritance is code reuse and extensibility. Inheritance enables us to create complex objects by allowing them to inherit members from simpler objects, thereby rapidly developing complex systems by combining objects together. Rather than having to write a new super object, two well-tested objects can be combined together, reducing both development and testing time.

4. The class you are writing will overload or replace the public method by the same name in the inherited class.

5. Because the variable yourLamp is a CSuperLamp object, the order of construction is CLamp -> CSuperLamp for construction, and then ~CSuperLamp -> ~CLamp for destruction.

6. CSuperLamp is called a derived class, because it inherits from CLamp.

Lesson 15: Answers

1. A base class is a class from which all other related classes inherit.

2. Declaring a member function virtual allows this function to be overloaded in a derived class to modify the function's behaviour in some way.

3. Overriding (or overloading) a function in a derived class means to declare a function with the same signature as in the base class, but modify its implementation in the derived class.

4. You would choose to overload or override a function or method in a derived class to modify the functionality of the original base class function, without having to rewrite or reinvent code. It also allows other classes that inherit from the base class to make use of this overloaded functionality through further inheritance.

5. An abstract base class is a class definition that only declares the interface and has no implementation. Abstract base classes are used to create a generic interface from which other objects can inherit.

6.

   a. The C++ new operator allocates memory on the heap for an object or data structure.

b. The C++ delete operator deallocates or frees memory previously allocated using the new operator.

7. The -> operator enables the user of an object to access the object's public members. For example, if a variable x is declared as of type CLamp, then code of the form x->OnOffButton(), etc., allows us to access the public members of x.

8. We might want a function that takes a pointer to a base class object, in order for that function to perform some generic operation on the object without having to know exactly what kind of derived object was passed to it. For example, a function might be written to take a shape object, and to ask the shape to describe or draw itself. The function does not need to know exactly what kind of shape is passed to it, only how to call base class members such as Draw(), Describe(), Perimeter(), Area(), etc.

9. A base class pointer allows you to access any public members of the base class interface, even if they are overloaded in a derived class object.

10. A class that inherits from multiple classes enables the creation of a super class, which combines the functionality of the classes from which this class inherits.

Lesson 16: Answers

1. The purpose of multiple inheritance is to combine the functionality of multiple classes together into a super class. This aids software reuse, extensibility, rapid system development, aids in testing and debugging and is ultimately more cost effective than creating code from scratch.

2.

```
CLightAndSiren ::OnOffButton()
{
    if (IsOff())
        Play()
    else
        Stop();
    CLamp::OnOffButton();
}
```

Lesson 17: Answers

1. An object is the encapsulation of methods, functions and variables that collectively describe a single concept.

2. Inheritance is the ability of one class object to inherit members from another class object.

3. Multiple inheritance is where one class object inherits from more than one other class object.

4. Overriding or overloading a class member means that a particular member of a class has its functionality modified from the base class's implementation.

5. You must mark class members as virtual, if you want to overload or override them in a derived class.

6.

   a. Public, protected and private.

   b. Public means that any user of the object can access the member. Protected means that only the object's implementation and objects that inherit from this object can access the member. Private means that only this object's implementation can access the member.

7. An abstract class is a class definition with no implementation, i.e., an interface definition only.

8. An abstract class can't be directly instantiated, because it has no implementation. In order to instantiate such a class, a derived class must be written that has an implementation of the abstract class definition.

9. A base class is a class from which other related classes inherit. A base class may or may not be abstract.

10. The purpose of inheritance is to facilitate code reuse and extensibility by allowing one class to inherit functionality from another, without having to reinvent or rewrite code.

11. Declaring the implementation of a class member inline means the implementation of the class member is declared in the class header where the interface is defined, inline with the member declaration itself, rather than declaring the implementation in a separate file.

12. It is okay to declare the implementation of a class member inline when the implementation is extremely small, i.e., one line of code, and, when it is okay for the user of the class to know how the function is implemented.

13. The purpose of declaring multiple constructors for an object means the object can be provided with different kinds of information during instantiation.

14.

    a. Constructors get called from the base class downward, i.e., the base class constructor gets called, then the first derived class, then the next derived class, down to the last derived class.

    b. Destructors get called in reverse order to constructors, from the distant most derived class to the base class.

15. When multiple objects inherit from a base class such as the CRectangle, CCircle and CSquare class examples which derive from the CShape base class, the objects are said to be polymorphic.

16. We might want a function that takes a pointer to a base class object, in order for that function to perform some generic operation on the object, without having to know exactly what kind of derived object was passed to it. For example, a function might be written to take a shape object and to ask the shape to draw or describe itself. The function does not need to know exactly what kind of shape is passed to it, only how to call base class members such as Draw(), Describe(), Perimeter(), Area(), etc.

Lesson 18: Answers

1. The stack is a small dedicated part of memory used for storing information about the state of running programs. This includes the address of the place to return to when the current function finishes executing, the formal parameters of the function being executed and any local variables in the block of code being executed. In a typical program with many functions which call other functions, which in turn call more functions, the stack may contain many return addresses, so that as each function finishes the execution can continue at the instruction after the location from which that function was called. (This is known as stack unwinding.)

2. The heap is the main memory of the computer, and is used for storing the instructions and data of the program being executed.

3. The stack is used for storing program state and local variables, whereas the heap is used for storing program instructions and variables that are too large to be placed on the stack. Also, the stack is managed like a stack of papers; the first thing pushed onto the stack is the last thing popped off the stack. The heap, however, is able to be accessed randomly.

4. The Programmer is responsible for allocating and deallocating heap memory (unless the language has its own memory management).

5. The operating system manages the stack as the program executes, pushing the return address, parameters and local variables onto the stack, as a new function begins execution and popping these values off the stack when the function exits.

6. It is convenient to store small variables on the stack, because memory management is automatic. You don't have to remember to free it, as it is freed automatically when the function or block containing the declaration of the variable goes out of scope. Storing and accessing variables on the stack is also typically much faster than having to access main memory.

7. Variables stored on the heap can outlast the scope of a running function, and can be much larger in size.

8. If you forget to deallocate memory allocated on the heap in languages such as C++, where the programmer is responsible for resource management, you'll get a memory leak.

9. The Stack Pointer SP is used for managing where on the stack the next item may be pushed, or from where it is popped.

10. The Instruction Pointer IP is used to point to the address in memory where the next instruction to be executed is located.

11. A stack overflow is where the SP (Stack Pointer) wraps around to the start of the stack unintentionally due to programmer error, causing stack corruption. When this occurs, the program will typically crash or hang, because due to the corruption, a random address is likely to be copied back to the instruction pointer when the function returns, causing execution of memory content that may not even be valid instructions.

Lesson 19: Answers

1.

2^0=1   2^1=2   2^2=4   2^3=8   2 ^ 4 = 1 6   2 ^ 5 = 3 2
    2^6=64   2^7=128   2^8=256

2.

   a. 4=00000100

   b. 12=00001100

   c. 16=00010000

   d. 33=00100001

    e. 65=01000001

    f. 127=01111111

    g. 255=11111111

    h. 256=0000000100000000

    i. 30=00011110

    j. 75=01001011

3.

    a. 00000011=3

    b. 00000111=7

    c. 00001111=15

    d. 00110011=51

    e. 01010101=85

    f. 10000000=128

    g. 11110000=240

    h. 11000011=195

    i. 00111100=60

    j. 11111111=255

4.

    a. 10000000

    b. 11111111

    c. 11001100

    d. 11110000

6. Bitwise operators compare numbers at the bit level, whereas logical operators combine conditions to enable the testing of multiple conditions combined in different ways. For example: a|b means compare the numbers a and b at the bitwise level and return

a 1, if either of the bits at each given bit position is a 1. On the otherhand, a|b means if condition a is true or condition b is true, then the result is true.

7. 8 is 00001000. If we shift left by 3 bits (8<<3) the result is 01000000 which is 64.

8. 128 is 10000000. If we shift right by 4 bits (128>>4) the result is 00001000 which is 8.

Lesson 20: Answers

1. 0123456789ABCDEF

2.

$$1 \times 16 = 16$$

$$2 \times 16 = 32$$

$$3 \times 16 = 48$$

$$4 \times 16 = 64$$

$$5 \times 16 = 80$$

$$6 \times 16 = 96$$

$$7 \times 16 = 112$$

$$8 \times 16 = 128$$

$$9 \times 16 = 144$$

$$10 \times 16 = 160$$

$$11 \times 16 = 176$$

$$12 \times 16 = 192$$

$$13 \times 16 = 208$$

$$14 \times 16 = 224$$

$$15 \times 16 = 240$$

$$16 \times 16 = 256$$

3.

   a. 4=4H

   b. 12=C

   c. 16=10H

   d. 33=21H

   e. 65=41H

   f. 127=7F

   g. 255=FF

   h. 256=100H

   i. 30=1E

   j. 75=4B

4.

   a. A=10

   b. 10H=16

   c. c0=192

   d. ff=255

   e. 100H=256

   f. 20H=32

   g. a0=160

   h. 80H=128

   i. ff00=65280

   j. ffff=65535

Lesson 21: Review Answers

1. The stack is a small dedicated part of memory used for storing information about the state of the running program. This includes the address of the place to return to when the current function finishes executing, the formal parameters of the function being executed and any local variables in the block of code being executed. In a typical program with many functions that call other functions, which in turn call more functions, the stack may contain many return addresses, so that as each function finishes the execution can continue at the instruction after the location from which that function was called.

2. The heap is the main memory of the computer and is used for storing the instructions and data of the program being executed.

3. The stack is used for storing program state and local variables, whereas the heap is used for storing program instructions and variables that are too large to be placed on the stack. Also, the stack is managed like a stack of papers; the first thing pushed onto the stack is the last thing popped off the stack. The heap, however, is able to be accessed randomly.

4. The Programmer is responsible for allocating and deallocating heap memory (unless the language has its own memory management).

5. The operating system manages the stack as the program executes, pushing the return address, parameters and local variables onto the stack as a new function begins execution, and popping these values off the stack when the function exits.

6. It is convenient to store small variables on the stack, because memory management is automatic. You don't have to remember to free it, as it is freed automatically when the function or block containing the declaration of the variable goes out of scope. Storing and accessing variables on the stack is also typically much faster than having to access main memory.

7. Variables stored on the heap can outlast the scope of a running function, and can be much larger in size.

8. If you forget to deallocate memory allocated on the heap in languages such as C++, where the programmer is responsible for resource management, you'll get a memory leak.

9. The Stack Pointer SP is used for managing where on the stack the next item may be pushed, or from where it is popped.

10. The Instruction Pointer IP is used to point to the address in memory where the next instruction to be executed is located.

11. A stack overflow is where the SP (Stack Pointer) wraps around to the start of the stack unintentionally due to programmer error, causing stack corruption. When this occurs, the program will typically crash or hang, because due to the corruption, a random address is likely to be copied back to the instruction pointer when the function returns, causing execution of memory content that may not even be valid instructions.

12. $2^0=1$, $2^1=2$, $2^2=4$, $2^3=8$, $2^4=16$, $2^5=32$, $2^6=64$, $2^7=128$, $2^8=256$

13.

    a. 7=00000111

    b. 15=00001111

    c. 16=00010000

    d. 31=00011111

    e. 82=01010010

    f. 127=01111111

    g. 128=10000000

    h. 254=11111110

    i. 256=0000000100000000

    j. 192=11000000

14.

    a. 00000010=2

    b. 00001011=11

    c. 01001111=79

    d. 01100110=102

    e. 10101010=170

    f. 10001000=136

    g. 11110001=241

    h. 11100111=231

    i. 00111100=60

    j. 11111111=255

15.

    a. 10=A

    b. 12=C

    c. 16=10H

d. 33=21H

e. 65=41H

f. 127=7F

g. 255=FF

h. 256=100H

i. 30=1E

J. 75=4B

16.

a. A=10

b. B=11

c. c0=192

d. D1=209

e. 100H=256

f. 20H=32

g. a0=160

h. 80H=128

i. ff=255

j. ABCD=$(13*16^0 + 12*16^1 + 11*16^2 + 10*16^3)$=43981

17.

a. 1

b. 4

c. 8

d. 16

e. 32

f. 64

18. Binary is used inside a computer's CPU, because the transistors used for storing numbers only have two states, on and off. Combining the transistors to store numbers means that we must store the numbers in terms of 1s and 0s.

19. A single hex digit can represent 4 bits.

20. Using hex yields a much more compact view of the data, thus it is easier to read and work with.

Lesson 22: Answers

1. A stack is a data structure for managing items on a last-in-first-out basis. It is used when you want to track the state of a program by remembering the order in which operations occur, i.e., functions are executed, thus being able to return to the correct memory address of the next instruction to execute after the current function exits.

2. Our stack is limited to managing the int data type, and can only handle a maximum of 1000 items.

3. Currently the Pop and Top functions return a value, so there is no way of telling if we've reached the bottom of the stack. We could modify our class to return true or false (i.e., a boolean), so that the caller could check the result of the function to determine if the function succeeded. Of course if we did this, we'd need to pass back the actual value via a parameter, which was passed by reference, so that the Top or Pop functions could place this value into the parameter for the caller to make use of, if the return result was true.

4. The Top member simply returns the top most value of the stack without removing it. The Pop member first removes the top item and returns its value to the caller.

5. We'd need to change the value of the MAX_STACK_SIZE constant at the top of the code from 1000 to 5000. This, in turn, would make the array able to hold 5000 rather than 1000 integers.

Lesson 23: Answers

1. A stack means the first item added is the last item removed, just like a stack of papers. A queue means the first item added is the first item removed, just like a queue of people.

2. A stack is useful when we need to keep track of program state, and in fact is used to maintain the list of return addresses when multiple functions call other functions, and we need to know where to continue executing instructions when each function exits. (See Lesson 18.)

3. A queue is useful when you need to process items in the order in which they are received, but can't process them fast enough, and need to store the items for processing in the correct order.

4. Because we used an array to implement our queue, we are limited in the number of items that can be stored in our implementation. If we require more than 1000 items, our implementation will be insufficient to handle the number of items. If we only need 10 positions, 990 positions are wasted, and our implementation will be memory inefficient.

   Each time an item is dequeued, all of the remaining items in the queue must be moved up in the array, which is also inefficient.

5.

```
for (int n=0; n < m_nNextPos ;n++)
{
        m_nItems[n]=m_nItems[n+1]; // move each item left by one
}
```

For each location from 0 to the last used position in the array, copy the value of the item from the next position to the current position, thereby moving all items toward the start of the array by one.

For example:

- On the first iteration, move the item in position 1 to position 0.

- On the second iteration, move the item from position 2 to position 1.

- On the third iteration, move the item in position 3 to position 2, etc., until all items in the queue have been moved.

Lesson 24: Answers

1. If we do not first save a copy of the pointer to the next record in the chain, when we delete the current element, we would have no way of accessing the next record, since we'd no longer have any idea where in memory the next record was stored.

2. If we do not set m_pFirst and m_pLast to 0 in the constructor, they may contain random data, and thus point to some irrelevant part of memory. Attempting to access the memory through these pointers would yield unpredictable results. We'd probably crash our program, if we attempted to traverse the queue.

3. Rather than returning the queue's item values from functions, we could return true or false, so that we knew if the function was successful, and pass the value of the

queue item back via a parameter passed by reference to the functions. This would allow the functions to put a value into the variable passed into the functions, and also return a result that we could interpret as success or failure.

4. If we don't maintain a pointer to the first record, we couldn't dequeue any items, nor indeed, could we even tell what the value of the first item in the queue was. We could also not free the memory resources used by the queue, since we'd have no way of knowing where in memory the queue's first item was located. If we didn't maintain a pointer to the last queue item, we'd have to traverse the entire queue each time we wanted to find the end to enqueue a new item. While this is not so bad for small queue sizes, it might be lengthy and inefficient with a queue of thousands of items.

5. We need to save a copy of nVal, because the actual queue item is deleted or deallocated from memory. Once this is done, there is no guarantee that what is at the memory address of the deleted item is what you expect to be there.

6. The destructor of the class traverses the queue, deallocating the memory used by each item.

7. We might leave m_pLast pointing at the now deallocated memory of m_pFirst, which would mean that if we tried to access m_pLast, we'd have unpredictable results.

8. A doubly linked list is one in which each list item has a pointer to both its next and prior item in the list, so that the list can be traversed in either direction.

Lesson 25: Answers

1. A doubly linked list is particularly useful when you need to frequently insert items into the middle of a list. They are also good when the size of the list is not known, and may potentially be very large.

2. Unless you maintain a pointer to the last item accessed, and it is likely that you'll access the same item again, finding the item you are looking for can be very expensive. You will need to traverse the list every time you want to locate a particular item. For a fixed size list with few insertions and lots of lookups, an array is far more efficient.

3.

```
int nThisIndex=0;
sDoublyLinkedListItem* pCurrent=m_pHead;
while (pCurrent && nThisIndex < nIndex)
{
     pCurrent=pCurrent->pNext;
     nThisIndex++;
}
```

Given an index, this code traverses the list from the first item, counting the items traversed until it finds the item with the supplied index, so that a new item can be inserted, its value returned, or the item with that index deleted.

4.

```
// This block inserts a new item prior to the current one.
pNew->pPrev=pCurrent->pPrev; /* set pNew's pPrev pointer to point
to the same as the current item's previous item. */
pNew->pNext=pCurrent; /* set pNew's pNext pointer to point to
the current item. At this point, the new item points to the prior
and current item, but the prior item doesn't know about the new
item, and the current item doesn't know about the new item. */
pCurrent->pPrev=pNew; /* set the current item's pPrev item to
the newly inserted item. */
if (pCurrent->pPrev) /* test if there is a prior item before
trying to access it. */
      pCurrent->pPrev->pNext=pNew; /* Set the prior item's pNext
pointer to point to the newly inserted item. */
/* Now the new item is correctly inserted with its pPrev and
pNext pointers pointing to the correct items, the prior item now
pointing to the new item and the current item now knowing that
the new item is prior to it in the list. */

/* This fragment deletes the item pointed to by pCurrent, but first
makes the necessary changes to the prior and next item to remove
the links, and ensure that the item being deleted is no longer
pointed at by either the prior or next items in the list. */
sDoublyLinkedListItem *pPrev=pCurrent->pPrev; /* Declare a new
variable pPrev to point at the prior item in the list. */
sDoublyLinkedListItem* pNext=pCurrent->pNext; /* Declare a new
variable pNext to point at the next item in the list. */
if (pPrev)// test if pPrev is valid before accessing its members.
      pPrev->pNext=pNext; /* make pPrev's next pointer point at
the item following pCurrent, bypassing pCurrent. */
if (pNext)// Check if pNext is valid before accessing its members.
      pNext->pPrev=pPrev; /* Make the item following pCurrent's
pPrev pointer point to the item before pCurrent, bypassing
pCurrent. */
/* At this point, the item pointed to by pCurrent is not referenced
by any other item in the list, only the variable pCurrent still
points to its memory. */
      delete pCurrent; /* Now deallocate the item pointed to by
pCurrent. At this point, pCurrent's memory has been deallocated
and pCurrent is invalid. We should not try accessing it from
here. To avoid anyone accidentally accessing the memory via this
pointer, we could set it to 0, since we test any pointers to be
non-zero before using them to ensure they are valid. */
```

5. We could have extracted the code to find an element with a given index into its own private class member function, which given an index, returned a pointer to the appropriate record. For example:

its class header signature would look like

```
private:
sDoublyLinkedListItem* GetItemWithIndex(int nIndex) const;
```

and its body would look like

```
sDoublyLinkedListItem* CDoublyLinkedList::GetItemWithIndex(int nIndex)
const
{
    int nThisIndex=0;
    sDoublyLinkedListItem* pCurrent=m_pHead;
    while (pCurrent && nThisIndex < nIndex)
    {
        pCurrent=pCurrent->pNext;
        nThisIndex++;
    }
    return pCurrent; /* either NULL if not found or a valid pointer
    if found. */
}
```

Functions that use this such as GetAt would be modified to look like this:

```
int CDoublyLinkedList::GetAt(int nIndex)
{
    sDoublyLinkedListItem* pCurrent=GetItemWithIndex(nIndex);
    if (!pCurrent) /* check the pointer returned to see if it is
    non-zero. */
        return 0;
    return pCurrent->nVal;
}
```

6. Remember, the first item in the list has index 0. Each time an item is deleted, the following item takes the place of the one deleted. This means that when item 1 is deleted, the item with value 2 is now in item 1's place. Then, when item 2 is deleted, you will be actually deleting the item with value 3, and thus the item with value 4 will be moved into its place. The upshot is that each odd item will be removed from the list.

Lesson 26: Answers

1.

    a. A tree is a data structure that implements a tree of items. Starting at the root, the root may contain one or more branches to other items (or nodes), which in turn contain branches to more nodes etc.

    b. A leaf node is a node with no branches.

    c. The root is the starting node, or the node with no parents and from which the tree branches out.

2. Recursion is the process of a function calling itself.

3. You need a stopping condition for a recursive function, otherwise you'll eventually get a stack overflow. Each time a function is called, the return address is pushed onto the stack. As we learned in Lesson 18, the stack is a finite resource.

4.

```
if (nDepth > nMaxDepth)
    return; // This returns without calling itself recursively
            again.
```

5.

```
void AddBranches(cBinaryTreeNode* pRoot, int nRootVal, int nDepth,
int nMaxDepth)
{
    if (pRoot==NULL)
        return; // nothing to do, no root passed to us.
    if (nDepth > nMaxDepth)// stopping condition
        return; // otherwise we won't stop!
    pRoot->SetNodeValue(nRootVal); // set the value of the node
    // Create new left and right nodes to go under this subtree root
    cBinaryTreeNode* pLeft =new cBinaryTreeNode;
    cBinaryTreeNode* pRight =new cBinaryTreeNode;
    nDepth++; // increment depth as we're about to add these nodes
    at next level
    /* Set the left and right branches of the root to the newly
    created nodes. */
    pRoot->SetLeftBranch(pLeft);
    pRoot->SetRightBranch(pRight);
    /* Call ourself recursively to add branches beneath each left
    and right branch. */
    AddBranches(pLeft, nRootVal+1, nDepth, nMaxDepth);
    AddBranches(pRight, nRootVal+2, nDepth, nMaxDepth);
}
```

6. The destructor of the cBinaryTreeNode class deletes the left and right branch nodes, which in turn calls their destructors, which in turn delete their left and right branch nodes. This recursive process deletes all nodes in the tree.

7. While our class doesn't make use of the parent node, it could be used for walking up the tree from any given node to its parent, in order to calculate a node's depth, or simply to find another branch to traverse.

8. As nodes are added to the tree, we could make each node keep track of its own depth, and then add a function, so the user of the class could query a node for its depth. This might be done as follows:

   a. Add another member variable to the class in the class declaration called m_nNodeDepth.

   b. Initialize this variable to 0 in the constructor.

   c. Add a public member called GetNodeDepth to return m_nNodeDepth.

   d. When Set Parent is called on a node, the node whose parent is being set would ask the parent for its depth, and set its own to the parent's depth plus 1.

9. Binary trees are most useful when sorting and searching through very large collections.

Lesson 27: Answers

1. A Hash Map is very fast for looking up key-value pairs. No searching is required, just a function to calculate the unique key from the key string being looked up.

2. Besides the memory required for the Hash Table and the complexity of implementation, a Hash Map can't be iterated sequentially in a predictable sequence as an array can.

3. The main reason to use a Hash Map is for time-critical applications where the speed of lookup is critically important.

4. A Hashing function is a function that transforms a key string into a unique index into the Hash Table.

5. Since the Hash function must return a unique index, typically the range of indices is very large, and thus the Hash Table requires lots of memory. This memory is just for the index and does not count the allocations for the actual key values. In order to conserve memory, especially in a sparsely populated array, it is more efficient to allocate blocks (or buckets) of memory for ranges of values as they are needed.

Lesson 28: Review Answers

1. A stack is a data structure that enables first-in, last-out data access, much like a stack of papers. Stacks are most useful when needing to manage the state of an application, where tracking the order of operations and being able to undo or unwind the operations in the reverse order they were performed is required.

2. A queue is a data structure that enables first-in, first-out data access. A queue is generally used when operations must be performed in the order data arrives, but where the processing of that data may be slower than the data arriving, requiring queuing.

3. A stack allows first-in, last-out data access, whereas a queue allows first-in, first-out data access.

4. A linked list is a list of items or nodes, where each node has a pointer to the next node in the chain. Linked lists are particularly useful and memory efficient when many insertions and deletions must be performed on the data in the list.

5. A doubly linked list means that each node has both a pointer to the next node and a pointer to the prior node in the list. You'd use a doubly linked list, where a linked list is required, and where backward traversal of the list is also needed.

6. You'd use a regular array over a doubly linked list when you know the number of items in the list, the number of items doesn't change often and where direct indexed access is required for speed of lookups.

7.

```
// This block inserts a new item prior to the current one.
pNew->pPrev=pCurrent->pPrev; /* set pNew's pPrev pointer to point
to the same as the current item's previous item. */
pNew->pNext=pCurrent; /* set pNew's pNext pointer to point to
the current item. At this point, the new item points to the prior
and current item, but the prior item doesn't know about the new
item. The current item doesn't know about the new item. */
pCurrent->pPrev=pNew; /* set the current item's pPrev item to
the newly inserted item. */
if (pCurrent->pPrev) /* test if there is a prior item before
trying to access it. */
    pCurrent->pPrev->pNext=pNew; /* Set the prior item's pNext
pointer to point to the newly inserted item.
Now the new item is correctly inserted with its pPrev and pNext
pointers pointing to the correct items, the prior item now point-
ing to the new item and the current item now knowing that the
new item is prior to it in the list. */
```

```
/* This fragment deletes the item pointed to by pCurrent, but first
makes the necessary changes to the prior and next item to remove
the links, and ensure that the item being deleted is no longer
pointed at by either the prior or next items in the list. */
sDoublyLinkedListItem *pPrev=pCurrent->pPrev; /* Declare a new
variable pPrev to point at the prior item in the list. */
sDoublyLinkedListItem* pNext=pCurrent->pNext; /* Declare a new
variable pNext to point at the next item in the list. */
if (pPrev)// test if pPrev is valid before accessing its members.
        pPrev->pNext=pNext; /* make pPrev's next pointer point at
the item following pCurrent, bypassing pCurrent. */
if (pNext)// Check if pNext is valid before accessing its members.
        pNext->pPrev=pPrev; /* Make the item following pCurrent's
pPrev pointer point to the item before pCurrent, bypassing
pCurrent.
At this point, the item pointed to by pCurrent is not referenced
by any other item in the list, only the variable pCurrent still
points to its memory. */
delete pCurrent; // Now deallocate the item pointed to by pCurrent.
/* At this point, pCurrent's memory has been deallocated and
pCurrent is invalid. We should not try accessing it from here. To
avoid anyone accidentally accessing the memory via this pointer,
we could set it to 0, since we test any pointers to be non-zero
before using them to ensure they are valid.
*/
```

8.

   a. A tree is a data structure that implements a tree of items. Starting at the root, the root may contain one or more branches to other items (or nodes), which in turn contain branches to more nodes etc.

   b. A leaf node is a node with no branches.

   c. The root is the starting node, or the node with no parents and from which the tree branches out.

9. Recursion is the process of a function calling itself.

10. You need a stopping condition for a recursive function, otherwise you'd cause a stack overflow. Each time a function is called, the return address is pushed onto the stack. As we learned in Lesson 18, the stack is a finite resource.

11. A binary tree is most useful for search intensive applications such as dictionaries.

12. The main advantage of a Hash map over a regular array is that the keys used for indexing do not need to be numeric, because a Hash function maps the string key to an index into the array. This allows very fast indexed access to the structure, similar to using numeric indices into a regular array.

13. The disadvantages of a Hash Map are the memory required for the Hash Table and the complexity of implementation. A Hash Table also can't be traversed like an array, since its only access is via a key that must be known beforehand, in order to store or retrieve a value from the Hash Table.

14. You'd use a Hash Map over other data structures when you have a list of key-value pairs, which must be accessed via their key instantly, and where sequential searching is not required.

15. A Hashing function converts an arbitrary string to a unique index into a Hash Table.

Lesson 29: Answers

1. The Bubble Sort algorithm is much slower than the Quick Sort algorithm.

2. The Bubble Sort algorithm is much slower than the Quick Sort algorithm, because it must keep traversing the same list of N elements until no swaps are necessary. The Quick Sort algorithm does not need to keep traversing the same list, as the number of unsorted elements is reduced by each recursive call.

3. It is better to sort data before searching for an item, because once sorted it is faster to use a Binary Search than a Sequential search to locate a match.

4. Sorting would not be necessary if:

    a. You use a Hash Map for storing your dataset.

    b. You only need to search elements once, and the overhead of sorting would thus not be necessary.

    c. The number of elements is relatively few, thus the overhead of sorting might be worse than a linear search.

5.

    a. You'd need to test 1,000,000 elements at most.

    b. You'd need to test at most 20 elements. (Keep dividing by 2 counting each division until you reach 1.)

6.

Step 1: halfway point is 5, check 5, 5 is lower than 7.

Step 2: halfway point between 5 and 10 is 7 (using integer division), which is our desired number.

It would thus take two steps to find 7 in an array containing the numbers 1 through 10, using Binary Search.

7. If you had millions of items to search, you might end up with a stack overflow using a recursive Binary Search.

```cpp
int BinarySearchNonRecursive(int nVal, int arr[],int nSize)
{
      int nLowerIndex=0;
      int nUpperIndex=nSize-1;
      int nMidIndex;

      while (nLowerIndex<=nUpperIndex)
      {
            nMidIndex=(nLowerIndex+nUpperIndex)/2;

            if(nVal==arr[nMidIndex])
            {
                  return nMidIndex;
            }
            else if(nVal < arr[nMidIndex])
                  nUpperIndex=nMidIndex-1;
            else if (nVal > arr[nMidIndex])
                  nLowerIndex=nMidIndex+1;
      }
      return -1;
}
```

Lesson 30: Answers

1. A template is a pattern or framework that allows the parameterization of the type used with the function or class.

2. Code reuse: Templates allow the same code to be used with different classes or object types. This reduces testing and debugging time.

3. A template argument is the actual type used in the declaration of a variable of the given class (between the <>).

4. CArray<float> myFloatArray;

Lesson 31: Answers

1.

   a. Syntax errors are grammatical errors in the code, such as missing or extra punctuation, mistyped keywords, variable names or function names, references to variables that are out of scope, passing the wrong number or wrong type of parameters to functions, etc. Such errors are always flagged by the compiler or interpreter, and are usually the easiest to solve.

   b. Logic errors are errors in your algorithm; the code actually compiles without errors, but it does not do what you expect. These are generally easy to find and solve using the tools that come with the compiler, such as the ability to run your code line by line, and see the values of variables as they change.

   c. Runtime errors are errors that occur when the program is in use by your customers or end users. These usually manifest in terrible ways, such as the program crashing, or hanging up or malfunctioning in some unexplained and random way. Such errors are typically caused by buffer over/underruns or stack corruption. Runtime errors are usually the most difficult and expensive to fix. Since the Programmer is usually not there to see the customer's computer crash, and even if he/she were, since the version of the program is typically the release and not the debug version, no debugging information would be provided at the time of the crash to aid in resolving the fault. Such runtime errors are also often not predictably repeatable, since the fault causing the crash depends on a very specific sequence of events to cause the memory to become corrupt in just the right manner to cause the crash.

2. It is better to catch errors earlier in development, because the later you catch them the more expensive it is to fix them. If you find and fix your errors during development, it means that other developer's time is not wasted trying to solve the problem you created, and the productivity of your end users is not negatively affected by your design flaw or bug. Every time someone else gets involved in the errors in your code, the cost escalates.

3.

```
bool TodayIsHotter (// missing closing parenthesis
{
      bool bRes=true//missing semicolon
      int x=GetTemperatureToday();
```

```
        int y=GetTemperatureYesterday();
        return bRes || x > y; // Logic error!
}
```

    a. Two syntax errors; a missing closing parenthesis on the first line, and a missing semicolon on the third.

    b. One logic error on the second to last line.

    c. The function will return true regardless of x and y, because bRes is initialized to true, and the return result is thus always true (true or something else always evaluates to true.)

4.

```
bool CalcSumOfFirstTenInts()) //extra closing parenthesis
{
        int nCounter=1;
        int nRunningTotal=0;
        while (nCounter <= 10)
        {
                nRunningTotal=nRunningTotal+nCounter;
        }
        return nRunningTotal;
}
```

    a. One syntax error; first line contains an extra closing parenthesis.

    b. one logic error in loop; counter is not incremented, and thus the loop will never exit!

    c. The function will not return, because the loop will never exit, since nCounter is not incremented, and thus the loop execution condition will never evaluate to false.

5. There is a semicolon after the loop condition that would be interpreted as the statement to be iterated. The {x++;} body would not be iterated at all, but would simply be executed once the loop terminated. The loop, however, would not terminate, because x would remain less than 10 forever, since there is nothing in the body of the loop to change it. This is a very nasty logic error. You'd think it would be considered a syntax error, but it is perfectly legal to have an empty statement, i.e., a semicolon with no instruction before it.

Lesson 32: Answers

1.

    a. Range checking: checking the values entered by the user to ensure they are within the expected range of values.

    b. Bounds checking: Ensuring that when accessing the elements of an array during loop iteration, you do not go beyond the end of the array's allocated area of memory by accessing a range higher than the last array subscript or lower than the array's first subscript. Remember, in C++ and many other languages, arrays are zero-based; the first element is at subscript 0, and the last at n-1, where n is the number of elements in the array.

    c. Parameter validation: Checking that the parameters passed to a function are within the expected range of values required by the function, in order for the function to operate correctly.

2.

```
// put alphabet into szTemp
char szTemp[26]="\0";
for (int nIdx=1; nIdx <=26; nIdx++)
{
    szTemp[nIdx]=64+nIdx;
    /* bad, this will leave the first element empty and access beyond
    the end of the array, causing a memory overwrite, because arrays
    are zero-based, not one-based */
}
```

The loop should have been written:

```
for (int nIdx=0; nIdx < 26; nIdx++)
{
    szTemp[nIdx]=65+nIdx;
}
```

3.

```
CLamp* pLamp=0;
CLamp* pLamp2; // bad, no initialization, points to random memory.
CLamp pLamp3=0;
pLamp=new CLamp;
pLamp->OnOffButton();
delete pLamp;
pLamp->OnOffButton(); /* bad! pLamp has already been deleted (dangling
reference)! */
```

If (pLamp2) /* pLamp was never properly initialized so this will most likely succeed errantly. */
pLamp2->OnOffButton(); /* bad, object was never instantiated, thus calling a method on this pointer will most likely cause a crash because pLamp2 points to random memory. */
pLamp3->OnOffButton(); /* null pointer error, pLamp was not instantiated and was initialized to 0. It was also not tested for null before use.*/

4.

```
int RemainderFromDivision(int nDividend, int nDivisor)
{
    if (nDivisor ==0)
        return 0; // avoid a divide by zero error!
    int nQuotient=nDivisor/nDividend; // integer division will round
    Int nMaxMultiples=nQuotient*nDividend;
    Int nRemainder=nDivisor-nMaxMultiples;
}
```

Lesson 33: Answers

1.

```
CLamp* p=new CLamp(); // instantiate a CLamp object
p->OnOffButton(); // Turn the lamp on
int nBrightness=0;
// gradually increase the brightness of the lamp
while (nBrightness < 10)
{
    p->SetBrightness(nBrightness++);
    Wait(20);
}
/* The below assignment of p to a new instantiation of a CLampAndSiren
object will overwrite the pointer p, and cause a memory leak, since
the original instantiation of the CLamp object originally pointed to
by p has not yet been deallocated. The original CLamp object will be
left on at its highest brightness until the program exits. */
p=new CLampAndSiren(); // woops memory leak!
p->OnOffButton();
wait(30);
// Create an array of 5 CLamp object pointers
CLamp* pLampArray[5];
// instantiate the 5 lamps to new objects
for (int n=0; n < 5; n++)
{
    pLampArray[n]=new CLamp();
}
```

```
/* turn each lamp on and off in turn

The below loop will cause a bounds error, because it actually accesses
array locations 1 to 5, rather than 0 to 4. It will thus only turn
lamps 2 through 5 on, and then on the last iteration cause an unini-
tialized memory location to be treated as a CLamp pointer, and most
likely cause a crash. Remember arrays are 0-based, not 1-based. */

for (int j=1; j <=5; j++)
{
    pLampArray[j]->OnOffButton();
    wait(5);
    pLampArray[j]->OnOffButton();
}
for (int k=0; k < 5; k++)
{/* The below two lines are around the wrong way. This will cause a
memory leak, since each array location's CLamp pointer is set to 0
without being deallocated. Then, we attempt to delete a NULL pointer,
causing a NULL pointer error. Fortunately, the deletion of a null
pointer won't cause our program to crash in this instance, but if we
had attempted to access the lamp's methods on the null pointers, we
would certainly cause something unpredictable to happen. */
    pLampArray[k]=0; // Woops, memory leak!
        delete pLampArray[k]; // Woops, null pointer error.
}
```

Lesson 34: Answers

1.

a. Syntax error: A grammatical error in your program code, such as missing or extra punctuation symbols, mistyped keywords, references to variables that are out of scope, function calls with the wrong type or number of parameters, etc.

b. Logic error: Your code is grammatically correct, but logically flawed; it doesn't do what you intended it to do. Logic errors include wrong calculation, loops that iterate too many or too few times, misunderstanding the problem you are trying to solve and hence solving the wrong problem, etc.

c. Runtime error: An error in your program while being used by the end user, such as a program crash, loss of data, a program hang, etc.

d. Buffer Overrun: A buffer overrun is where you unintentionally write past the end of an allocated region of memory, thereby corrupting other data or program instructions.

e. Buffer Underrun: A buffer underrun is similar to a buffer overrun, except it is caused by writing before the beginning of the intended memory region.

f. Stack corruption: Stack corruption is usually the result of a buffer overrun or underrun, and describes the situation where stack data such as variables or return addresses have become corrupted, causing your program to crash or malfunction. These are the hardest kinds of runtime errors to fix because they may result in different symptoms, and the symptoms may appear seemingly randomly.

g. Exception: An exception is an error thrown by your program and is usually caught by an exception handler, which is a special block of code written to recover gracefully from runtime errors.

h. Range checking: Range checking is the practise of ensuring that user input or parameters passed to functions are in the expected ranges of values. For example, if a function performs a division calculation, you should check that a divide by 0 error will never occur.

i. Subscript validation (or bounds checking): Whenever array access is performed, either to read or write data to an array, you must check that the array subscript or index is within the array's legal limits, or you will cause stack (or heap) corruption. Remember, arrays are typically 0-based, thus if an array has N elements, its subscripts go from 0 to n-1.

j. Pointer validation: Pointer validation is simply the practise of checking that a pointer is non-zero before calling a method on it. Of course, you must ensure that the pointer is initialized to 0 before use, so that it doesn't start out pointing at random memory that you assume to be a valid object. You then must ensure your pointer points to an instantiation of an object before calling a method, by using the new or other appropriate keyword to create an instance of that object. When you've finished with the object, destroy it with delete and set the pointer to 0, so that you don't try accessing the deleted object's methods.

k. Null pointer error: This is simply an error caused by attempting to access a method on a pointer variable that has been initialized to 0, thus does not yet point to an instantiation of any object.

l. Dangling reference: A dangling reference is where a pointer is left pointing to an object that has since been destroyed. If methods are called on this pointer, unpredictable results will occur. If the pointer now points to memory allocated to another object, and the programmer tries to deallocate the pointer's memory, nasty things will probably happen in the program, such as heap corruption.

m. Memory Leak: A memory leak is where memory allocated to an object is not deallocated. This may be because the programmer forgot to deallocate it, or because a pointer's value is accidentally overwritten before the object to which it points has been deallocated (causing a subsequent deallocation using the overwritten pointer to fail). This results in the memory allocated to the object being unavailable until the program exits. If sufficient memory leaks occur in a program, the program will eventually run out of memory, and most likely terminate unexpectedly. If a program is meant to run continuously, such as aviation tower monitoring software or life support software, it is critical that there are no memory leaks or other memory corrupting errors, which might unintentionally cause the system to go down.

2. Comments mark syntax errors:

a.

```
if GetPassword()) // missing opening ( after if
    RunProgram() // missing ; after )
else
    PrintError();
```

b.

```
if (NetworkReady())) // extra closing ) at end of line
    SendData();
```

c.

```
int main(int argc, char* argv)
( // should be { not (
    for (int n=0; n < argc; n++)
    {
        cout << "Parameter " << n << "=" << argv[n] << endl;
    }
    return 0 // missing ; at end of line
) // Should be } not )
```

3. Comments mark logic errors:

a.

```
while (n < 10); /* erroneous ; empty loop body, infinite loop
will occur. */
    { // This block will never execute!
        cout << "n=" << n << endl;
    }
```

b.

```
    int aEvenNumbers[10];
    int nEven=2;
    for (int n=0; n <=10; n++) /* Should be n < 10, not n <=10, will
cause bounds error. */
    {
        aEvenNumbers[n]=nEven;
        nEven*=2;
    }
```

c.

```
    int max(int a, int b)
    {
        if (a > b); // ; will cause empty statement.
            return a; /* a will always be returned because of
empty statement in if above. */
        else
            return b; // Will never execute due to empty statement
in if.
    }

    void test()
    {
        cout << "Enter two numbers: ";
        cin >>a >> b;
        cout << "The maximum of " << a << " and " << b " is " <<
max(a, b) << endl;
        return 0;
    }
```

4. Pointer errors marked with comments:

a.

```
    CLamp* p=new CLamp;
    pLamp->OnOffButton();
    pLamp=0; // Memory leak, pLamp not deleted
```

b.

```
    CLamp* pLamp=new CLamp;
    pLamp->OnOffButton();
    delete pLamp;
    if (pLamp->IsOn()) /* dangling reference, pLamp not zeroed after
    deletion. */
        pLamp->OnOffButton();// dangling reference, pLamp not zeroed
```

```
                   after deletion.
           pLamp=0;
```

c.

```
       void Describe(cShape* pShape)
       {
               if (pShape==0)
                       return;
               cout << "The shape is a " << pShape->Name() << endl;
       }

       void test()
       {
               CShape* pShape1; /* Uninitialized! Will likely cause a
               crash when described. */
               CShape* pShape2=new CRectangle(50,100);
               Describe(pShape1);
               Describe(pShape2);
               // Memory leaks, pShape1 and pShape2 not deleted.
       }
```

Lesson 35: Answers

1. A macro is a pattern that is replaced by the code it represents. The compiler actually looks for the parameterized pattern in your code, substitutes your parameters for the parameters in the pattern and then substitutes the entire pattern with the code that the pattern represents. No type checking of the pattern is performed; it is simply a text substitution mechanism. Once the pattern has been replaced, the compiler then compiles the resultant code. A function, on the other hand, is compiled as is, without any text substitution. The standard convention is to use uppercase and underscore characters for macro names, and mixed case characters for function names.

2. One way of protecting against the contents of a file being included multiple times, when several files include common headers, and other files include these files, is to use an

```
#ifndef UNIQUE_HEADER_ID
#define UNIQUE_HEADER_ID
// header file
#endif //UNIQUE_HEADER_ID
```

block around the header contents. This way, when the first file includes the header, the symbol UNIQUE_HEADER_ID is undefined. It is thus defined and the content included.

When another file attempts to include this header, if the UNIQUE_HEADER_ID is defined, it does not include it again.

3. One advantage of using the #define directive to define a symbol to represent a literal value in your code is so that you can simply change the value of the literal, rather than having to find and change every instance of that literal in your code. Also, the symbol representing the literal can be given a meaningful name, which helps the reader to understand the purpose of the literal value.

4. One danger of using the #define directive to define a symbol representing a literal value, rather than using a constant variable declaration, is this is not a type safe mechanism, thus compiler errors can sometimes seem cryptic, and code harder to debug.

5. a. A compiler directive which can be used to conditionally include different files depending on the value of a defined symbol is the #ifdef #else #endif directive.

   For example:

   ```
   #ifdef WIN_64
   #include <64bit.h>
   #else
   #include <32bit.h>
   #endif
   ```

   b. This is very useful when you want to compile a program for different operating system platforms, such as 32 bit or 64 bit windows, which require different headers for the different operating system versions.

Lesson 36: Answers

1. CKJBibleApp

2. publically inherits from CWinApp

3. InitInstance and OnAppAbout

4. a. DECLARE_MESSAGE_MAP() is an MFC macro that combined with macros in the class's implementation file, declares message handlers that map Windows messages to event handlers. These are used to activate menu items and other UI controls.

   b. This is a macro.

   c. Macros are usually all uppercase with underscores between the words, as opposed to mixed upper and lower case, which is the convention for function or method names.

5. Afx_msg void OnAppAbout(); (Note, afx_msg is defined as part of a message handler's function signature used by MFC for type checking parameters.)

6. OnAppAbout is executed when the About option is chosen from the Help menu.

7. InitInstance initializes any variables and resources used by the application.

8.

CloseAllDocuments	Closes all open documents.
DoMessageBox	Implements AfxMessageBox for the application.
DoWaitCursor	Turns the wait cursor on and off.
ExitInstance	Override to clean up when your application terminates.
HideApplication	Hides the application before closing all documents.
HtmlHelp	Calls the HTMLHelp Windows function.
InitInstance	Override to perform Windows instance initialization, such as creating your window objects.
OnDDECommand	Called by the framework in response to a dynamic data exchange (DDE) execute command.
OnIdle	Override to perform application-specific idle-time processing.
PreTranslateMessage	Filters messages before they are dispatched to the Windows functions TranslateMessage and DispatchMessage.
ProcessMessageFilter	Intercepts certain messages before they reach the application.
ProcessWndProcException	Intercepts all unhandled exceptions thrown by the application's message and command handlers.
Run	Runs the default message loop. Override to customize the message loop.
SaveAllModified	Prompts the user to save all modified documents.
WinHelp	Calls the WinHelp Windows function.

9. InitInstance.

10. The CWinApp Class provides a base from which a Windows application can be derived.

Endnotes

1. See Appendix 11 for more information on the living cell.

2. See Appendix 12 for more information on the human brain.

3. Gen 1:27-28, Psalm 8:5-8

4. Gen 2:20

5. Deut. 6:7-9

6. Psalm 119:11

7. Gen 1:31

8. Exod. 31:18, 17:14 ; Deut. 17:18, 27:8 ; Isa. 30:8; Jer. 30:2, 36:2, 36:28; Hab. 2:2; Rev. 1:11, 1:19, 21:5

9. Psalm 115:3, 135:6, 138:2; Dan. 4:35

10. http://www.colsoncenter.org/the-center/columns/indepth/17348-johannes-gutenberg-c1398-1468; http://en.wikipedia.org/wiki/Gutenberg_Bible; http://inventors.about.com/od/gstartinventors/a/Gutenberg.htm. Accessed on 4 July, 2012.

11. James Nickel, *Mathematics: Is God Silent?*, 14.

12. Johannes Kepler, *Epitome of Copernican Astronomy & Harmonies of the World*, trans. Charles Glenn Wallis (Amherst: Prometheus Books, 1995), 245.

13. Cited in Max Caspar, Kepler, trans. C. Doris Hellman (New York: Dover Publications, 1993), 374.

14. Galileo Galilei, *Discoveries and Opinions of Galileo*, trans. Stillman Drake (Garden City: Doubleday, 1957), 183.

15. Ibid., 196.

16. Blaise Pascal, Pensées (number 425).

17. *Christian Influences in the Sciences* by Daniel Graves 7/7/1998 www.rae.org/pdf/influsci.pdf accessed on 13 December, 2011.

18. Loemker, Leroy, (1969). *Leibniz: Philosophical Papers and Letters*. Reidel., 717.

19. Magill, Frank (ed.). *Masterpieces of World Philosophy*. New York: Harper Collins (1990).

20. Newton, *The Principia,* 440.

21. Faraday, as cited in Jones (1870), Vol. II, 471.

22. Faraday, as cited in Eichman (1993), 93-94.

23. http://en.wikipedia.org/wiki/George_Boole, http://understandingscience.ucc.ie/pages/sci_georgeboole.htm both accessed on 14 December, 2011.

24. William Kneale, 1948, 'Boole and the Revival of Logic', Mind, New Series, Vol. 57, No. 226. (Apr., 1948), 158.

25. Maxwell, as cited in Bowden (1998), 288; and in Williams and Mulfinger (1974), 487.

26. http://www.radio-electronics.com/info/radio_history/gtnames/fleming.php Accessed on 13 December, 2011.

27. http://en.wikipedia.org/wiki/Category:Christian_creationists Accessed on 13 December, 2011.

    Also see *Christian Influences in the Sciences* by Daniel Graves (7/7/1998), accessed on 13 December, 2011.

28. http://www.brainyquote.com/quotes/authors/j/john_ambrose_fleming.html Accessed on 13 December, 2011.

29. Christian Knowledge Society: London (1904).

30. Marshall Morgan and Scott, (1938), 114 pages, ASIN: B00089BL7Y - outlines objections to Darwin.

31. Marconi, as cited in Maria Cristina Marconi (1995), 244.

32. Marconi, as cited in Popov (1992), 298.

33. *John von Neumann: selected letters* by John Von Neumann, Miklós Rédei, 197, and Gambling on God: Essays on Pascal's Wager. Jeff Jordan, Lanham, Md. u.a. (Rowman & Littlefield, 1994), introduction.

34. http://www.uncommondescent.com/biology/john-von-neumann-an-ider-ante-litteram/ accessed on 7 December, 2011. Also see John Von Neumon, *Theory of Self-Reproducing Automata*, (1966), University of Illinois Press, Urbana.

35. *Things a Computer Scientist Rarely Talks About* by Donald E. Knuth (Stanford, California: Center for the Study of Language and Information, 2001), xi+257. (CSLI Lecture Notes, no. 136.)

36. I called Lynn Ritchie, Dennis's sister in England on 11 February, 2012 to try and confirm the veracity of this post, but she said that to her knowledge he had no belief in God.

37. http://www.topix.com/forum/religion/christian/TCSVQBO0183A5Q8B0 accessed on 11 February, 2012.

38. https://plus.google.com/101960720994009339267/posts/ENuEDDYfvKP #101960720994009339267/posts/ENuEDDYfvKP accessed on 11 February, 2012.

39. Ibid.

40. http://cm.bell-labs.com/cm/cs/who/dmr/ accessed on 11 February, 2012.

41. Exerpt from an email from Dr Bjarne Stroustrup to Joseph Stephen, received on 10 February, 2012.

42. Exerpt from an email from Dr Bjarne Stroustrup to Joseph Stephen, received on 13 February, 2012.

43. Email correspondence with Prof. David Powers on 13 December, 2011.

44. Psalm 111:10; Proverbs 2:1-5, 9:10

45. *The Sufficiency of Scripture—The Key To Revival,* Chapter 3, by Joseph Stephen, (2010), Winepress Publishing.

46. Cited in M.J. Behe, *Darwin's Black Box: The Biochemical Challenge to Evolution,* The Free Press, New York, (1996), 24.

47. Sir James Gray, *chapter in Science Today,* (1961), 21, professor of Zoology, Cambridge University.

48. Carl Sagan, *"Life" in Encyclopedia Britannica: Macropaedia* (1974), 893-894.

49. Peter Gwynne, Sharon Begley, and Mary Hager, *"The Secrets of the Human Cell,"* in Newsweek, (August 20, 1979), 48.

50. Sarfati, J., Design in living organisms (motors: ATP synthase), Journal of Creation 12(1):3–5, (1998), creation.com/motor.

51. Adapted from http://creation.com/atp-synthase accessed on 18 December, 2011.

52. Adapted from http://creation.com/design-in-living-organisms-motors-atp-synthase accessed on 19 December, 2011.

53. http://www.ncbi.nlm.nih.gov/pubmed/14630314 accessed on 19 December, 2011.

54. Adapted from http://creation.com/atp-synthase accessed on 18 December, 2011.

55. Adapted from http://hauns.com/~DCQu4E5g/DNA.html accessed on 19 December, 2011.

56. Adapted from http://creation.com/dazzling-design-in-miniature-dna-information-storage-creation-magazine accessed on 19 December, 2011.

57. Michael Denton, *Evolution: Theory In Crisis* (1985), 264.

58. The late biochemist and atheist author Dr. Isaac Asimov.

59. C. Judson Herrick, *Brains of Rats and Man: A Survey of the Origin and Biological Significance of the Cerebral Cortex* (New York: Hafner Publishing Co., 1963), 382 and see Paul G. Roofe, p. x of the introduction to the same edition, 5, 7-8.

60. Michael Denton, *Evolution: A Theory in Crisis* (Bethesda, Maryland: Adler and Adler Publishers, 1986), 310.

61. Arthur Ernest Wilder-Smith.

62. http://www.sciencedaily.com/releases/2012/08/120829094209.htm
PLoS Computational Biology Prabhakar B, Dektar KN, Gordon DM (2012) The Regulation of Ant Colony Foraging Activity without Spatial Information. PLoS Comput Biol 8(8): e1002670. doi:10.1371/journal.pcbi.1002670
http://www.ploscompbiol.org/article/info%3Adoi%2F10.1371%2Fjournal.pcbi.1002670

63. Adapted from Evidence News 23/12 - 12th September 2012 by John Mackay www.creationresearch.net

64. An exact solution for 15,112 German towns from TSPLIB was found in 2001 using the cutting-plane method proposed by George Dantzig, Ray Fulkerson, and Selmer M. Johnson in 1954, based on linear programming. The computations were performed

on a network of 110 processors located at Rice University and Princeton University. The total computation time was equivalent to 22.6 years on a single 500 MHz Alpha processor.

In May 2004, the travelling salesman problem of visiting all 24,978 towns in Sweden was solved: a tour of length approximately 72,500 kilometres was found, and it was proven that no shorter tour exists. The work was carried out on a cluster of 96 dual processor Intel Xeon 2.8 GHz workstations at Georgia Tech's School of Industrial and Systems Engineering, running as a background process. The cumulative CPU time used in this calculation was approximately 84.8 CPU years on a single Intel Xeon 2.8 GHz processor. (David Applegate, AT&T Labs - Research; Robert Bixby, ILOG and Rice University; Vašek Chvátal, Rutgers University; William Cook, Georgia Tech; Keld Helsgaun, Roskilde University. Details at http://www.tsp.gatech.edu/sweden/) In March, 2005, the travelling salesman problem of visiting all 33,810 points in a circuit board was solved using Concorde TSP Solver: a tour of length 66,048,945 units was found, and it was proven that no shorter tour exists. The computation took approximately 15.7 CPU-years (Cook et al., 2006).

In April 2006 an instance with 85,900 points was solved using Concorde TSP Solver, taking over 136 CPU-years (Applegate et al., 2006).

65. This assumes a 1GHZ processor can execute 10^9 instructions per second. This is by way of example only, and does not reflect the actual execution performance, since most processors do not execute one instruction per cycle on every cycle. The calculation of 9×10^{46} years is based on (3×10^{64} operations)/(10^9 instructions per second), which approximates 3×10^{54} seconds, which approximates 9×10^{46} years. This also assumes the simplest "brute force" solution to the TSP, which has no optimisations and requires every node to be compared to every other node to calculate the distances between nodes. Much more efficient algorithms have been devised, but this example should suffice to demonstrate the complexity of the basic problem.

66. Tiny brained bees solve a complex mathematical problem, Queen Mary—University of London, www.qmul.ac.uk, 25 October, 2010.

67. Lihoreau, M., Chittka, L., and Raine, N., Travel optimization by foraging bumblebees through readjustments of traplines after discovery of new feeding locations, The American Naturalist 176(6):744–757, 2010.

68. http://www.qmul.ac.uk/media/news/items/se/38864.html.

69. Lihoreau, M., Chittka, L., and Raine, N., Travel optimization by foraging bumblebees through readjustments of traplines after discovery of new feeding locations, The American Naturalist 176(6):744–757, 2010.

70. ibid.

71. — Richard Dawkins, *River Out of Eden: A Darwinian View of Life* (1995).

72. http://www.geekosystem.com/bees-havent-solved-traveling-salesman-problem/

73. Isaiah 55:9; 1 Corinthians 1:25

74. 1 Corinthians 1:27

www.ingramcontent.com/pod-product-compliance
Lightning Source LLC
Chambersburg PA
CBHW080353060326
40689CB00019B/3989